RESURRECTING
the Gospel of Christ

EDMOND LABBE

Printed in the USA

ISBN 978-0-615-36352-3

∼ *Contents* ∼

～ *Dedication* ～

I t's with the most heartfelt expressions that I dedicate this book to Joan, my beautiful and wonderful wife of forty-five years. She has sacrificed a great deal to follow me from place to place in search for answers to life's dilemmas. What an incredible companion she has been; not just a happenstance in my life, but a purposed and incredible partner planned for me from the foundation of the world. It is beyond words to express what God has given me in my lifetime; and to you, my dear, incredible, wonderful wife and friend, all the expressions in the world could not adequately articulate the love and gratitude I have for you. It is my prayer that you and I will kneel together on that wonderful day when Jesus breaks the atmosphere of this world and takes us to be with him, where home and family and friends will never be separated again.

⌁ *Preface* ⌁

To all who express a desire to examine this document, I would ask your earnest patience as I acknowledge my great deficiency in being a writer, scholar, or having the advantage of great intellect. I am a simple man in retirement, educated the hard way in northern New England. My dear and wonderful mother raised me in a family of very little education, along with my five brothers and two sisters. I have only a high school education and very little academic training beyond that. I have been a mechanic most of my life, and lived in the beautiful state of Vermont the majority of my married life. I have two sons, one daughter, and many wonderful grandchildren. In 1978, after a terrible back injury, and having been educated in a religious system that could only supply unclear answers to my most important questions, I turned to the only source one can depend on for truth and righteousness: the Word of God. For the last thirty years, with the Bible in one hand and a Strong's Concordance in the other, I have learned about the value of life and the price our heavenly Father has had to pay to educate humanity and the entire universe pertaining to righteousness unto life, and to redeem this misguided creation from rebellion of the principles that can only keep a universal creation in perfect harmony. I have been a Bible instructor, pastor, and evangelist and retired in 2002 as the result of an injury acquired while baptizing a candidate for the heavenly kingdom.

It is my greatest desire to express to you all the wonderful things I have learned from the Word of God, and to leave in your hands the decision as to whether or not they are for you. I pray that this information may be a blessing to you as it has been for me, and that you read and study this whole manuscript before you make your decision.

∼ *Introduction* ∼

R evelation, the last prophetic book written for this generation, is complete in its final warning pertaining to the issues and events presently taking place on Planet Earth. At this present time we are in the critical hour predicted by Jesus. "And there shall be signs in the sun, and in the moon, and in the stars; and upon the **earth distress of nations**, with perplexity; *the sea and the waves roaring;* Men's hearts failing them for fear, and for looking after those things which are coming on the earth: for the powers of heaven shall be shaken" (Luke 21:25, 26). To the believer as well as the unbeliever, the certainty of man's origin and responsibility will soon be made clear at the appearing of He who has the right of legislative universal authority. Soon heaven will open and, behold, a white horse will be seen and He that sits on him, who is called the Faithful and True Witness, *will come to judge the entire world in life-giving righteousness.* It is then that Jesus will come and call to accountability all who have failed to appropriate the right to life as a citizen of Christ's heavenly kingdom (Revelation 19:11).

The principle subject in the preparation of this book is that we, in this final generation, may understand the three most critical issues that face each one of us in light of the biblical statements that apply to every man, woman, and child born in this world since the days of creation.

1. **"It is appointed to men once to *die,* but after this the judgment"** (Hebrews 9:27).

2. **"For we must all appear before the judgment seat of Christ"** (2 Corinthians 5:10).

3. **"Because he hath appointed a day in which He will judge the world in righteousness by that Man whom He hath ordained; whereof He hath given assurance to all men, in that He hath raised Him from the dead"** (Acts 17:31).

Since the fall of mankind into sin (Romans 5:12), the instructions given him from the mouth of his Creator has been lightly understood or completely disregarded. In times past, God has winked at man's ignorance (Acts 17:30). But in this final generation, in the light of God's Word being available to most of God's creation, a call to repentance is demanded. There will be no excuses when Jesus comes the second time to receive unto Himself the kingdom prepared for Him from the foundation of the world (Matthew 25:34). The world must give account for its participation in the rebellion against the authority and principles that govern life in the government and universal kingdom of our Lord and Savior Jesus Christ.

The one principle subject I pray may impress your understanding from this book is the principle term defined in the Bible as *life-giving righteousness*. Isaiah says, "When thy judgments are in the earth, the inhabitants of the world will learn righteousness" (Isaiah 26:9). But many, scripture says, will have learned it too late. The term *righteousness* is critical to all of God's creation. Righteousness is defined as goodness, virtue, honesty, morality, justice, decency, and uprightness. In scripture it is used in terms as good, just, justified, justification, right, and righteous. It is a term used to define Adam at creation, as created *in nature and character* of divine righteousness, justified as righteous and has a legal moral standing with God in a mental, moral, and physical state. Righteousness is the principle characteristic of life according to the code of conduct that governs life in God's universal kingdom. "Let us hear the conclusion of the whole matter: Fear God, and keep His commandments: **for this is the whole duty of man**. For God shall bring every work into judgment, with every secret thing, whether it is good or whether it is evil (Ecclesiastes 12:13, 14).

Righteousness is the central principle in the law of God, defined in God's universal moral code of being and conduct. David said, "My tongue shall speak of thy word: for all thy commandments are righteousness" (Psalm 119:172). Righteousness is the standard of life and character demanded by God and His moral code that governs
life in the universe (James 1:25; 2:12; Exodus 20:1-17). It is not just in the keeping of God's commandments that righteousness is demanded. But this righteousness, which was supplied to man at creation, must be maintained in order for any created being to have the rights to live and continue to live in God's universal kingdom. Righteousness is the express written term describing the divine character of God, the standard of divine character He supplies to man, and is characterized as His standard of morality in sustaining eternal life.

It's not difficult to see and understand the words of Jesus when He said, "**Except your righteousness shall exceed the righteousness of the scribes** and **Pharisees**, ye shall in no case enter into the kingdom of heaven" (Matthew 5:20). "But seek ye **first** the kingdom of God, and **His righteousness**, and all these things shall be added unto you" (Matthew 6:33). The apostle Paul, in defining the central principles of God's universal kingdom, says, "For the **kingdom of God** is not meat and drink; **but righteousness, and peace, and joy in the Holy Spirit**" (Romans 14:17).

No created being, whether holy or unholy, sinful or sinless, has of himself the righteousness demanded as the divine standard of life in the universal kingdom of God. This is the principle issue of discussion in this volume, and is the foremost issue in who does and does not have the right to life at the second coming of Christ (Acts 17:31; Revelation 14:6, 7; 19:11).

⌒ *Chapter One* ⌒
Adam Created in Righteousness

Creation of Man and Time

It is in clear, distinct tones that scripture records the creation of our world and the universe: "In the beginning God" (Genesis 1:1). In these four critical words, God has appointed, as part of man's path of faith for everyone who will accept it, the path to eternal life. Our creation, as well as the creation of this planet, is based on principles of divine creative authority. The universe is not, according to God's divine word, a happenstance, or just a formation of things evolved from nothing, but a complete and direct product from the mouth of our divine Creator (John 1:1-3).

According to the Bible, our planet has a sacred chronology, an approximate life span of about 6,000 years. This, my friends, is a simple biblical time line of our existence and should be accepted by faith in a time when everything from evolution to atheism is being used by the adversary of souls to prepare this generation for the final conflict between God and man.

When our planet was created, the record states that, "In six days the Lord made heaven and earth, the sea, and all that in them is, And God saw everything that He had made, and, behold, **it was very good**. And the evening and the morning were the sixth day. Thus the heavens and the earth were finished, and all the host of them" (Genesis 1:31-2:1; Exodus 20: 8-11). When Jesus created our planet, everything was done in divine order as to its time, place, and location in the universe (Hebrews 1:1, 2). Earth was created in **six literal days** by the Lord Jesus Christ (Psalm 33:6-9). And along with its physical appearance, Jesus created the system of time based on His divine authority and purpose. It was Jesus who created the day, the week, the month, and the year that governs time and life in the universe. It was Jesus who created night and day, and the four seasons, for man's existence in perfect divine order (Genesis 8:22). All this was done for man's existence in God's work of extending His kingdom in a vast universe of unimaginable space. This knowledge is critical to those who believe and want a solid foundation for their existence.

God's Original Plan and Bill of Rights

When Jesus created our world, the last physical thing He created was man. "Male and female created He them, and blessed them and **called their name Adam,** in the day when they were created" (Genesis 1:27; 5:1, 2). It is vital and critical to understand that at the time of their creation they were not just let loose to roam and do anything they would choose or purpose to do. Alternatively, they were instructed "to be fruitful, and multiply, and replenish the earth, and subdue it: and have dominion over the fish of the sea, and over the fowl of the air, and over every living thing that moves upon the earth" (Genesis 1:28). In addition, they were given **dominion in righteousness, under heaven's universal bill of rights** with instructions and directions in their responsibility and duty as stewards of God's creation.

In formulating the character of man at creation, Adam and Eve were endowed with incredible wisdom above all under their dominion. Before sin, Adam and Eve were perfect in nature, being, and quality of intellect. They were guided by the complete indwelling power and knowledge of the Holy Spirit of God to impress and guide them with power and righteousness through all eternity. They had no evil propensities to sin, nor evil thoughts, desires, or passions. They were completely free from every aspect of sin and the knowledge of sin.

When Adam and Eve were created, their makeup contained a **bill of rights by declaration in character,** with privileges under divine appointment. In scripture, a bill of rights is defined as **garments of salvation, a robe of righteousness** (Isaiah 61:10). As long as they maintained this divine state of being, Adam and Eve would maintain citizenship in God's heavenly kingdom. This bill of rights, Christ's robe of life-giving righteousness, garments of salvation, have always been the principle issue in one's rights to eternal life. It has always been a free gift, given freely by Jesus, the Creator of the universe. However, along with this incredible privilege of life given to Adam and his descendants, the universal principle of freedom of choice was also conveyed (Genesis 2:15-17). **Adam was given the right of willingness to exist under and abide by divine principles,** since liberty of conscience has always been a condition of existence in the kingdom of God.

Men, as well as other created beings such as angels in heaven, were created with the same capacity to understand and maintain the conditions and principles that govern life in God's universal kingdom. Freedom of the right to choose life or death, righteousness or unrighteousness, Christ or Satan, has always been one of the most important principles of God's governing nature and character.

In order for Adam and Eve to maintain their existence through all eternity, they would have to pass the **test of righteousness** based on faith, love, and obedience. In the first week of creation nothing was born, but was created from the mouth of our Divine Creator (Genesis 1-2:1-3). After the creation of Adam and Eve, human life came through the conception of man; all were born of man (Genesis 2:4). After sin entered this world (Romans 5:12), man was given another chance to embrace the righteousness of Christ, the fundamental principle that establishes the right to eternal life. But it's important to understand that we as individuals may not want to live under God's principles of divine order, under God's loving hand of life-giving righteousness that must be maintained in order for life to be perfectly harmonious throughout the universe.

Friends, we see the principle of choice every day in our homes, in our community, our country, and all over this world. Moreover, when Jesus created this planet He never planned to force any man to obey Him because He said so. **Life is a choice**, and yes, God created us to live, a choice He made because of His divine right and character as Creator of the universe. But as He placed Adam and Eve in the beginning under divine grace, a choice to live or die under divine governing principles, we in our lifetime have the same liberty of conscience, the same heavenly privilege to choose our own destiny. Life has always been a choice and will continue to be a choice throughout all eternity.

When Satan and his angels fell from heaven (Luke 10:18) it was a choice they made of their own free will under the principle of **liberty of conscience**, to sustain life under divine righteousness and the governing principles of God's universal kingdom (Exodus 20:1-17). Or death in opposition to Gods standards of life. When man was created on this planet we were given the same choice: "**To whom you yield yourselves servants to obey**, his servants ye are to whom ye obey; whether of sin to death, or of obedience to righteousness" (Romans 6:16).

The Test of Righteousness

The simple test of man's choice to retain the right to eternal life came in the Garden of Eden. "And the Lord God commanded the man, saying, of every tree of the garden *thou may freely eat:* But of the tree of the knowledge of good and evil, thou shall not eat of it: for in the day that thou eat thereof thou shall surely die" (Genesis 2:16, 17). It was Adam's failure, as the head of the human family, that placed humanity in the terrible condition that has defiled him and separated him from God (1 Timothy 2:14). Adam's willful transgression of God's code of conduct, *"thou shall not"*

(Genesis 2:17; Exodus 20:1-17), placed each one of us under a declaration of **unrighteousness**, under the condemnation of the principles that govern life in God's universal kingdom (Romans 3:9-19).

This eternal divine code of conduct, defined in scripture as the Ten Commandments (Exodus 20:1-17) demands not only a heavenly bill of rights from its author, but also character obedience to the principles of divine righteousness. When Jesus commanded Adam, *"thou shall not eat,"* He was implying the governing principles of life to a man and woman He created in righteousness, and upon whom He imparted divine love. *"Thou shall not"* is said or implied ten times in the biblical record of law defined as the Ten Commandments (Exodus 20:1-17).

When Adam sinned (Romans 5:12) and committed willful transgression, he made a choice based on the universal principle of liberty of conscience, or the right to choose, between righteousness or unrighteousness, life or death, Christ or Satan as his authoritative ruler. No evil propensities resided in Adam when he consciously made the terrible decision to sin and die (Romans 5:12). By his willful disobedience, Adam subjected all of his future descendants to this terrible death decree and the sinful, corrupt condition existing in all of mankind (Genesis 3:19; Romans 3:10-18).

Adam was created without any desire for wrongdoing in his nature of being. It must have been as difficult for him to do wrong as it is for us to do right under the pressures of this present evil world. Oh, if only he had called Jesus to council him in what he should do after Eve gave him the fruit of the forbidden tree (Genesis 3:6). How many terrible experiences would have been prevented in our lives and in the lives of our children? It was Adam's choice to willfully transgress the principles of life under the simplest test and condition afforded to the human family. When Adam sinned shortly after creation, he willfully and deliberately disconnected humanity from Christ's righteousness and the principles that governs the moral fiber of God's divine being.

The kingdom of God exists throughout the whole universe under divine principles of life, governed by heaven's bill of divine righteousness. From the fall of Lucifer and his angels (Isaiah 14:12; Revelation 12:4), along with the inhabitants of Planet Earth, our world has been a test in experimental governments, revealing the principles and nature of sin under the direct influence and dominion of Lucifer, the adversary of God and man (Luke 4:6). This world is only a test, which will utterly fail under earthly governments and principles. Planet Earth has been the theater of the universe in educating the human family and the universe about God's divine governing principles of life and the right of every creature to choose or not choose eternal life, according to their own free will. History has demonstrated the nature of man's sinful condition given to him after the fall, which has been recorded in the books of the Bible from Genesis through Revelation.

From Righteousness to Unrighteousness

God's kingdom exists under laws and regulations to sustain life just as earthly governments do: principles, laws, and regulations created in order to maintain life in perfect harmony. Do we as citizens of the United States have rules and regulations along with a bill of rights that grants each citizen legal precedence and privileges in the affairs of this nation? Principles of righteousness in government have always existed in heaven before the fall of heavenly angels and man (Revelation 12:4, 12). If a citizen of the United States violates the code of conduct defined under our bill of rights, he will eventually lose the right of citizenship by exportation or by a decree of death. It was Adam's act of unrighteousness that placed the human family under a divine death decree.

This decree after the fall is recorded: **"As it is written there is none righteous** [legal for life]**, no not one; there is none that understands** [their condition]**, there is none** [of their own] **that seeks after God.** They are all gone out of the way, they are together become unprofitable, there is none that doeth good, no not one." "For all have sinned and fallen short of the glory (righteousness) of God (Psalm 97:6) for the wages of sin is death." Unrighteousness is man's condition before God, a state of being that will only lead to the death of any man who fails in his lifetime to seek first the kingdom of God and his righteousness (heaven's bill of rights), and all of life's privileges will be add unto you (Romans 3:23; 6:23; Matthew 6:33).

We are all in a terrible condition here on Planet Earth. We are all under the dominion of sin, Satan, and his cohorts unto the destruction of all humanity and this planet. About 6,000 years ago the devil acquired us out of the hands of Jesus by deception (Genesis 1-7; Luke 4:6). It's amazing to see from the study of God's Word how Jesus came here as a baby two thousand years ago. He lived in human nature that needed redeeming for thirty-three years (Galatians 4:4, 5) without sinning mentally, morally, physically, or spiritually, to produce the *bill of rights* Adam lost by his willful sinful transgression. Then Jesus died to provide, for each one of us, **a** *death certificate with our name on it, a bill of sale for all our sins,* and finally a passport, *a rite of passage* from citizenship of this sinful world, to citizenship in Christ's heavenly kingdom (Philippians 3:20). Then, the Bible says, he rose from the dead and went to heaven as our advocate, our lawyer in the judgment hour of Revelation 14:6, 7 and Daniel 7:9-14 (see also Acts 17:31; Hebrews 9:27; 2 Corinthians 5:10). There He provides everything the principles of God's eternal code of conduct demands from each one of us at judgment time, in order for us to have the right to live forever with Jesus in His future kingdom (Exodus 20:1-17).

It's vital to understand Jesus did not commit any act which God said "thou shall not" (Genesis 2:17; Exodus 20:15), nor did He steal or manipulate His principles of righteousness in order to redeem man back out of the hands of the great deceiver (Luke 4:6; 2 Timothy 2:26). He paid the ultimate price to redeem man without breaking one principle of His divine code of conduct (Exodus 20:1-17) and in return was granted the right to redeem, reclaim, and restore man and Planet Earth to its original state in the future (Revelation 21:1), a race and planet He already owned by creation (John 1:10).

~ *Chapter Two* ~
The Gospel: The Remedy
for Sin After the Fall

The Fall

"And when the woman saw that the tree was good for food, and that it was pleasant to the eyes, and a tree to be desired to make one wise, she took *(thou shall not)* of the fruit thereof, and did eat, and gave also unto her husband with her; and he did eat. And the **eyes of them both were opened, and they knew that they were naked** and they sewed fig leaves together and made themselves aprons" (Genesis 3:6, 7). From Genesis through Revelation, the principle application of the word *naked* applies to man's condition after the fall. To be naked means to be void of divine righteousness, void of any rights to life before God, void of any legal standing as children and citizens of God's heavenly kingdom.

"And they knew that they were naked" applies not only to their physical condition after the fall, but to the new characteristic of being or nature of their human heart. This act of becoming naked represents a state of *not only being in unrighteousness, but being unrighteous*, in an unrighteous state of mind, character, personality, and immoral nature of being. When Adam sinned, he became contentious and suspicious, a being with a self-centered nature defined as cunning, crafty, and sly from the heart. He acquired a destructive nature bent towards one's own unrighteous, sinful, self-centered desires and passions that became part of his human heart, and the heart of his future descendants (Mark 7:20-23).

The Results

Immediately after their fall from righteousness, Adam and Eve's nature revealed itself through accusations of one another and even accusing God of bearing some responsibility for their actions (Genesis 3:11-13). It's not difficult to understand why we do what we do if we believe that after Adam sinned, man's heart became "deceitful above all things, and desperately wicked, who can know it" (Jeremiah 17:9).

In our day, as the restraining power of the Holy Spirit is gradually being withdrawn, the reality of what is in the hearts of men is now again being fully materialized as it was in the days of Noah (Matthew 24:37), which is directly attributable to the withdrawal of the Holy Spirit at the time of Adam's sin. Jesus said, "That which cometh out of the man, that defiles the man. For from within, out of the heart of men, proceed evil thoughts, adulteries, fornications, murders. Thefts, covetousness, wickedness, deceit, lasciviousness, an evil eye, blasphemy, pride and foolishness: All these evil things come from within, and defile the man" (Mark 7:20-23).

When Adam sinned, the law of God, which is the code of conduct that governs life in the universe, demanded a complete judicial withdrawal of man's divine right to life. This left man not only with the knowledge of sin but with the destructive nature of sin. Not only was man now in a complete self-destructive mode towards himself, he would also have this withering nature towards all his surroundings. He had fallen under the standards of the positive and negative demands of God's governing judicial principles, God's universal divine code of conduct the Ten Commandments.

After the fall, these ten governing universal principles demanded from Adam the removal of heaven's bill of rights, afforded to him and his posterity at creation with all its righteous benefits. In yielding to the temptations of the adversary of souls (Genesis 3:1-7), Adam now knew "that to whom ye yield yourselves servants to obey, his servants ye are to whom ye obey; whether of sin unto death, or of obedience to righteousness" (Romans 6:16). When Adam sinned and lost our bill of rights to life, the ultimate judgment for his offense was given. "And unto Adam he said, Because thou hast hearkened unto the voice of thy wife, and hast eaten of the tree, of which I commanded thee, saying, Thou shall not eat of it: cursed is the ground for thy sake; in sorrow shall thou eat of it all the days of thy life; In the sweat of thy face shall thou eat bread, *till thou return unto the ground;* for out of it was thou taken: for dust thou art, and unto dust shall thou return" (Genesis 3:17-19).

Wherefore, as by one man sin entered into the world, and death by sin; and **so death passed upon all men,** for that all have sinned (Romans 5:12). After the ultimate judgment for man's transgression was given, the full and immediate penalty for the wages of sin was not **immediately** executed ("the wages of sin is death") (Romans 6:23). It's important to understand that "the Lord Jesus Christ is the same yesterday and today and forever" (Hebrews 13:8). "Keeping mercy for thousands, forgiving iniquity, transgression and sin, and that will by no means clear the *guilty*" (Exodus 34:7). When Adam fell from righteousness, and Planet Earth lost her heavenly bill of rights, God's eternal plan to save the human family from the fall was instated (Revelation 13:8). Although the death penalty was delayed in man's fall from divine righteousness, everything would change and begin a downward destructive journey. The earth and all its inhabitants, along with nature, would suffer under the curse of sin.

With the sentencing of Adam, God universally revealed and instated the **plan of salvation, the gospel** for Planet Earth. *"And I will put en-mity between thee and the woman, and between thy seed and her seed; it (Jesus Christ) shall bruise thy head, and thou (Satan) shall bruise his heel"* (Genesis 3:15). When Adam sinned, he unknowingly chose a nature at to-tal enmity (hatred and antagonism) with the character and will of God. This united the human family in complete harmony with the rebellion that began in heaven (Revelation 12:7). In order to save mankind through the plan of salvation, the same degree of enmity attributed in man towards God by sin was now placed in man by Jesus towards Satan and his confed-eracy, who at that time inherited dominion over Planet Earth (Luke 4:6).

This enmity would place the human family in the middle of the great controversy between Christ and Satan. In this position all, in their proba-tionary lifetime, may of their own free will individually chose life or death, Christ or Satan, righteousness or unrighteousness. The gospel, given after the fall, is everything to us. It must be understood in the light of what it cost God to save mankind and educate the universe (Ephesians 3:10) about the malignancy and nature of sin. The gospel, the good news *of and about* Jesus Christ, has always had a specific definition according to the testi-mony afforded us by the apostle Paul, expressed in his letters to the early Christian Church. In defining the mystery of the gospel (Ephesians 6:19), Paul makes it vitally clear that the gospel has a specific order of reception of faith to them who choose to "obtain like precious faith through the righ-teousness of God and our savor Jesus Christ. Vital for the *beginning of one's walk of faith, from faith to faith,* a mystery today still vague to many believ-ers (Romans 1:16, 17; Colossians 1:5; 2 Peter 1:1, 2).

The Truth of the Gospel

In his narrative presenting the mystery of the gospel, Paul is very specific in his recorded statements applying to *"**the truth of the gospel of Christ.**"* In Colossians 1:5 he is definite about hearing *"**the truth of the gospel.**"* In Galatians 2:14 he is insistent about walking in *"**the truth of the gospel.**"* In Galatians 2:5 he is emphatic about continuing in *"**the truth of the gospel.**"* And finally in Ephesians 1:13 he is absolute about the *"**word of truth, gospel of your salvation.**"* These texts imply a distinct and spe-cific truth about the gospel message; one must *hear, walk, continue and stay absolute* in its meaning, power and purpose, which is imperative to our salvation. Paul said, "Though we, or an angel from heaven, preach any other gospel to you than that which we have preached to you, let him be accursed" (Galatians 1:8), thereby signifying a direct and specific meaning to be conveyed as the gospel.

Do you ever wonder why there are so many different denominations and gospel theories in our day? The **truth of the gospel** produced by Jesus Christ was being perverted, the apostle Paul said in the early Christian church (Galatians 1:7). Paul penned to the Corinthian church, "For I am jealous over you with godly jealousy: for I have espoused you to one husband that I may present you as a chaste virgin to Christ. But I fear, lest by any means, as the serpent beguiled Eve through his subtlety, so your minds should be corrupted from the simplicity that is in Christ. For if he that cometh preaches another Jesus, whom we have not preached, or if ye receive another spirit, which ye have not received, or another gospel, which ye have not accepted, ye might well bear with him" (2 Corinthians 11:2-4).

It is here, Paul says, as Satan beguiled Eve on the issue pertaining to our life-giving righteousness, our bill of rights as citizens of God's universal kingdom, that the central attack for man's redemption takes place. Jesus said, in Matthew 24:14, "**And this gospel** of the kingdom **shall be preached in all the world,** for a witness unto all nations; **and then shall the end come,**" knowing that the truth of the gospel from his time to ours would be perverted by the adversary of souls, but restored to its proper meaning and representation just before Jesus comes again in the clouds of heaven.

There are three distinct verses in scripture defining the truth of the gospel according to the apostle Paul: Romans 1:16, 17; Galatians 2:14-16, and Galatians 3:8. The first, in Romans 1:16, 17, says, "**For I am not ashamed of the gospel of Christ: for it is the power of God unto salvation to everyone that believeth; to the Jew first, and also to the Greek.**" It is here the apostle Paul defines the gospel as *the Power of God unto salvation.* For in the gospel we find what God needs to save us because of Adam's fall, which is the "righteousness of God" (Romans 1:17). Secondly, in Galatians 2:14-16, Paul communicates to Peter that it's the "truth of the gospel that justifies a man or makes a man just before God." Also, in his letter to the Galatians, Paul teaches that God "preached before the gospel to Abraham" (Galatians 3:8), in order that the heathen, the nations around him, would be blessed through the gospel message of life-giving righteousness.

It is in these three scriptures that Paul teaches what the gospel is, says, and does. In scripture, salvation is defined in many different ways. Here we see that what saves us is the gospel; but who saves us, scripture says, is the Lord Jesus Christ. So, what is the difference between Jesus, the man of salvation, and the gospel, the product of salvation? The difference is this: **Jesus is the *who*; *the man* or *personification* of righteousness that produced the gospel** and **the gospel is *the power* or *product* of Christ's all-important atonement.** Did not Jesus come here two thousand years ago and produce what the gospel is? Could Jesus, in his feeding of the five thousand, feed the multitude if He did not produce the food they needed? The truth of the gospel that saves us was produced by the life, death, and resurrection of Jesus Christ. It's not difficult to see why the dragon voice in Jesus' day tried to kill baby Jesus shortly after His birth, knowing what Jesus had to produce in order to save each one of us (Revelation 12:4; Matthew 2:13).

The gospel or atonement for man's salvation, or the product for saving man, was in three phases. The Bible makes clear that Jesus lived a perfect life without sinning mentally, morally, physically, or spiritually, for every second, every minute, every hour, of every day of his entire human life (1 John 3:4; Hebrews 4:15). In this first phase of the atonement, Jesus, by his righteous life, produced for all of us a heavenly robe of divine righteousness, a *bill of rights* that Adam took from us at the fall (Genesis 3:6). Did not Jesus say He had finished "the work," the first phase of the atonement, just before His hour of trial had come in the garden of Gethsemane (John 17:4)? In Matthew 5:17, Jesus said that He had come not to destroy the law but to fulfill its entire demands placed on man because of Adam's sin. The Ten Commandments are God's written code of conduct that Adam violated when he participated with Eve in eating of the forbidden fruit of the tree of knowledge of good and evil (Genesis 3:2-6).

The "thou shall not" (Genesis 2:17; 3:3; Exodus 20:1-17) given to Adam and Eve at creation because of Adam's sin have positive and negative demands on each one of us, necessary to reinstate us as sons and daughters of God and citizens of Christ's heavenly kingdom (Matthew 6:33; Romans 5:9-11; Philippians 3:20). Jesus came to produce for us a perfect character in righteousness, exemplifying the divine code of conduct fulfilling the first positive phase of the atonement for man. The first stipulation in heaven's code of conduct necessitates for our reinstatement into God's divine kingdom is a heavenly bill of rights, the judicial heavenly deed of righteousness Adam willfully, deliberately, and knowingly threw away shortly after creation (Genesis 3:6; 1 Timothy 2:14).

Friend, do you truly want to go to heaven and live forever in Christ's heavenly kingdom? Paul says that outside of the divine righteousness of Christ—that is, without Christ's righteousness, heaven's judicial bill of rights—we are aliens from the commonwealth of what constitutes the covenant of promise; we have no hope, and are without God in the world (Ephesians 2:12). The kingdoms and nations of this world are about to come to their prophetic end, and any man, woman, or child who fails to appropriate the full components of Christ's atonement cannot stand and cannot enter into heaven when Jesus comes again (Revelation 6:17). We complain that immigrants are always coming into our country without first being naturalized, adopted, or established as citizens, because they have no rights. This same condition applies to all of us when it comes to man having the right to enter God's universal kingdom. No naturalization into the kingdom of God and His righteousness in our lifetime (Matthew 6:33) means no legal judicial right to enter Christ's kingdom when He comes the second time in righteousness (Revelation 19:11).

The atonement Jesus produced for us is complete in providing for all what is necessary to receive the right to eternal life, from Adam's time to the last baby born just before Jesus returns the second time. *By His perfect life of obedience (Hebrews 5:8, 9), Jesus produced the bill of rights God and heaven demands from us to become sons and daughters of God, in order to become legal citizens of God's glorious kingdom.* This divine bill of rights, the righteousness of Christ, must be appropriated by every man, woman, and child in order for God to accept any obedience whatsoever. No commandment-keeping, even in its purity of behavior, is legally acceptable outside of Christ, our righteousness. Paul says, "When we were enemies, we were reconciled to God by the death of his Son, much more, being reconciled, **we shall be saved by his life**" (Romans 5:10). We are saved first by the righteous life of Christ, not just by his death; as so many have this misconception of the plan of salvation. The death of Christ is the secondary phase of the atonement and has different applications pertaining to our salvation. It is through Jesus' righteous life we are officially authorized in righteousness.

Scripture describes for us Christ's terrible agony as a human in his ordeal in the Garden of Gethsemane as He enters into the second phase of the atonement. There He must, for the glory of God and all of mankind, make the most troubling decision of His human life. "**For he hath made him to be sin for us,** who knew no sin; that we might be made the righteousness of God in Him (2 Corinthians 5:21). In this critical hour for Jesus and mankind He must, as a human being, and of His own free will, choose to produce for man the penalty and wages for sin (Romans 6:23). It is here, because of Adam's sin, Jesus must satisfy the two negative demands of God's law placed on us by Adam's sin. First, by His death He must produce a *death certificate* for the human race (Galatians 2:20), and second, a *bill of sale* for the sin of the world (John 1:29). Can you imagine how holy and demanding the law of God is (Exodus 20:1-17; Matthew 5:17-20)? They are the principles that define God's character and govern the standard of life in His universal kingdom. Of these principles He cannot and will not compromise in their requirement.

It is not difficult to see why Paul says, "Wherefore the law is holy, and the commandment holy, just, and good" (Romans 7:12). It was in the garden of Gethsemane that the human nature of Jesus was so severely pressed by the terror of the conflict that it convulsed as drops of blood protruded from his body (Luke 22: 43, 44). I believe we will forever study, and probably never completely understand, the nature of this part of the atonement. How broad are its concepts to understand. It was in the garden of Gethsemane that Jesus cried out in anguish, "Abba, Father," and willingly **chose to accept for each one of us imputed transgression** (Mark 14:35; Luke 22:42, 43). There He committed himself to supply everything the sinner needs to be saved from the time of Adam's transgression (1 Timothy 2:14).

This He chose to accept in order to save every child born from the time of Adam, consciously knowing He must suffer a terrible death and be separated from the presence of his Eternal Father. Friends, when Jesus went through the experience of Gethsemane and died for us on that cruel cross, he produced for us:

1. A death certificate with our name on it (Galatians 2:20).

2. A bill of sale for the sins of the world (1 Corinthians 15:3; Isaiah 29:16)

How wonderful is the truth of the gospel, defined in the New Testament and telling us how breathtaking Jesus is! Why is it that in this generation, when Jesus is just about to come, that the **"truth of the gospel"** is so misinterpreted and the people of the world are left in a stupor as to its beauty? I believe there are too many ministers in the Christian church educated only to communicate the death of Jesus. As important and central as it is, that message alone is lacking in the complete understanding of what the gospel provides through the ministry of Christ's life, death, and resurrection. The plan of salvation requires an understanding of, and an application of, each aspect of Christ's ministry (2 Thessalonians 1:7, 8).

The Bible says that in this generation the final gospel message, called the **"everlasting gospel"** (Revelation 14:6, 7), is calling this world to understand the judgment hour message of Daniel 7:9-14, a judgment that comes upon this final generation as it did in Noah's day when only eight souls were saved by water (1 Peter 3:20). Why? Because they knew not the time of their visitation as did the generation at the time of the first coming of Christ (Luke 19:44). This final gospel message calls for our generation to *fear God*, and *give glory to him*; for the hour of *His judgment* is come; and worship *Him* that made heaven and earth and the seas (Revelation 14:6, 7) in the light of the glorious gospel of Christ (2 Timothy 1:8-10).

How can this everlasting gospel concept of fear, glory, judgment, and worship be conveyed and understood by this final generation when the concept of what the gospel **is, says,** and **does** is not fully defined by the ministry and understood by the members constituting the Christian church? Through the definite article of the **"truth of the gospel"** (Galatians 2:5, 2:14; Colossians 1:5; Ephesians 1:13), God can call man what he is not, in order to save him from what he is. O, how we should endeavor to search for the riches of the goodness, forbearance, and longsuffering of God. It would not take long for humanity to understand the true concept of what constitutes true repentance (Romans 2:4).

Friends, we must understand especially in this final generation the wonderful merits of the Gospel of Christ.

Christ's faithful life produced for us:

1. A bill of rights for all mankind (2 Timothy 4:8).

2. Our new title or identity as children of God (John 1:12).

3. A judicial right to be saved by grace through the righteousness of Christ (Romans 5:1, 2, 21; 2 Peter 1:1, 2).

4. The right to be sealed with the Holy Spirit (John 3:5-8; Ephesians 1:13; 4:30).

5. The right to repentance and acceptance in the judgment hour (Daniel 7:9-13; Acts 17:30, 31; Revelation 14:6, 7).

By His faithful death Jesus produced:

6. A death certificate in our name (Galatians 2:20).

7. Peace with our Heavenly Father through the shedding of the blood on His cross (Colossians 1:20).

8. A bill of sale for all our sins (1 Corinthians 15:1-3; 1 Peter 1:18, 19).

9. Justification by faith through the imputed righteousness of Christ that covers the sins of the World. (Romans 4:1-8; John 15:22; 1 John 1:9; 2:1-2)

By His Resurrection Jesus produced:

10. **An advocate with the Father at judgment time (Daniel 7:9-14; 8:14; Revelation 14:6, 7).**

Justifying for us the rite of passage or a passport into the kingdom of God when Jesus comes again (Hebrews 4:14; 1 Thessalonians 4:13-16; 2 Peter 1:11; 1 John 2:1).

In order to produce these ten wonderful merits of the atonement, Scripture defines an authoritative expression vital to the production of man's justification unto life, called "the power of God," which identifies Christ, the cross, and the gospel as three distinct but *not* separate subjects in understanding the atonement and plan of salvation.

- First, the Bible says Christ is called *"the power of God"* (1 Corinthians 1:24).

- Second, centrally and accordingly, the cross is called *"the power of God"* (1 Corinthians 1:18).

- Third, and accordingly, the gospel is called *"the power of God unto salvation"* (Romans 1:16).

Unequivocally, Jesus, the primary figure in understanding the power of God in the restoration of man, must first of all be believed (Acts 16:31), received (John 1:12), and obeyed (Hebrews 5:9), especially in light of His universal position as God, *the power of God unto salvation*. Secondly, the cross, the central figure and wonder of the atonement, the fundamental central factor of the *power of God*, will forever be the subject of amazement and study by the redeemed throughout all of eternity. And third, the gospel theme of accredited or imputed life-giving righteousness is the *power of God*, the product of Jesus' life, death, and resurrection in the salvation of man, and is emphatically the cleansing power of God that will ever safeguard and rid the universe from the malignancy of Satan and sin.

My friends, Jesus, the cross, the gospel, the "power of God" unto salvation," manifested for our reinstatement as sons and daughters of God, are altogether critical in the plan of salvation, and must be understood and presented collectively to the believer in Christ, our life-giving righteousness.

The life and death of Jesus, which are the first two phases of our gospel atonement, are indispensable together, but they would be of no value to us unless we understand what the final phase of what the gospel provides in light of Christ's resurrection. Remember, Paul said, "that Jesus Christ of the seed of David was raised from the dead *according to my gospel* (2 Timothy 2:8). Friends, is Jesus in heaven? Does the Bible say He was resurrected and taken to heaven? Paul says *He is seated at the right hand of God* (Hebrews 8:1, 2) and is the only high priest who can morally offer to our Heavenly Father the merits of the atonement, necessary for our salvation in again establishing us as citizens of God's heavenly kingdom. The scriptures say Jesus "was delivered for our offenses, and *was raised again for our justification*" (Romans 4:25). When Jesus died and was resurrected He was taken to heaven to justify us (to make us right) with the indispensable merits (intrinsic value) of His atonement. He is our representative, high priest, judge, lawyer, and our only advocate acceptable with the Father. The apostle John says, "My little children, these things I write unto you, that ye sin not. And if any man sin, we *have an advocate with the Father*, Jesus Christ the righteous" (1 John 2:1).

It is vitally critical for all of us to recognize that God is so Holy, so pure, so undeniably divine and morally righteous in character and purpose. And we so undeniably immoral and unrighteous that even when we try to speak to Him in sincerity of heart our words and motives are so defiled with sin that they are scripturally declared immoral and unacceptable (Jeremiah 17:9; Mark 7:20-23). Isaiah says, "But your iniquities have separated between you and your God, and your sins have hid His face from you, that He will not hear" (Isaiah 59:2). The resurrection of Christ according to gospel order (2 Timothy 2:8) is all inclusive in the gospel commission of Christ (Matthew 28:19, 20). And because of man's fallen condition (Romans 3:23), God the Father cannot and will not accept our petitions but through all the divine merits of Jesus Christ's life-giving atonement (Romans 5:11), necessary for every aspect of our salvation.

It is only through the righteous hands of Jesus (1 John 2:1), the only righteous man defined in scripture as the only "name under heaven given among men, whereby we must be saved" (Acts 4:12). Nothing petitioned outside of Christ, our life-giving righteousness, can be or will be acceptable in the judgment hour message of Revelation 14:6, 7; Acts 17:31; Daniel 9:7-14. But many will have "not sought the Lord nor inquired of Him" (Zephaniah 1:6), but have chosen to reside in iniquity, their present state of unrighteousness (Matthew 7:20-23).

⌁ *Chapter Three* ⌁
The Gospel Commission

The theme of the atonement, the great gospel commission given to the apostles at the end of Jesus' ministry (Matthew 28:19), was never predestined to present salvation by just a name or a title suitable to the God-man Jesus Christ. The name Jesus Christ is characterized as "Jehovah saves the anointed one," the only name associated with the cross and the truth of the gospel; the only name under heaven given among men, whereby we must be saved (Acts 4:12). However, the adversary of souls, "he that deceives the whole world" (Revelation 12:9), uses this as the only factor in the gospel message to formulate unbiblical gospel fabrications. Just because one believes in the name of Jesus, or accepts the name of Jesus, or calls upon the name of the Lord, does not biblically constitute one's salvation. Jesus was specific when He said to His apostles, "Go ye into the entire world, and preach the gospel to every creature" (Mark 16:15).

It took our Savior three and one half years to educate and train twelve men in these wonderful truths of the gospel, and it was only after His death and resurrection that they understood its power, peace, and purpose. Then, and only then, did they unite to share its wonderful truths (Acts 2:1). Jesus said, "Go preach the gospel to every creature teaching them what the gospel *is*, what the gospel *says* and what the gospel *does*" (Mark 16:15), thus making the disciples officially authorized apostles. They were disciplined and qualified in the truth of the gospel and in gospel order, so that they could teach everyone who was willing to observe all the things He commanded them (Matthew 28:19). Jesus told His disciples that as they brought the gospel of peace in His name, they were officially authorized by the Father to convey the same gospel peace after His resurrection (Romans 10:15; John 20:21).

They were officially authorized to remit or retain the sins of man under the merits of the gospel of Christ, under heaven's bill of rights into justification by faith, to restore humanity through the product of the atonement, as citizens of Christ's heavenly kingdom (John 20:23). Jesus said that everyone who comes to Him of their own freewill has the right to confess his sins to Him according to gospel order and heaven's bill of rights on a continual basis for the salvation of his soul. Jesus, the only begotten Son of God, was authorized before the foundation of the world to be the Savior of the world. He lived a perfect life as a son of man and was justified in heaven's court room (John 5:22-27) after His resurrection, to forgive all that come to Him for life (1 John 1:9). Jesus is telling us that He knows our infirmities and has passed through all the temptations the adversary of souls can assail upon us. He has made a way of escape for every trial (Hebrews 4:15). Then Jesus sent His apostles to invite the world to believe and obey the truth of the gospel, and He would fill all that believed with the same fullness of the Holy Spirit that He gave His disciples after His resurrection (John 20:14-21).

Can you imagine Paul's enthusiasm when he said, "Let us therefore **come boldly to the throne of grace** that we may obtain mercy, and find grace to help in time of need" (Hebrews 4:16). But be sure, friends, back then the gospel commission demanded obedience to the gospel by getting into the water (Mark 16:16; 1 Peter 3:21). Only those who believed and obeyed the gospel by being baptized (Galatians 3:26, 27; Colossians 2:10-13) could truly claim Christianity through the life-giving merits of the atonement of Christ, the intrinsic value of:

Jesus Christ, the power of God (1 Corinthians 1:24)

The Cross, the power of God (1 Corinthians 1:18)

The Gospel, the power of God (Romans 1:16)

Jesus Christ scripturally produced for us the ten wonderful merits of our atonement in order to save us from our unrighteous condition (Romans 3:10). "Therefore [in light of], being justified by faith, we have peace with God through our Lord Jesus Christ" (Romans 5:1). Justification is the product of the merits of our Lord and Savior's atonement, "**by whom also we have access by faith into this grace** wherein we stand. And rejoice in the hope of the glory [righteousness] of God" (Romans 5:2). Friends, the truth of the gospel is not just to believe in a name given to the son of God. The name Jesus also represents what we must be in character, to be accepted, and have the rights to life in the kingdom of God. Some preach Jesus, some grace, some faith, and some the cross. The Bible uses these different words as opening doors in our understanding of critical points of salvations.

However, many in past generations have not understood these concepts illustrated in scripture, and there are many believers who have never seen scripture. In the judgment, Jesus will decide and "wink at" the sincere believer who down through the ages did not know and did not have access to these specific truths of the gospel, but were drawn and convicted by the Holy Spirit into understanding and maintaining the only righteousness they knew in their lifetime (Acts 17:30).

Paul said, "For not the hearers of the law *are* just before God, but the doers of the law shall be justified. For when the Gentiles, which have not the law, do by nature the things contained in the law, these, having not the law, are a law to themselves: Which show the work of the law written in their hearts, their conscience also bearing witness, and their thoughts the mean while accusing or else excusing one another *in the day when God shall judge the secrets of men by Jesus Christ according to my gospel*" (Romans 2:13-16). Especially will the Christian church of the last two millennia of Earth's history be judged accordingly, who predominantly, with the scriptures in her hand, failed to present and maintain these specific gospel truths given to us in Jesus' day.

"Now if any man build upon this foundation [**the gospel of Christ**], gold, silver, precious stones, wood, hay, stubble; **Every man's work shall be made manifest**: for the day shall declare it, because it shall be revealed by fire; and the fire shall try [test] every man's work of what sort it is" (1 Corinthians 3:12, 15).

GOSPEL ORDER

The foundation of the gospel of Christ is biblically defined in three progressive judicial or legal principles in the institution of gospel order in the orderly process of establishing a believer in the "truth of the gospel" (Colossians 1:5; Ephesians 1:13; Galatians 2:14, 5).

The first and primary principle in gospel order the apostle Paul defines as *faith* (Hebrews 11:1-3, 6) or the "*law of faith*" (Romans 3:27) which must be obeyed (Romans1:5; 16:26) by the believer in Christ.

The second is *righteousness by faith*, or what the apostle Paul defines as the "*law of righteousness*" (Romans 9:31, 32), which also must be obeyed (Romans 1:5; 16:26).

The third is *justification by faith* (Romans 5:1), God's official declaration of the Christian's standing as a born-again child of God, a citizen (Philippians 3:20), heir to the kingdom of God (Matthew 6:33).

Gospel order must be understood in light of man's moral fall from righteousness, his present state of unrighteousness as Paul defines *"there is none righteous, no, not one" (Romans 3:10)*. This means man has no rights, no righteousness, to be anything, to do anything, or to have any say in anything in any part of the universe, which creatively belongs to God and God alone (Psalm 50:10-13).

Righteousness by faith

Unless man by faith believes, receives, accepts and obeys what God defines and demands as life-giving righteousness, man will continue to be immoral (unrighteous) in his probationary lifetime and must eventually be eradicated from life.

Please understand righteousness is what Jesus Christ is, has, says, and does in light of his godliness, holiness, righteousness, and divine oneness with the Father of the universe (John 10:30). According to scripture the right to eternal life is only derived and sustained through the creative and redemptive activity of Jesus the living Christ, by Jesus Christ, through Jesus Christ, Lord (*Supreme Authority, Creator, Controller, God, Master*) of the universe. In order for man to have the right to eternal life in God's universal kingdom he must believe, and receive the righteousness of Christ (Philippians 3:9) as his sole *bill of rights* to life in the kingdom of God (Matthew 5:20, 6:33; Philippians 3:8-11).

Justification by Faith

Justification by faith, the next principle in line with righteousness by faith, is critical to the believer's understanding of God's plan of salvation. The word justification means to be acquitted or in a state of acquittal. Released, set free, *made right with God*, just, justified or *innocent of unrighteousness* in God's eyes. Only because Jesus Christ came two thousand years ago as a man and produced everything God's principles of life (*God's code of being, nature, and conduct*) demands from us because of Adam's sin can we be justified. In simple words, a Christian is justified by faith or is under the covering of justification by faith (Romans 5:1) when they first believe, receive, accept, and obey the gospel message of righteousness by faith into justification by faith. The believer is justified as a newborn (born again) child of God, a new citizen of Christ's heavenly kingdom (Philippians 3:20). Unless one is established in righteousness by faith into justification by faith, mankind has no legal right to eternal life. Isaiah said, "In righteousness shall thou be established ... this is the heritage of the servants of the Lord and their righteousness is of me, saith the Lord (Isaiah 54:14, 17).

The biblical foundation of the gospel message in every age from Adam to the present everlasting gospel message of Revelation 14:6, 7 is:

1. "Faith" which must be obeyed (Romans 1:5; 16:26)
into
2. Righteousness by faith, which also must be obeyed
into
3. Justification by faith, which also must be obeyed

This was produced by Christ's life, death, and resurrection in a signed and sealed gospel covenant agreement in compliance with gospel order.

Many today have no concept of gospel order, claiming salvation by faith alone. Ask the apostle Peter if salvation is by faith alone? He will gladly tell you that real faith, *"precious faith," is only obtained "through the righteousness of God and our Savior Jesus Christ" (2 Peter 1:1)*. Paul's statements to Christians apply as much today to the ministry as it did in his day. There is a great injustice being done to the gospel, to the atonement produced for us by Jesus Christ; a great injustice is being done to the truth of the gospel and to the people hungering and thirsting for life-giving righteousness (Matthew 5:6).The apostle Paul made it very clear that many in his day as well as ours would become "false apostles, deceitful workers, transforming themselves into the apostles of Christ. And no marvel; for Satan himself is transformed into an angel of light. Therefore it is no great thing if **his ministers also be transformed as the ministers of righteousness;** whose end shall be according to their works" (2 Corinthians 11:13-15).

Many in this generation are presenting a fabricated gospel, defining salvation through just the name of Jesus as one's sole right to salvation (Acts 16:31). Others point to the death of Jesus alone as the only critical product of the atonement that saves mankind, pointing to His shed blood without reflecting on His life-giving achievements or the merits produced for our right to life. They present only a few merits of the atonement, while denying or leaving the atonement not half understood by most members in the church. It's not difficult to understand why Jesus said, "Take heed that no man deceive you. For many will come in my name, saying, I am Christ [*I am Christian*] and will deceive many" (Matthew 24:4, 5).

"My people are destroyed for lack of knowledge: because thou hast rejected knowledge, I will also reject thee, that thou shall be no priest to me: seeing thou hast forgotten the law of thy God, I will also forget thy children (Hosea 4:6). When Jesus comes, Paul says *only those who know God biblically and are obeying the truth of the gospel will be saved.* "And to you who are troubled rest with us when the Lord Jesus shall be revealed from heaven with his mighty angels, in flaming fire **taking vengeance on them**

that know not God, and that **obey not the gospel** of our Lord Jesus Christ" (2 Thessalonians 1:7, 8).

Friend, do you know the specific truths about the gospel of Jesus Christ, in order that you might stand in His presence when He comes the second time (Revelation 6:17)? It's critical to test everything by the Bible; it is not safe to trust your salvation to any denomination or any man, and that especially includes me.

Do you really know Jesus biblically?
Jesus as Creator (Hebrews 1:1-3)

Jesus as God (John 1:1-10)

Jesus as Councilor (Genesis 4:6)

Jesus as the Great I Am (Exodus 3:13, 14; John 8:58)

Jesus the Lawgiver (Exodus 20:1-17; John 14:14; 1 John 2:3, 4)

Jesus as Lord (Romans 1:3)

Jesus as Redeemer (Galatians 4:4, 5)

Jesus as Mediator (1 John 2:1)

Jesus as Commandment Keeper (John 15:10)

Jesus as King of kings and Lord of lords (Revelation 17:16)

Do you know the "truth of the gospel" message the apostle Paul defines as "my gospel," "that gospel which I preach among the gentiles?" (Romans 2:16; 16:25; Galatians 2:2; 2 Timothy 2:8.)

The apostle Paul says, "The gospel of Christ is the power of God unto salvation"

Revealing
"The righteousness of God"

From
"Faith to faith"

From
Righteousness by faith into justification by faith
(Romans 1:16, 17)

Revealing the righteousness Jesus needs in the judgment to justify (or make right) before God the children of His heavenly kingdom. (Psalm 9:8; John 1:12; Romans 3:26; Acts 17:31; 2 Corinthians 5:10)

Today we have many churches, many ministries, and many confusing gospel denominations; it's been that way since the reformation of the six-teenth century became stagnant (Revelation 3:8-10). It's not scriptural that any church can claim to preach the truth of the gospel unless they biblically understand and present the mystery of the gospel revealed to us by the apostle Paul, hidden to many from the foundation of the world (Galatians 1:11, 12; Ephesians 3:4, 5; Colossians 1:25-29). No church can convert a church member or unbeliever without the *truth that defines what the gospel is, says, and does,* in justifying an individual to stand in the day of Christ (Revelation 6:17).

It is biblical that God has a church in this generation; He calls her the remnant church (Revelation 12:17). But even this last-day remnant, the end-time representative of the church produced in Jesus' day, can't justify anyone unless the "truth of the gospel" is totally conveyed in one unit-ed gospel tone of *righteousness by faith into justification by faith.* Paul says it is "God that does the justifying," or makes a person right with God (Romans 8:33). How can the truth of the gospel be conveyed to the world just before Jesus comes when the representative members of the church do not, together in the same mind and in the same judgment, speak the same thing (1 Corinthians 1:10) when it comes to obeying the gospel in order to be justified (*made right*) by faith into the imputed righteousness of Christ in order to be saved when he comes again (2 Thessalonians 1:7, 8).

The church is only the boat that carries the passengers who have pass-ports and gospel rights to be on the vessel heading towards the promised land. The church is responsible that the passengers have the right creden-tials based on gospel order before anyone has the right to board the vessel. **Every generation since the time of Adam has had a sign of faith based on the present truth in order to get into the gospel boat of justified be-lievers** (2 Peter 1:10-12), along with a seal of imputed righteousness in order to get into heaven when Jesus comes the second time. Scripture is very clear that the baby Christian church in Jesus' day only allowed justi-fied believers who obeyed the *present truth* of the gospel (Mark 16:15, 16) to enter the church and then, and only then, "the Lord added to the church daily such as should be saved" (Acts 2:38-47).

Being born an Israelite, being born a Christian in the household of faith, being born in any faith or denomination, will not justify anyone in approaching and obtaining the merits of our crucified and risen Savior. The unrighteous act of Adam's transgression is a testimony to all genera-tions as to what God demands from all of us, as well as all created beings, under the inflexible principles of God's divine government. God's law of righteousness, the principles defining His divine character, have never, can never, and will never be changed (Exodus 20.1-17). *"Jesus Christ the same yesterday, and today, and forever"* (Malachi 3:6; Hebrews 13:8).

After Adam sinned and received the judgment for his willful transgression, Jesus conveyed to him the plan of salvation (Romans 5:12). Scripture says that the Lord said to the serpent, Satan, "And I will put enmity between thee, and the woman, [the church] (2 Corinthians 11:1-3) and between thy seed [unrighteousness] and her seed [Christ our righteousness] (Galatians 3:16), it shall bruise thy head, and thou shall bruise his heel (Genesis 3:15). And then the Lord God [Jesus Christ] made coats of skins and clothed Adam and Eve (Genesis 3:21) with a covering of imputed righteousness in order to save them and someday present them *faultless* before the presence of His glory (Jude 24). For they, and all that respond to gospel order in their lifetime, will be found *without fault* before the throne of God at judgment time (Revelation 14:7).

Now is the time to understand our condition before God and take the necessary steps demanded by God for our salvation. Paul says, "Wherefore, my beloved, as ye have always obeyed, not as in my presence only, but now much more in my absence, *work out your own salvation with fear and trembling*, For it is God which works in you both to will and to do of his good pleasure" (Philippians 2:12, 13). Just before Paul is about to close the book of Romans he says, "Now to him that is of power to establish you according to my gospel, and the preaching of Jesus Christ, according to the revelation of the mystery, which was kept secret since the world began, But now is made manifest, and by the scriptures of the prophets, according to the commandment of the everlasting God, made known to all nations for the obedience of faith" (Romans 16:25, 26). Please, friends, obey Jesus (Hebrews 5:9) and live, but more so believe, accept, and obey the gospel (1 Peter 4:17; 2 Thessalonians 1:8) and be sure of it.

⌐ *Chapter Four* ⌐
The Gospel and the Antediluvian World

After Adam sinned and lost our heavenly bill of rights, he received the gospel and the promise that someday Jesus would come and save the world (Genesis 3:15). Also after Jesus announced the fate of the human family (Genesis 3:17-19) he applied the symbol of appropriating the benefits of the gospel upon Adam and Eve. And "unto Adam also and to his wife did the Lord God make coats of skins, and clothed them" (Genesis 3:21). It was at this critical time after Adam's transgression that the sacrificial system was given, a parallel of the ceremonial law given to Israel after the Exodus that Jesus would use to educate the first generation of human being in the cost of rebellion and God's ultimate cost to save mankind. To Adam and his early posterity a system of faith based on trust and obedience would be afforded them in order for them to maintain the **robe of righteousness** now imputed to them, as long as they maintain the sign, the sealing system of sacrifice.

The coats of skins Jesus clothed our first parents with, Isaiah says, were "**garments of salvation**, he hath covered me with **the robe of righteousness**" (Isaiah 61:10). In those early days the mystery of God (Revelation 10:7), the mystery of the gospel (Ephesians 6:19), was just beginning to educate man and the universe in the principles that must be maintained under the universal government and kingdom of God. The principle teaching of the sacrificial system given to Adam and his posterity (descendants) is represented in the actions of Cain and Abel, forecasting the issues that brought the terrible destruction of the great flood some fifteen hundred or so years after creation. Critical to every one of us is to "study to show thyself approved unto God, a workman that needs not to be ashamed, rightly dividing the word of truth" (2 Timothy 2:15).

What happened between Cain and Abel is a sign, a symbol, a testimony of an era that parallels the generation living just before Jesus comes again. What happened between Cain and Abel will happen again on a universal, worldwide scale. Just before Jesus comes, a major group of Christians will persecute a specific group of Christians, called the **remnant** (Joel 2:32;

Revelation 12:17), the biblical vintage of the "woman clothed with the sun" (Revelation 12:1), that are biblically grounded in obedience to the present truth of the gospel of Christ (1 Peter 4:17). In order for a believer to be saved when Jesus comes, faith in line with *obedience to the truth* of what constitutes the gospel of Christ (Romans 1:5; 16:26; Galatians 2:14) must be maintained. Both sons of Adam were educated as to the issues and condition of man's fall from grace. "And in the process of time it came to pass that Cain brought of the fruit of the ground an offering unto the Lord. And Abel, he also brought of the firstlings of his flock and of the fat thereof. And the Lord had respect unto Abel and to his offering: But unto Cain and to his offering He had not respect. And Cain was very angry and his countenance fell (Genesis 4:4, 5).

Two brothers, two worshipers, came to offer their gifts before the Lord. Each brought an offering believed acceptable; each with a sacrifice critical in its representation. "And the Lord had respect unto Abel and to his offering." Scripture says, *"By faith Abel offered to God a more excellent sacrifice than Cain, by which he **obtained witness that he was righteous,** God testifying of his gifts: and by it he being dead yet speaks"* (Hebrews 11:4). The offering of Abel was in accordance with the gospel order of his generation and the theme of justification by faith. In order for Cain and Abel to be saved in their generation, the gospel order that was communicated to them by their parents had to be believed, accepted, and unmistakably maintained through the ordinance of sacrifice.

Sin is a terrible thing. It has not only condemned us, but our "iniquities have separated between you and your God and your sins have hid His face from you that He will not hear us" (Isaiah 59:2). If we fail to understand and comply with gospel requirements, God cannot and will not allow us to live eternally in His kingdom. It is only through the righteous merits of Christ's atonement, defined by the "truth of the gospel" (Romans 1:16, 17; Galatians 2:14-17; Ephesians 1:13; Colossians 1:5) that we are acceptable and answerable to heaven's authority.

Abel's offering was in compliance with gospel order, principally because of the specifics of his offering. Paul said, "Without the shedding of blood there is no remission" (Hebrews 9:22). Friend, the blood of Christ is everything to us. **It is a representation of the life and death of Jesus Christ.** Scripture says, "Being justified by His blood" (Romans 5:9) represents not only the blood that was shed for us in death, but blood that lived in righteousness to produce a bill of rights, in a human body without ever sinning; This is the same blood that was shed in death in order to produce a death certificate, a bill of sale and a passport for every human *who believes and obeys* gospel truth.

Abel brought a blood sacrifice and was accepted according to gospel order. "God testifying of his gifts: and by it he being dead yet speaks" (Hebrews 1:4). By it Abel is still speaking to every generation, from Adam to our time. Believe the truth of the gospel and live. Accept the truth of the gospel and live. Obey the truth of the gospel in your lifetime and live. It's the only offering God the Father will accept in righteousness.

"But unto Cain and to his offering he had not respect. And Cain was very angry, and his countenance fell" (Genesis 4:5). Cain's offering is today like many who worship the Lord under one or two pretentious verses of scripture that negate continuing concepts of faith. Many today misapply particular verses of scripture to concede to the concept that faith alone saves a believer in Christ, thus leading many to contradict many gospel principles that today have been hidden under the rubbish of error.

Today this generation has a specific gospel message, called in the book of Revelation the *"everlasting gospel."* This is a critical, life-saving message that must be believed and obeyed prior to Christ's second coming (Revelation 14:6). "Saying with a loud voice, **Fear God**, and **give glory** to Him; for the hour of **His judgment is come:** and **worship Him** that made heaven, and earth, and the sea, and the fountains of waters" (Revelation 14:7). In these critical statements the phrase *"fear God"* is not given to man for his own personal interpretation. Also, *"give glory to Him"* and *"the hour of His judgment is come"* must be as well properly understood in the light of worshiping Him, not just because we go to church and praise Him in song, sermon, or testimony.

We are to fear God and give Him glory, for the hour of His judgment is come, and worship Him in light of Christ's final gospel message given to this final generation. Today, the "Christian Universal Church" is in darkness, as was the church in Jerusalem in Jesus' day. This church is in a stupor of misunderstanding, filled with misconceptions of Christ and his gospel mission, scripturally unable to define what the truth of the gospel of Christ is, says, and does for the sinner. They are confused as to the specifics of how scripture interprets, *"Fear God and give glory to Him for the hour of His judgment is come and worship Him"* in light of Christ's gospel commission (Matthew 28:19, 20; Revelation 14:6, 7) which must be properly and chronologically given to this final generation of believers.

Friend, did Cain bring an offering before the Lord? Yes, he did, but did he bring the right offering? No. Did he believe? Yes, he did. James says, "The devils also believe and tremble." Someday Cain will tremble along with the many that follow in his footsteps. Will Cain be judged by faith in the judgment hour by noncompliance to the right sacrifice and gospel order? And will we be judged, by faith interpreting scripture to suit our own Jesus, our own gospel, our own ten commandments, our own grace, our own creed, and our own church affiliation that he or she believes is the right one (Proverbs 3:5; 14:12)? John says that when Jesus comes again, who will be able to stand (Revelation 6:17)?

Paul says, "For we must all appear before the judgment seat of Christ; that every one may receive the things done in his body, **according to that he hath done, whether** *it be* **good or bad**" (2 Corinthians 5:10). We will be judged whether it be good, done biblically under divine righteousness, under the sign and seal of the imputed righteousness of Christ (Revelation 7:2, 3; 14:6, 7), or whether it be bad, done by faith but not under the merits of Christ our righteousness. False works will be rejected as illegal unrighteous works of faith, because they were not done according to gospel order, but presented in iniquity and unrighteousness (Matthew 7:21-23). Only those with clean hands and pure hearts shall be able to stand under the gospel grace God has provided for this generation.

Paul says, "Stand therefore, having your loins *girt about with truth,* and *having on the breastplate of righteousness*; and your feet *shod with the preparation of the gospel* of peace (Ephesians 6:14, 15). The truth of the gospel must be **believed** (Mark 1:15), **received** (1 Corinthians 15:1), and **obeyed** (2 Thessalonians 1:8; 1 Peter 4:17) in order for one to be accepted and saved in life-giving righteousness. Cain was a believer and doer, but not according to gospel order or gospel righteousness. "But whilst thou know, O vain man, that faith without [biblical imputed, righteous] works is dead" (James 2:20)?

Cain said no to blood sacrifice by offering his own personal bloodless sacrifice. He got angry and changed his attitude towards God, resulting in the death of his brother and the death of thousands years later in the great flood. How wonderful to see that after the rejection of Cain's offering, the Lord comes to him (Genesis 4:6) to appeal to his senses about the importance of gospel order.

Jesus says to him, *Cain, if you, according to gospel order, bring the right sacrifice, will I not accept you and your offering? If you don't bring the blood offering that represents my life, death, and resurrection in righteousness, sin—the decree of unrighteousness placed upon man at the fall—lies at the door of your right to eternal life* (Genesis 4:6, 7).

Cain, understand from the heart that man allowed sin to enter the kingdom I created for him in the beginning. "The wages of sin is death" (Romans 3:23).

Cain, recognize that according to divine righteousness and my Father's code of conduct, which has always existed, the law of the Lord of creation demanded your father's immediate death after he **willfully** *sinned. Life is in the blood* (Leviticus 17:11-14, Deuteronomy 12:23), *and blood must be sacrificed in order for me to reinstate eternal life on Planet Earth in the future, according to the judgment-hour message of Revelation 14:6, 7 and Daniel 7:9, 10.*

Cain, appreciate the blood sacrifice I ask you to bring, because it represents the blood sacrifice I will shed on man's behalf, which I need in divine righteousness at judgment time (Revelation 14:6, 7) to save you and all of mankind from the wages of sin, which is death. I need divine righteousness in order to restore you and all of mankind to the sinless nature I created at the beginning, before the fall.

Cain, my kingdom is perfect in divine order, in principle, and judicial righteousness. In order to maintain life in the universe, sin, unrighteousness, and rebellion to the standards that govern life in the universe cannot be entertained.

Cain, when Adam willfully chose sin and death it broke my heart and the great heart of my Father, who in the beginning planned with me all of creation. After sin entered the world, my divine Father and I introduced the plan of salvation, which had been ordained before the foundation of the world (1 Peter 1:18-20). *We are not in any way responsible for earth's condition because of sin, but we have divinely chosen to take upon ourselves the wages of sin, which is death, in order to meet the expense for that wage and to give you and all mankind another choice in divine righteousness.*

But "Cain raised up against Abel his brother and killed him" (Genesis 4:8). How incredible is Jesus! Again he comes to council Cain in his transgression (Genesis 4:9, 10), but again Cain chooses not to "bring forth therefore **fruits** worthy of repentance" (Luke.3:8). Jesus did for Cain as He does for all of us when we fall in sin, or choose to willfully sin. He revealed to Cain his rebellious attitude and the sin of killing his brother, but Cain turned away and "went out from the presence of the Lord, and dwelt in the land of Nod, on the east of Eden (Genesis 4:16). Jesus didn't force or compel Cain's decision in any way, but afforded him liberty of conscience.

When one comes to the position of hearing and understanding our sinfulness and sins, in perspective to the truth of the gospel of Jesus Christ, he or she must respectively respond in the positive to the gospel message of his generation. Cain's sin was the **willful** rejection of the truth of gospel order, as well as his unwillingness to be saved by obedience to the faith, by bringing the proper blood sacrifice in order to appropriate life-giving righteousness (Romans 6:16; 16:25, 26). Cain is the father of the many who, down through the ages, "have gone the way of Cain" (Jude 11). Blood sacrifice was the sign given to Adam and his posterity after the fall (Genesis 3:21), a sign and seal of their belief, acceptance, and obedience to the gospel presentation of that era, which would continue long after the flood, to the time of Abraham.

Paul said in his day, "I am not ashamed of the gospel of Christ: for it is the power of God unto salvation to everyone that believeth." It is for everyone who:

First, takes the opening step of faith and believes the truth of the gospel of Christ (Mark 1:15)

Second, accepts and receives the truth of the gospel of Christ (1 Corinthians 15:1)

Third, obeys the truth of the gospel of Christ (1 Peter 4:17)

"For therein, [for in the gospel] is the righteousness of God revealed from faith to faith: as it is written, the just, [the justified, those made righteous by obeying the truth of the gospel] shall live by faith" (Romans 1:17). At the second coming of Christ, Paul says that only those who know God and are obeying the gospel of Christ will not suffer the flaming fire of God's vengeance (2 Thessalonians 1:7, 8).

"And it came to pass, when men began to multiply on the face of the earth, and daughters were born unto them … There were giants in the earth in those days; and also after that, when the sons of God [the born again Christians] (John 1:12; 3:7) came in unto the daughters of men [those not born again] and they bare children to them, the same became mighty men which were of old, men of renown. … "And GOD saw that the wickedness of man was great in the earth, and *that every imagination of the thoughts of his heart was only evil continually.* … And the Lord said, "I will destroy man whom I have created from the face of the earth; both man, and beast, and the creeping thing, and the fowls of the air; for it sorrows me that I have made them" (Genesis 6:1-7). A little over fifteen hundred years after creation, God had to intervene to stop man's destructive nature, which was under the complete influence and dominion of Satan. All because of Cain's willful transgression and failure to present God's righteous plan of salvation through gospel order to his posterity,

Cain's rebellion produced within the first two millennia of earth's history a deplorable, unfit, destructive generation educating the universe in the principle subject pertaining to our eternal right to eternal life, Christ our life-giving righteousness. Deceived **because of their unwillingness to be-**

lieve and obey gospel order by the adversary of souls (2 Corinthians 4:3, 4), all but a few of that ungrateful generation came under the complete domineering control of Satan.

Only a few in that antediluvian era were accountable to Jesus and the gospel, and were under the guiding influence and indwelling power of the Holy Spirit. "And the Lord said unto Noah, Come thou and thy entire house into the ark; for thee have I seen righteous before me in this generation" (Genesis 7:1). It was Adam, Seth, Enos, Cainan, Mahaleleel, Jared, Enoch, Methuselah, Lamech, and Noah before the flood that are represented as the born again sons of God (John 1:12), who did not marry the unconverted daughters of men (Genesis 6:1, 2), and "who call upon the name of the Lord" (Genesis 4:26) in imputed divine righteousness by blood sacrifice and taught the principles of gospel order to their posterity.

About the middle of the second century B.C., Jesus called Noah to prepare an ark and warn that generation of God's judgments, soon to fall upon that rebellious age. "And Noah found grace in the eyes of the Lord. Noah was a just man and perfect in his generation, and Noah walked with God" (Genesis 6:8, 9). Noah, scripture says, was just—a justified man—a man God could look upon and make the positive judicial statement: "His righteousness is of Me, saith the Lord" (Isaiah 54:17). Noah was not just or righteous of his own; he was obeying the gospel in his generation. He was fulfilling the requirement necessary in the application of life-giving righteousness.

"And Noah built an altar unto the Lord; and took of every clean beast and of every clean fowl, and offered burnt offerings on the altar" (Genesis 8:20). Not only was he obedient to the law of faith (Romans 3:27), in line with the law of righteousness (Romans 9:31), but, "By faith Noah, being warned of God of things not seen as yet, moved with fear, prepared an ark to the saving of his house; by the which he condemned the world, and became heir of the righteousness which is by faith." He become in character what righteousness in Christ is in action (Hebrews 11:7).

The wonderful statement made after the flood, after Noah made sacrifice to God, should excite us to look a little deeper into the wonders of Jesus' prefigured atonement for all mankind. "And the Lord smelled a sweet smell" (Genesis 8:21), a magnificent representation of the sweet smell of the life-giving righteous life, death, and resurrection of Jesus Christ. A sweet smell of the prefigured atonement; representing the travail and satisfaction of Christ's soul, in the salvation of every willing believer in every generation that takes hold of the plan of salvation and obeys it (Isaiah 53:11). This may not have been understood by Noah and his family after the ark came to rest upon the mountains of Ararat (Genesis 8:4), but it speaks to us clearly in this generation of the wonderful thoughts of our heavenly Father towards those who have accepted and obeyed gospel order and represent respectfully the "travail of the soul of Christ" (Isaiah 53:11) for the souls of the righteous.

I believe it did not take Noah long to leave the ark and offer blood sacrifices. The fear of that terrible time and experience must have been incredible and unimaginable. Especially in critical warning times, as before the great flood, the exodus of Israel from Egypt, the first and finally the second coming of Christ, the word *fear* is presented in scripture to capture every generation in the unimaginable coming events. The apostle Paul says at the time of the rise of the early Christian church, "Let us therefore *fear*, lest, a promise being left us of entering into his rest, any of you should seem to come short of it. For to us was the gospel preached, as well as to them: but the word preached did not profit them, not being mixed with faith in them that heard it" (Hebrews 4:1, 2).

At that time the apostle Paul was speaking of the generation that had come out of Egypt and "always continued to err in their hearts, not having the *necessary fear* and not willing to learn and know the principles of the gospel of Jesus Christ (Hebrews 3:10). The word fear associated with gospel order does not just represent respect, it is the definite article as to frighten, to be alarmed, to be sore afraid, exceedingly reverenced, afraid like terror. Sin is not allowed to exist in God's presence. Sin is not only what we are, but what we do by the nature of our sinful, self-centered, unrighteous condition (Romans 3:10; Mark 7:20-23).

Even the good that we do, because of our sinful nature, is unacceptable before God because of man's fall from righteousness (Romans 3:23; Jeremiah 17:9; Matthew 7:22, 23). Scripture is clear: be fearful in contemplating any irreverence in approaching the God of the universe, especially in coming to Him in any way outside of the indisputable, unquestionable righteousness of Christ. We are again in this final gospel dispensation of time a fearless, irreverent Christian generation, thinking we can come before the Father of the universe without gospel order.

The Bible says to be fearful, friend, of how we call upon the name of the Lord, because truly "the god of this world hath blinded the minds of them which believe not, lest the light of the glorious gospel of Christ, who is the image of God, should shine to them" (2 Corinthians 4:4). Be fearful, God says. No justification through the imputed righteousness of Christ means no salvation. In the judgment, God will say He called "heaven and earth to record this day against you, that I have set before you life and death, blessing and cursing: (**righteousness and unrighteousness**) *therefore choose life,* that both thou and thy seed may live" (Deuteronomy 30:19).

Just before Jesus comes again, the final gospel message (Revelation 14:6-12) will be given to every nation, kindred, tongue, and people, "saying with a loud voice, **Fear God**." *Fear God* and believe the truth of the gospel, *fear God,* and accept the truth of the gospel, *fear God* and obey the truth of the gospel which is presently being given in this final generation.

Fear God if you do not have the life-giving righteousness Jesus needs *to present you faultless* before the throne of God, before the presence of His glory with exceeding joy, in order to save you in the judgment hour (Revelation 14:6, 7; Jude 24).

Fear God if you have "trodden underfoot the Son of God, and hath counted the blood of the covenant, wherewith he was sanctified, an unholy thing, and hath done despite to the Spirit of grace" (Hebrews 10:29).

Fear God, "For if we sin willfully after we have received the knowledge of the truth [the truth of the gospel], there remains no more sacrifice for sins" (Hebrews 10:26).

Scripture says, "For we know him that hath said, Vengeance belonged to me, I will recompense, says the Lord. And again, The Lord shall judge his people. It is *a fearful thing* to fall into the hands of the living God (Hebrews 10:30, 31). My friend, I am not saying fear God to make people fear of not having any hope; only fear if you have not heeded this generation's signed and sealed passport into the glorious kingdom of our Lord and Savior Jesus, the living Christ.

After the terrible destruction of the great flood, "God blessed Noah and his sons, and said unto them, **be fruitful, and multiply, and replenish the earth**" (Genesis 9:1). The same statement Jesus made to Adam before the fall was now repeated to Noah under the same principles, but now under terrible conditions. **He did not say**, be fruitful, and multiply, and replenish the earth, subdue it, and have dominion over it (Genesis 2:28). Instead He told them to be fruitful, and multiply, and replenish the earth, without having dominion over it, for the authority and dominion of our planet was in the hands of Satan, delivered to him after the fall (Luke 4:6). The adversary of souls would now, after the flood, have greater wisdom and understanding of how to defeat man in the great controversy over life-giving righteousness. The generations of the first two millennium years of earth's history revealed a great and mighty race of beings, fresh from the hands of Jesus our Creator, **who willfully and deliberately chose death over life, unrighteousness over righteousness, Satan over Christ.** The next generation of human beings would be of smaller stature, considerably more deficient in moral and mental capacity, and their life span would decrease dramatically (Genesis 11:10-32).

It is evident that the antediluvian generation's rejection of blood sacrifices, their **sign of faith in present truth** essential in their day in obeying the truth of the gospel and receiving their "**seal of the imputed righteousness of Christ**" (1 Peter 3:20, 21; 2 Peter 1:1, 12), was the test question in the first two thousand years of earth's history. A mighty generation failed to comprehend, accept, and obey, which brought to humanity a lesser moral ability to comprehend, perceive, and obey what the Bible calls **the truth of the gospel of Christ** (Romans 2:8, 9; Galatians 2:14; Ephesians 1:13, 14; Colossians 1:5).

∽ *Chapter Five* ∽
The Gospel Preached to Abraham— An Introduction to Circumcision

"And the scripture, foreseeing that **God would justify (make right) the heathen** through faith, **preached before the gospel to Abraham**, saying, in thee shall all nations be blessed" (Galatians 3:8). A little over four hundred years after the great flood, Abram, the father of faith, was called by Jesus to remove himself and his family from his relatives and the area of his birth (Genesis 12:1-4). He was to be the father of Israel, the nation Jesus would create and authorize to reveal the governing principles of his universal kingdom to the nations surrounding them. Abram was called with the future promise that the seed Jesus Christ, promised to Adam to redeem the world, would come through his ancestry (Galatians 3:16).

Prior to the call of Abram, most of the descendants of Noah were influenced by Satan to establish on the earth a centralized city under the governing power of a chosen few. Scripture defines this city as Babel (Genesis 11:1-9), detained and confounded at its birth by heaven's providence (Genesis 11:7, 8). Babel will find its complete fulfillment when **MYSTERY, BABYLON THE GREAT, THE MOTHER OF HARLOTS AND ABOMINATIONS OF THE EARTH** (Revelation 17:5) is influenced by the Mystery of Iniquity (2 Thessalonians 2:7) into uniting the nations of this world with the religions of this world, under one religious head for the battle of Armageddon (Revelation 16:16). This one Christian denominational power that apostatized from the truth of the gospel in the middle of the second century (Revelation 2:8, 9) will, through the **legislative and judicial authority of the nations** of this world, set up Babel or Babylon's final controlling influence over the peoples of the earth. "Yet he **(the man of sin the son of perdition and his apostate denominational activity)** shall come to his end, and none shall help him" (Daniel 11:45).

In the calling of Abram, scripture identifies Abram's faithfulness in his accountability to gospel order; In preaching the gospel to Abraham, Jesus communicated to him its meaning and purpose that **God would justify (make right) the heathen** (who are willing) through faith. "For therein, is the **righteousness of God revealed** from faith to faith: as it is written, the just **(the made right with God)** shall live by faith (Galatians 3:8; Romans 1:17). Imperative, Abram was to make known in his generation gospel order to forecast "that God would justify (make righteous) the heathen **(the unsaved nations)** through faith, if they would respond to gospel order. "For there is one God and one mediator between God and men, the man Christ Jesus; "**Who will have all men to be saved** and to **come to the knowledge of the truth**" (1 Timothy 2:5).

In every generation, when the **truth of the gospel** for their time is conveyed and understood, all must come to God through all the prefigured merits of our life-giving, crucified, and risen savior. Justifying the nations or heathen, sometimes translated gentiles, through the gospel represents appropriating heaven's bill of rights for those who choose in their lifetime to live under heaven's legislative and judicial powers. When Jesus appeared unto Abram (Genesis 12:7) it was in light that Abram was faithful in the gospel message of his day; Abram was obeying gospel order in that he was conveying the right sacrificial offering to the Lord. "And he (Abram) built an **altar unto the Lord**, who appeared unto him" (Genesis 12:7). Scripture testifies as Abram moved from place to place he built altars of sacrifice to the Lord. "And he removed from thence unto a mountain on the east of Bethel, and pitched his tent, having Bethel on the west and Hai on the east: and there he **built an altar** unto the Lord, and c**alled upon the name of the Lord**" (Genesis 12:8). After his return from Egypt because of his blunder in lying to Pharaoh about Sarah being his sister instead of his wife (Genesis 12:9-13:1), Abram came back "unto the place of the altar, which he had made there at the first: and there Abram **called on the name of the Lord**" (Genesis 13:1-4).

Most Christians today believe Romans 10:13, "**For whoever shall call upon the name of the Lord (Jesus) shall be saved**," constitutes the right to life-giving righteousness unto eternal life. There are many today being taught to just call on the name of Jesus and you're saved, but this verse is taken erroneously out of context. Abram called upon the name of the Lord, but it profited him nothing unless he brought a blood sacrifice in obedience to gospel order of his day. In the beginning stages of one's faith, not many Christian believers understand this principle. They are accepted by their timely belief and faith in the Lord Jesus Christ, but accountability to gospel order is based on one's faithfulness in their lifetime, to personally **grow scripturally in grace "from faith to faith"** (2 Peter 3:18; Romans 1:17) and be aware of the availability of understanding the "truth of the gospel" (Galatians 2:14-17), as well as the governing ideology of what the gospel is, says, and does (Psalm 119:172-174). When Abram removed his tent and came and dwelt in the plane of Mamre, which is in Hebron (Genesis 13:18), there again he built an altar to the Lord. There he followed gospel order and called upon the name of the same Lord under divine judicial righteousness.

Many a Christian in the judgment hour (Daniel 7:9-13; Acts17:31; Revelation 14:6, 7) just before Jesus comes will find his or her name blotted out of the Lamb's book of life (Revelation 3:5) for failure to seek in their lifetime a biblical understanding of present gospel truth (2 Peter 1:12). In order for Adam, Seth, down through Abram, to be accepted in precious faith through the righteousness of Christ (2 Peter 1:1) by calling on the name of the Lord, they had to offer blood sacrifices (Genesis 4:26; 8:20; 12:8; 13:4, 18). They had to maintain gospel order. Saying no to obedience to gospel order meant no justification unto eternal life.

There is no bill of rights for **those living among earth's kingdoms that are temporarily living outside of heaven's life-giving legislative and judicial powers**. Rejecting **righteousness by faith into justification by faith** into the imputed righteousness of Christ means **no salvation,** but **weighed in the balances and found wanting** at **judgment time** (Daniel 5:26, 27; 7:9, 10; Acts 17:31). The wanting of Christ's righteousness in the progression of righteousness by faith into justification by faith will find many a name in the judgment message of Daniel 7:9-14; Acts 17:31; and Revelation 14:6, 7 without legal standing and representation in heaven's tribunal just before Jesus comes again (Matthew 28:19, 20; 1 Peter 4:17, 18; Hebrews 8:1-6).

"And he, Abram, believed in the Lord; and he counted it to him for righteousness" (Genesis 15:6). Here we see a verse that many believe constitutes and transfers life-giving righteousness. It is true that Abram believed in the Lord, and the Lord counted it to him for righteousness. "Counted it to him for righteousness" does not declare one officially just or made right, until accounted to him for righteousness has a legal forensic right of transfer in a time application (James 2:20-23). Paul writes a complete chapter on this concept in Romans chapter four. But before we go there, let's look at Abram's early walk of faith, from "faith to faith" (Romans 1:17), as he asks God a question. "And Jesus said unto Abram, I am the Lord that brought thee out of Ur of the Chaldees, **to give thee this land to inherit it**" (Genesis 15:7). The next verse reveals in Abram the same humanity, the same doubt and unbelief revealed in all of us. And Abram asks, "Lord God, **whereby shall I know that I shall inherit it**" (Genesis 15:8)?

Can you believe Abram was completely like us and made the same statement we all make under the theme of righteousness by faith into justification by faith? Yes, Abram was a man of faith in the Lord Jesus

Christ, but he wanted evidence, some kind of indication, sign, or symbol from God that His promise to him was going to happen. Can you just believe the boldness of him? Do we as Christians doubt our Creator with the same mindset almost every day? I have many friends that ask me when God is going to give them a sign, seal, or evidence of his acceptance. Everyone wants a sign. It was the same with Abram's generation as it was in Jesus' day. Jesus said, "A wicked and adulterous generation seeks for a sign; and there shall no sign be given to it, but the sign of the prophet Jonah and he left them, and departed" (Matthew 16:4). After Jesus' triumphal entry (Matthew 21:6-10) he spent the last three days and nights of his ministry teaching in the heart of the Israel, **the temple in Jerusalem**, the heart of the earth, (2 Chronicles 7:16; 1 Kings 9:1-3). He instructed as many as were receptive that he **was the only sign of salvation afforded that generation** (John 12:32; John 13:19; John 14:1, 10-12). And then after his crucifixion, death, and resurrection he was later taken to heaven to administer his atonement work in the heavenly sanctuary (Act 1:9; Hebrews 8:1, 2).

Friend, the **only true divine sign** acceptable to God by faith in every generation is the timely **sign of personal salvation. The biblical evidence that points to what Jesus had to do to save believers in every generation.** The first divine sign given to man after sin entered the world was blood sacrifice (Genesis 3:21). And how many in those early days of earth's history believed and obeyed it unto their salvation? Only when we see the redeemed after Jesus comes again will we know.

After Abram asks the believer's unkind, distrustful question (Genesis 15:8), Jesus said, "Take me a heifer of three years old, and a she goat of three years old, and a ram of three years old, and a turtledove, and a young pigeon"(Genesis 15:10). He wanted Abram to **make the blood sacrifice** according to the evidence given to his ancestors as a sign of the promise made to them of imputing to them their rights of being under divine guidance through the imputed righteousness of Christ. After Abram accepted God's judicial evidence of life-giving righteousness (Genesis 15:10-17), "**in the same day the Lord made a covenant with Abram**, saying. 'Unto thy seed have I given this land, from the river of Egypt unto the great river, the river Euphrates'" (Genesis 15:18). And for the **first time in scripture, blood sacrifice is specified as a sign** of an arrangement or contract between God and those that would represent Christ through gospel order that reveals the life-giving righteousness of Christ.

In the same day the Lord made a covenant with Abram, saying blood sacrifice is the covenant sign between God and Abram, a contract not to be broken based on Abram's **obeying the covenant contract by sacrificing and waiting** (Revelation 14:12) for God to deliver the promised land and the **promised seed**, the child called Isaac. Isaac was to be born through Sarah, his elderly wife beyond the age of childbearing (Genesis 17:19; Romans 4:19, 20). Isaac was a symbol of the promised seed, Jesus Christ (Galatians 3:14-16).

Terrible Mistake

Scripture records: "Sarai Abram's wife bare him no children: and she had a handmaid, an Egyptian, whose name was Hagar. And Sarai said unto Abram, 'Behold now, the Lord hath restrained me from bearing: I pray thee, **go in unto my maid; it may be that I may obtain children by her.**' And Abram hearkened to the voice of Sarai. And Sarai Abram's wife took Hagar her maid the Egyptian, **after Abram had dwelt ten years in the land of Canaan**, and gave her to her husband Abram to be his wife"(Genesis 16:1-3). This record of Abram is a mighty testimony to all of us in the lesson of taking God at his word and waiting for God's providence in fulfilling His covenant pertaining to gospel order (Revelation 14:6-12). Abram's first error was in Egypt, when he lied to Pharaoh (Genesis 12:18, 19) about Sarai being his sister instead of his wife, after God allowed circumstances to lead him there for the principal purpose of revealing to the Egyptian nation the principles of God's kingdom (1 Timothy 2:4). Abrams's second mistake was creating an order of descendants with a dominant mindset in the Middle East (Genesis 16:12), countering the work of the gospel of Christ from Abram's day to the second coming of Christ.

Again, another appointed leader making another terrible choice deterrent to gospel order. Abram's error is a parallel of Adam's choice (Genesis 3:6) in counseling with human flesh in the critical issues of appropriating and sustaining life without a "thus saith the Lord." Adam's failure placed man on a collision course, which almost destroyed the entire human race in the first two millennia of earth's history (1 Peter 3:20). Now Abram's choice in yielding to Sarah's council without heaven's guidance placed God's chosen in the Middle East, and the world, in the next four millennia of earth's history in greater jeopardy than desired. Abram's failure is also a parallel to Adam's steps in forfeiting the covenant of life-giving righteousness that Jesus made with him at creation (Genesis 2:15-17).

When Abram's faith faltered in waiting for the promised seed, the covenant contract made between him and Jesus (Genesis 15:6-18) was nullified. Again, Jesus foreseeing man's inability to "seek ye first" the council of God, interceded his eternal plan to interpose on Abram's behalf at that critical time in earth's history. "And when Abram was ninety years old and nine, twenty-four years after his calling, the Lord **(Jesus)** appeared to Abram and said unto him, 'I am the Almighty God; **walk before me, and be thou perfect'"** (Genesis 17:1). How gracious is our Lord and Savior, Jesus Christ? Knowing the deficiency in man after two thousand years of sinful decline, he didn't come to Abram with any negative accusations or condemnation, but said, "Walk before me, and be thou perfect and **I will make my covenant between me and thee, and will multiply thee exceedingly**" (Genesis 17:1, 2; Psalm 51:17).

And then, **"Abram fell on his face"** in acknowledgement of his sin, "and God talked with him, saying, as for me, behold, my covenant is with thee, and thou shall be a father of many nations" (Genesis 17:3, 4). Friend, how precious is the God we serve? How wonderful is Jesus in his long-suffering with us. Abram, knowing the critical elements of his covenant contract with Jesus, now knows what he has done and bows in humble submission before the Lord (Genesis 17:3). Critical to man's understanding was the first millennial sign given to Adam after the fall (Genesis 3:11) by Jesus pertaining to gospel order. For over two thousand years, blood sacrifice was God's covenant sign, seal of faith, and obedience to the truth of the gospel. After Abram's error in judgment, Jesus does not rebuke him, but says plainly, "My covenant is with thee" (Genesis 17:4). Although Abram failed, Jesus renewed his part of the negotiated covenant. In God's providence, as man progresses in his downward progress of sinfulness, Jesus in every generation must intercede on man's behalf to increase his understanding in the plan of salvation.

It's critical to study and contemplate this time of Abram's life, and his calling in biblical history, especially from Genesis 12 through 22:1-19. There is much controversy in our day over what constitutes the covenants in the Old and New Testament, as to what Jesus gave the patriarchs of old pertaining to gospel order. Some believe the Old Testament is the old covenant and the New Testament is the new covenant. Some also believe the law of Moses, including the Ten Commandments, are the old covenant regulation, and faith in Jesus Christ represents what the apostle Paul defined as the new covenant. But a thorough study from Genesis to Revelation would reveal, "**For it is written,** that **Abraham had two sons**, one by **(human performance)** a bondmaid, **the other** by **(the providence of God)** a freewoman. But he *who was* of the bondwoman was born after the **flesh**; but he of the freewoman *was* by **promise**. Which things are allegories, **(a metaphor)**: for **these are the two covenants**" (Galatians 4:22-24).

Friends, its critical to understand **Abraham had two covenants** in his lifetime. The first covenant Jesus made with Abram was at his calling, a new covenant contract based on his faith in believing what God had promised him in **land and seed**, in order to create out of his loins the nation of Israel (Genesis 12:2; 13:14-17; 15:5, 6). Jesus, the promised seed, is central to the covenant contract made between Abram and God at the beginning of his calling (Galatians 3:16). This covenant was made with Abram at the age of seventy-five years (Genesis 12:4), to be conceived with Sarah his wife when they were both "old and well stricken in age" (Genesis 18:11). What started as a new covenant of faith between Abram and God became, through an arrangement made by Sarai and Abram, the old covenant of works of the flesh (Galatians 5:19).

"Now the works of the flesh are manifest, which are *these;* Adultery, fornication, uncleanness, lasciviousness" (Galatians 5:19). Friends, polygamy and slavery may have been to Abram and Sarai acceptable and legal in their lifetime, but the scriptures are clear: "Nevertheless the foundation of God stands sure, having this seal, The Lord knows them that are his. And, Let everyone that names the name of **Christ** depart from **iniquity (legal injustice)** (2 Timothy 2:19).

Injustice is defined in the scriptures as man establishing for himself illegal bylaws so he may live according to his carnal intentions. **Injustice** is defined as **abortion, polygamy, slavery, legislation uniting church and state, alcohol trafficking, gambling,** etc. These may be legalized under man's governing principles, but are illegal under heaven's judicial and moral principles of divine righteousness. Polygamy is iniquity, a legal injustice, like it or not. In the eyes of God, polygamy is iniquity. When Abram and Sarai decided to assist God by the works of the flesh to fulfill the new covenant promise of producing a child, God said, "Sarah thy wife shall bear thee a son indeed; and thou shall call his name Isaac: and I will establish my covenant with him for an everlasting covenant, *and* with his seed after him" (Genesis 17:19). "What therefore God hath joined together, let not man put asunder" (Mark 10:9). Jesus afforded to Adam at creation one legal wife in the beginning (Genesis 2:23-25).

When Abram took Sarai's handmaid as a wife (Genesis 16:3), he broke the new covenant made with Jesus at the beginning of his calling and nullified its divine legitimacy. Abram was seventy-five years of age when Jesus made the new covenant contract with him. He was eighty-five when "he went into Hagar" (Genesis 16:4) and broke the covenant, but was not told of his blunder until fourteen years later (Genesis 17:1, 2). Twenty-four years of time had passed, with God dealing with Abram's sinful nature in order to teach him instructions "from faith to faith (Romans 1:17) that leads to justification unto life in the earth made new (Romans 5:1-5; Revelation 21:1-5). All was prearranged according to gospel order, per God's divine plan in saving a fallen race.

After this long process of instructing Abram in patience and righteousness, Jesus said, "I *am* the Almighty God; walk before me, and be thou perfect. And I will make my covenant between me and thee, and will multiply thee exceedingly" (Genesis 17:1, 2). And then and only then after Abram's long, **misconceived walk of faith** did Jesus addresses him and make another covenant contract, under another covenant sign and seal, now called circumcision (Genesis 17:10, 11; Romans 4:11).

Scripture reveals Abram had two covenants: one made at the beginning of his calling, and another made twenty-four years later, after his blunder in producing an unrighteous heir (Genesis 16:11, 12). Paul paralleled these two covenant concepts in the life of Abram when he says, "For this Agar is Mount Sinai in Arabia, and answered to *Jerusalem which now is*, and is in bondage with her children through *animal sacrifices*" (Galatians 4:25, 26). This was written about A.D. 57, and ceased when the temple in Jerusalem was destroyed A.D. 70 by Roman aggression (Hebrews 8:13). Here Paul parallels the mindsets of God's people in every generation when they take a faith-based covenant contract in a sealed agreement between God and man and make it a "works of the flesh" issue. This was the mindset of Abraham, the mindset of the Israelites at the time of the exodus, and was also the mindset of God's people at the time of the first coming of Christ. It is still a mindset present today in many Christian households.

The first covenant God made with Abram at the beginning of his walk of faith was based on the concept of animal sacrifices, which was fulfilled by the temple ceremonial services in Jerusalem at the first coming of Christ. The apostle Paul says that instead of instructing Israel to give up their sin, the sacrifices only made them more tolerant towards sin. The mindset became such that if you sin, just sacrifice and your sins are covered. It was a cycle of futility. Paul said unbelief and misunderstanding the ceremonial system kept the descendants of literal Israel in bondage (Galatians 4:25) from the time of the Exodus even up to the day he wrote the book of Galatians. Sin and confess, it is just as powerless today as it was back than to supply the necessary righteousness unto justification that obtains divine power for victory over man's besetting sins. The **old covenant temple animal blood sacrifices (Hebrews 9:9)** were replaced by the new covenant blood of Christ (Matthew 26:28), a heavenly temple sacrifice of Christ on the cross. This produced the "better covenant," which was established on better promises. The blood of Christ was offered on man's behalf in the sanctuary in heaven (Hebrews 8:1, 2; 6; 9:12).

These better promises are based on the new temple services in the heavenly sanctuary (Hebrews 8:1, 2) after the ascension of Christ, to continue the atonement process for man's redemption until the close of man's sinful history prior to Christ's second coming. It is a new and better covenant "which the Lord pitched, and not man (Hebrews 8:2). "Not by the blood of goats and calves, but **by Jesus' own precious blood,**" Jesus entered into the new covenant Holy Place of the heavenly sanctuary after "having obtained eternal redemption for us" (Hebrews 9:12). Paul clarified what the new covenant biblically represents when he said, "And for this cause he is the mediator of the New Testament **(the new covenant),** that by means of death, for the redemption of the transgressions *that were* under the first testament **(old covenant temple animal sacrifice),** of which they that were called might receive the promise of eternal inheritance" (Hebrews 9:6, 15). This scripture is stating and clarifying that the old temple covenant animal services were forever canceled by Jesus (Matthew 23:37-39), completely fulfilled at his death (Matthew 27:51; Mark 15:38). They had become old and were decaying, the apostle Paul said. In his day they were ready to vanish away. They were a prophecy fulfilled at the destruction of Jerusalem (Hebrews 8:13).

The new/old covenant controversy is just words to keep the minds of men busy over secondary truths until there is no more time for men to be converted in righteousness in the born again experience (John 3:5-8). To do away with covenant laws, principles that men do not want to practice, men love to find just the right verses in scripture to do away with any laws or codes that inhibit their sinful nature. The law of Moses has been and still is the main target, that old covenant written by Moses that inhibits our perceived rights. Christian scholars and Christians today love to manipulate and misapply principles of biblical righteousness and right doing, to which the scriptures say in the end will lead many "unto their own destruction" (2 Peter 3:16).

The covenant described in Hebrews 8:7-9 was the covenant of promises God made with Abraham, Isaac, and Jacob, the fathers of Israel. The covenant that God made with Abraham was a faith-based covenant of promises, based on faith in the operation of God (Colossians 2:12). It was made pertaining to **land** and **seed,** which man "cannot disannul," and was fulfilled in 1451 B.C. when Israel crossed the Jordan and entered the **promised land** (Joshua 1-4). Jesus Christ, the promised seed (Galatians 3:16), was fulfilled years later in A.D. 27, when John the Baptist announced and baptized "the Lamb of God who takes away the sin (iniquity) of the world" (John 1:29). When Abram heard and believed in the promises of God in receiving land and seed (Genesis 15:4-7), it was enough for God to covenant with him the sign and seal system of animal sacrifices in God's atoning plan of salvation (Genesis 15:9, 10, 18).

The Law of Moses is biblically defined in the Old Testament in three judicial codes: the *civil*, the *ceremonial*, and the *health* code, all written by Moses and then placed specifically **in the side** of the ark of the covenant of God (Deuteronomy 31:24-31). The law of God, the **moral code** defined as the Ten Commandments (Exodus 20:1-17), were not written by Moses but with the finger of God (Jesus), and placed **in the ark** of the covenant (Deuteronomy 10:1-5). The three specific codes were given by Jesus to Moses, and written by Moses to instruct man in the principles of right living in the light of his fallen condition. All codes were given to instruct man in his individual *responsibility to God*, his own *personal health*, *society*, *civil government*, and his *sacred sacrificial responsibility* in his atonement process in this life and the life to come.

Although the ceremonial temple code of animal sacrifices was done away at the cross, its *new covenant parallel* still exists in the light of Jesus' present administration in heaven, called by the apostle Paul the sanctuary of the true tabernacle, which the Lord pitched, and not man (Hebrews 8:1-6). The old covenant system of animal sacrifices given to Adam at the fall (Genesis 3:21), Abram at his calling, and Israel at the exodus were foreshadows of Jesus' future administration in heaven. This covenant will be administered in the day when our names appear before the judgment seat of Christ (2 Corinthians 5:10) so that our recorded (Revelation 20:12) sins in the day that Jesus begins the judgment (Acts 17:31; Revelation 14:7) may be "blotted out" (Acts 3:19).

It's not difficult for the human mind, under the influence of the adversary of souls, to take Old Testament codes, laws, and principles of right doing and call them old covenant works of the flesh. Please understand, my friends, we were all born with a carnal mind. Paul said, *"For to be carnally minded is death … Because the carnal mind is enmity against God: for it is not subject to the law of God, neither indeed can be"* (Romans 8:6, 7). The carnal mind hates rules, both God's and man's. If you don't believe it, just ask your children. Although Abraham's experience is a **testimony** in time to all of us **that righteousness by faith into justification by faith in Christ** is a faith issue. Established by God's providence in the time and life of his calling, Abraham did obey Jesus' voice, His commandments, His statutes, and His laws (Genesis 26:5; John 8:58).

It was about the time of Abram's blunder, in the beginning of the third millennia of earth's history, that Jesus **introduced circumcision to Abraham** (Genesis 17:10, 11). That new covenant seal of circumcision (Romans 4:11) was given to Abraham, revealing new characteristics in educating man in a greater comprehensive meaning of redemption. New insights were given into the promised seed, Jesus Christ (Galatians 3:16), who would not only have to sacrifice his righteous blood, but in the process **cut off, or circumcise,** what man is in human flesh. Human flesh, or human nature, is characterized as a sinful nature produced after the fall in result of Adam's sin and man falling under the condemnation of the law, the Ten Commandments.

The human race is void of life-giving righteousness, and must be educated in the gospel principles of "from faith to faith" (Romans 1:17) through their progression into justification unto life (James 2:20-23) demanded by God's principles of life (Exodus 20:1-17) in the restoration of the human family. The apostle Paul says, "When the fullness of the time was come, God sent forth his Son, made of a woman, **made under the law,**" made in a nature of flesh, because of sin, that needed redeeming. "To redeem them that were under the **(curse of the)** law, that we might receive the **adoption of sons**" (Galatians 4:4, 5).

Circumcision was introduced to Abram and all of us, that through man's own personal works of the flesh, no man can be justified or made right with God. Man is circumcised, cut off from ever trying to produce the purity of righteousness, the bill of rights heaven demands by God's eternal code of conduct, judiciously required for the salvation of man. The humanity of Jesus, made under the condemnation of the law (Galatians 4:4) cut off what sin is (**unrighteousness [1 John 5:17]**), does (**"for the wages of sin is death" [Romans 6:23]**), and says to all of us (**"your iniquities have separated between you and your God, and your sins have hid his face from you" [Isaiah 59:2]**). By the righteous life, death, and resurrection of Jesus Christ, **righteousness by faith into justification by faith** brought in Christ the emancipation proclamation to all of humanity.

It was the **faith of Jesus,** and the faith of Jesus **alone,** that produced the works in human nature necessary to create a new man (Ephesians 2:15), acceptable in character to God's governing ideology of heavenly conduct, the Ten Commandments. Through the wonderful faith and works of the man Christ Jesus, our heavenly Father has afforded every child of Adam the right to *appropriate the righteousness of Christ* (Philippians 3:9), heaven's divine bill of rights for the salvation of his soul. This must be done *in order for man to be justified* as sons and daughters of God (John 1:12, 13), legalized citizens of Christ's heavenly kingdom (Philippians 3:20).

Righteousness by Faith into Justification by Faith

The heavenly procedure of believing, receiving, and obeying the establishment and process of the born again (John 3:5, 6) experience, through *righteousness by faith in Christ unto justification by faith in the life of the believer,* must be understood today by the remnant people of God (Revelation 12:17). This concept is clearly defined in the scriptures as the walk of faith, "from faith to faith" (Romans 1:17). In the life and education of Abram unto Abraham, the father of unrelenting faith, how critical it is to understand *Abram's* instructions at the beginning of his calling in the expression of *"counted to him for righteousness"* (Genesis 12:1; 15:6; Romans 4:3). It is just as important to understand *Abraham's* all-important perfection of faith (Genesis 17:1; James 2:22) at the time of his all-important test of justification by faith (Genesis 22:1; James 2:21). This was a process from the time of his calling at the age of seventy-five (Genesis 12:4) to the time he offered his son Isaac to God thirty years later in his walk of faith (Genesis 22:1-12). Abraham justified his faith in the biblical model of justification unto life as a citizen in Christ's heavenly kingdom (Genesis 22:8, 9: James 2:21).

How many today are in confusion, struggling to understand the difference between the expression "righteousness by faith" and "justification by faith"? How critical it is to understand how one obtains *righteousness by faith* that leads to how one abides in *justification by faith*. How many today, as well as in the past, who have believed in justification by faith through continuous stumbling and falling have turned away from the faith once delivered to the saints? They turn away from the whole concept of continuing to be under the heading of justification by faith, or under the official title or designation justified or made right through the righteousness of God.

The question must be asked: Has Jesus, the cross, and the gospel of Christ lost the power of God unto salvation (1 Corinthians 1:24, 18; Romans 1:16)? Has grace lost its power over sin? It seems today many, like many in the past, have accepted *the lie* that where grace abounds sin did much more abound, which is a complete reversal of Romans 5:20. Why is this confusion in misunderstanding salvation continuing to exist, continuing to deprive many a confused soul, into giving up on the wonderful truth of the gospel of Christ? Who must take the responsibility for such a terrible condition among believers?

Was not Abraham counted, reckoned, imputed with life-giving righteousness because "he believed in the Lord" (Genesis 15:6) at the beginning of his calling? Were not Abraham's sins and blunders in time covered? Did not the apostle Paul say, "Even as David also describes the blessedness of the man, unto whom God imputeth righteousness without works, saying, blessed are they whose iniquities are forgiven, and whose sins are covered. Blessed is the man to whom the Lord (Jesus Christ [John 5:22]) will not impute sin (Romans 4:6-8). Does the statement, "If we confess our sins he is faithful and just to forgive us our sins and cleanse us from all un-righteousness (1 John 1:9) have no meaning to the believer in Christ our righteousness? Did not the great apostle John write, *"That ye sin not, and if any man sin, we have an advocate with the Father, Jesus Christ the righteousness"* (1 John 2:1). *Abraham was reckoned with righteousness by faith that covered his walk of faith during his all important education and training into justification by faith as a son of God into his present and future title as a citizen (Philippians 3:20) of Christ's heavenly kingdom.*

Jesus' example in his orderly walk of faith as a man must be critically studied. It was Jesus' orderly production of gospel order that produced righteousness by faith that leads to a Christian's right to be under the auspices of justification by faith. If righteousness by faith is not imputed and applied in the life of a believer, he or she cannot be justified to be called a son or daughter of God and have the right to be called a citizen of Christ's heavenly kingdom. How central it is to understand that without the righteousness of Christ there is no justification unto life. Paul made this significantly clear when he said, *"To declare, I say, at this time his righteousness: that he (Jesus) might be just, and the justifier of him which believeth in Jesus" (Romans 3:26).*

How judicial is Paul's statement, "Therefore as by the **offense** of one judgment came upon all men to **condemnation**; even so by the **righteousness** of one the free gift came upon all men **unto justification** of life" (Romans 5:18). How critical to believe and understand that Adam's offense (**sin of unrighteousness [1 John 5:17]**) put us under condemnation of God's governing principles. Christ's righteousness overturned Adam's offense into our justification unto life. Sin condemned us unto death; righteousness officially authorized us under the title of justification by faith unto life.

What the scriptures say was not written for Abraham alone, that righteousness was imputed so that Abraham was licensed under the certification of justification by faith. Was this for Abraham only? No. "But for us also, to whom **it shall be imputed, if we believe on him that raised up Jesus our Lord from the dead;** Who was delivered for our offenses, and was **raised again for our justification**" (Romans 4:24, 25). Jesus was raised from the dead, Paul said, according to his gospel (2 Timothy 2:8), as a man for man as the personified righteousness of God to justify every son and daughter of Adam *"who also walk in the steps of that faith of our father Abraham"* (Romans 4:12).

By Jesus' perfect, orderly life (Romans 5:10; Hebrews 5:8, 9) of producing acceptable judicial righteousness, the Christian can claim being justified by faith. We can claim justification unto life, have peace with God, and be indwelled by the sanctifying power of the Holy Spirit. It was Jesus and Jesus alone, through the operation of God according to gospel order of his generation, that produced the righteousness that justifies a child of Adam with the right of justification unto life. Jesus, our advocate in heaven today, justified the accredited righteous son and daughter of God with the merits of his all present, all perfect atonement (Romans 5:11).

Scripture defines true Christianity under the theme of righteousness by faith into justification by faith foreordained in Christ and characterized as it did in Abraham's walk of faith from "faith to faith." And this applies to the sincere biblical believer in Christ our righteousness. "Therefore being justified by faith" (Romans 5:1), therefore as one is declared righteous with God, through the imputed righteousness of Christ, one is legally justified as a legal citizen of heaven.

"And God said unto Abraham, **"Thou shall keep"** my covenant therefore, thou, and thy seed after thee in their generations. **This is my covenant, which ye shall keep**, between me and you and thy seed after thee; **every man child among you shall be circumcised"** (Genesis 17:9, 10). A new legal precedent was in Abraham's day authorized in heaven's judicial system in saving man. **Circumcision** was introduced as the **sign of faith**, a **seal** in not only being accounted with Christ's righteousness, but having God's bill of rights imputed, applied to our life's record in the prefigured process for man's atonement unto justification by faith (Romans 4:11). "And ye shall **circumcise** the flesh of your foreskin; and **it shall be a token (sign)** of the covenant betwixt me and you" (Genesis 17:11). Even God's directions in the method of circumcising was critical. "On the eighth day, of he that is born among you and those bought with money of any stranger which is not of thy seed, **must desire** (freedom of choice) to be circumcised: **and my covenant shall be in your flesh for an everlasting covenant"** (Genesis 17:13).

Any man from that time forward who did not follow these life-giving instructions, **could not** and **would not** be accepted in righteousness among God's chosen. The condemnation of being uncircumcised or cut off meant that you are **"without Christ,** being aliens, cut off from the commonwealth of Israel, and strangers from the covenants of promise, having **no hope**, and without God in the world" (Genesis 17:14; Ephesians 2:12). "And Abraham was ninety years old and nine, when he was circumcised in the flesh of his foreskin. And Ishmael his son was thirteen years old, when he was circumcised in the flesh of his foreskin. In the selfsame day was Abraham circumcised, and Ishmael his son. And all the men of his house, born in the house, and bought with money of the stranger, were circumcised with him" (Genesis 17:24-27). It was also along with the **renewing of the covenant** of promise to Abram, Jesus said, "Neither shall thy name any more be called **Abram**, but thy name shall be **Abraham**; for a father of many nations have I made thee" (Genesis 17:5).

∼ *Chapter Six* ∼
Romans' Sign of Faith, Seal of Righteousness

"**W**hat shall we say then that Abraham our father, as pertaining to the flesh, **hath found**,"; For if Abraham were justified by works he hath whereof to glory but not before God. For what says the scripture? **Abraham believed God and it was counted to him for righteousness**" (Romans 4:1-3). Here in this chapter Paul defines Abram's faith experience in a time frame of faith from the beginning of his calling at the age of seventy-five (Genesis 12:1-5) through the time his faith was being perfected at the age of ninety-nine (Genesis 17:1-27). From the beginning of his calling, Abram journeyed through unfamiliar territory into the land he was promised, and as he journeyed he was given instructions and knowledge in his walk of faith. "Because that Abraham obeyed my voice, and kept my charge, my commandments, my statutes, and my laws" (Genesis 26:5). Although Abram was being instructed in gospel order and the plan of salvation, Genesis 26:5 emphatically characterizes Abram as not unfamiliar with God's governing principles of righteousness (Exodus 20:1-17). These principles are necessary for all of humanity to come into "the unity of the faith and of the knowledge of the Son of God, **to a perfect man**, to the measure of the **stature** of the fullness of Christ (Ephesians 4:13).

Again in Genesis 15:5-7, the promise of land and seed is repeated, and in verse six says, "And he **believed in the Lord**; and he counted it to him for righteousness." Yes, the scriptures say he believed in the Lord, **and that faith in believing in the Lord at the beginning of his calling and his future promises accounted to Abram for life-giving righteousness.** Why does scripture define Abram being accounted with life-giving righteousness by **faith in believing in the God that justifies? (Romans 4:5).** First of all, it will never be understood by any man until he or she sees and understands that mankind after the fall became an unscrupulous, deplorable, degraded, unrighteous, unjustified, deceptive creature under the dominion of the god of this world, who put man in captivity to sin at his own will (2 Timothy 2:26; Romans 6:16). You may not want to believe these biblical definitions of man's nature (Jeremiah 17:9) and character, but all scriptures from Genesis through Revelation prove these terrible truths. Scripture says, "As it is written, there is none righteous no not one," There is none that understands (**truly knows their own condition**), there is none that seeketh (**on their own [John 6:44]**) after God. They are all gone out of the way (**of righteousness**), they are together become unprofitable (**useless in the universe**), there is none that doeth good, no not one (Romans 3:10-12; Mark 7:20, 23).

There is a frightful deception upon the human mind. Because man, especially those associated with the work of God, do not fully discern that millions and millions of souls, valuable in the sight of God as they are, are being deceived, neglected, and cruelly left to die outside of gospel righteousness (Romans 1:16, 17). The question can be asked, Why? It must be biblically understood that stature or position does not make a man valuable in God's eyes. God is not a respecter of persons or values one soul above another (Romans 2:11). When will true Christianity recognize that true value in the eyes of God is expressed in understanding what the truth of the gospel of Christ is, says, and does for every fallen son and daughter of Adam (Romans 5:12). Christians today need to understand that true integrity of character can only be attained and sustained by the complete indwelling power of the Holy Spirit in connection with receiving Christ's righteousness through gospel order.

Man is so immorally corrupt and unrighteous, void of any attribute of character, that God can only save him by accounting him with a declaration of life-giving righteousness by believing in God's divine intervention through the imputed life-giving righteousness of Christ. The purity of divine righteousness demanded by God's divine code of conduct that governs life in the universe. Righteousness is defended, safeguarded, and recorded in the biblical phraseology of the commandments in Exodus 20:1-17. God cannot and will not save any man outside of Christ's life-giving righteousness, the testimony to the law of God (Isaiah 8:20). His code of character conduct demands in a signed, sealed covenant contract (Isaiah 8:16) for the salvation of all men in every generation (2 Timothy 2:19).

If we would be like Christ, we must individually ask and seek (Matthew 7:7) for a character like Christ. We must, first as Jesus instructed, seek gospel righteousness, which is of utmost value with God the Father (Matthew 6:33). If we would be like Christ we must possess the complete indwelling power of the Holy Spirit. When the truth of gospel righteousness is studied, believed, accepted, and obeyed, then the true Christian will not possess any vestige of self-righteousness or importance above his fellow man, but weigh himself with the spirit of humility (1 Peter 5:6, 7) and the biblical wisdom that only comes from God through the study of God's word (Psalm 111:10; 1 Timothy 4:16; 2 Timothy 2:15).

It was because man became so completely corrupted, bankrupt of any value or merit in moral worth, to save himself from his immoral condition, that God the Father sent Jesus here to become a man in the nature that needed redeeming (Galatians 4:4, 5). Produced in that nature were all the attributes heaven's code of righteousness demands for man's reinstatement as sons and daughters of God. Yet in and with all these merits and benefits of Christ's life, death, and resurrection, God will only account or accredit to man these heavenly gifts by faith in the atonement of the Lord Jesus Christ. Friends, it's imperative to understand God only creates and sustains life in divine righteousness, and He **will not** in any way swerve from His divine principles that define His character. When one believes (Acts 16:31), receives (John 1:12), and obeys (Hebrews 5:9) the Lord Jesus Christ, the gospel personified, as his soul right of salvation, God credits him with an account in Christ's universal bank of life-giving righteousness, with enough righteousness to save him from his immoral state of being (Romans 3:10).

But it doesn't end here. Accounted righteousness is not imputed or transferred righteousness. It is righteousness that can only be transferred onto the life's record of the individual when he or she accepts God's official document of transfer from Christ's heavenly bank account to his lifetime recorded (Revelation 20:12) account in heaven's judicial hall of justice, called the heavenly sanctuary (Hebrews 8:1, 2). As one receives an inheritance of great monetary value in a bank account, they also receive a bank book with the name and seal of its establishment, along with a statement of the right of transfer of funds, so the gospel of **righteousness by faith into justification by faith** in Christ is exemplified. No one who has a monetary bank account would knowingly and willfully refuse a passbook or bankbook to his funds. When one believes from the heart (Romans 10:9) the truth of the gospel of Christ (Galatians 2:2; Colossians 1:5; Galatians 2:14; Ephesians 1:13) of his generation, **an account is open in Christ's heavenly bank of life-giving righteousness, along with the information of one's life's record, a documentation of his life, in heavens court of inquiry (2 Corinthians 5:10),** where the Christian's name is recorded in the Lamb's book of life (Philippians 4:3; Revelation 3:5).

But in order for this bank account of life-giving righteousness to be transferred from Christ's heavenly bank account to the individual's record, the Lord has provided a judicial bank book statement of transfer to every generation. To believers this process gives evidence that God **has not** and **will not** deviate from the heavenly principle that all created beings have a judicial divine right to accept His heavenly gift, liberty of conscience to choose righteousness or unrighteousness, life or death, Christ or Satan as their guide from "faith to faith' (Romans 1:17) of their own free will.

Friends, this is the born again experience that God needs to justify every individual who believes as sons and daughters of God (John 3:5-7). After Adam sinned, he received the sign of sacrifice (Genesis 3:21), an official transfer from Christ's heavenly bank account of righteousness, the bill of rights he lost by his willful transgression, now transferred upon his future life's record as garments of salvation. Friends, many an accounted Christian will in the judgment hour (Daniel 7:9-14; Acts 17:31; Revelation 14:7) be condemned in iniquity, in unrighteousness, because of their failure to follow gospel order in their lifetime. Jesus said, "Many will say to me in that day, 'Lord, Lord have we not done ... many wonderful works?'" Then he will say unto them, "Depart from me, I never know you, you **who are living in iniquity**, you who are living in violation, outside the law of life-giving righteousness (Matthew 7:23; Romans 9:31). These believers have never transferred their life-giving righteousness accredited from heaven's bank to their life's account for justification unto life (Romans 5:1-5).

The theme of righteousness by faith is not justification by faith. **Righteousness by faith** accounts a man with the sufficient quantity of heavenly righteousness God needs to save him in righteousness. **Justification by faith is a "faith to faith" (Romans 1:17) issue** that transfers Christ's faith-based righteousness onto man's recorded life record (Romans 4:11). But not only is this righteousness God needs to save him applied to his life record, but this righteousness is also needed to credit man's good lifetime works as righteous before God and the universe. Friends, it's important to understand Jesus is seated in authority in heaven's judgment hall (Hebrews 8:1-3) on man's behalf to justify in righteousness all of man's good deeds in order for God to accept him and give judicial right to his dealing on earth. We are so degraded that even our prayers to God have to be interceded by the Holy Spirit through groaning we do not comprehend or understand (Romans 8:25-27).

Righteousness by faith into justification by faith in Christ is a process. It was never designed to exalt the Christian believer above the simplicity and character revealed in the gentle life and firm character of Jesus Christ (Psalm 51:17). Righteousness by faith affords man the righteousness, peace, and joy in the Holy Ghost that exemplifies the life of Christ and the kingdom of heaven through gospel order (Romans 14:17). This is what true **righteousness by faith into justification by faith** truly says, does, and means to the sincere believer, but to many it seems to take forever to understand and characterize in a lifetime. It's evident that most Christians read the Bible instead of **studying "to show thyself approved to God, a workman that needs not to be ashamed, rightly dividing the word of truth"** (2 Timothy 2:15). To Adam after the fall, knowing the curse and condemnation of his sinful act, **righteousness by faith into justification by faith** (Genesis 3:21) must have been a joyous experience, but more so the most degrading, humiliating, and humbling experience to his unequivocal demeaning, immoral condition before God and the universe.

In his narrative of Romans chapter four, Paul makes is exceptionally clear that although Abram "believed God, and it was counted to him for righteousness," he afterward "**received the sign of circumcision, a seal of the righteousness of the faith** which he had yet being uncircumcised: **that he might** be the father of all them that believe, though they be not circumcised; **that righteousness might be imputed (accredited to their personal life's record) to them also**" (Romans 4:11). How can it be any more clear? Abram believed that the Lord Jesus Christ was going to give him land and the seed, a son called Isaac, a direct descendant of the seed to Christ, and it was accounted to him for righteousness in heaven's bank account. The righteousness of God revealed from faith to faith, as it is written, "the just, **(the made right with God)** shall live by faith" (Romans 1:17).

It is faith in the atonement of Christ that appropriates divine judicial righteousness that no man can claim of himself (Romans 3:10). Then Abram accepted the sealing sign of circumcision (Romans 4:11), authorized in his generation by Jesus. By Abram obeying it, he then and only then was imputed, or clothed, with the life-giving righteousness that saves at judgment time (Hebrews 9:27; 2 Corinthians 5:10; Acts 17:31). Jesus needs and must have this righteousness in place in the life of the believer in order to justify him in the judgment hour (Revelation 14:7). Paul says this process sealed the faith of Abram in justification unto life, then Abram became Abraham, the "father of circumcision to them who are not of the circumcision only, but **who also walk in the steps of that faith of our father Abraham**, which he had being yet uncircumcised" (Romans 4:12).

Paul said after Abraham received the specific covenant sign of circumcision, "being not weak in faith, he considered not his own body now dead, **when he was about a hundred years old**, neither yet the deadness of Sarah's womb: He **staggered not at the promise of God through unbelief; but was strong in faith, giving glory to God;** And being fully persuaded **(after twenty-four years)** that what he **(Jesus)** had promised, he was able also to perform" (Romans 4:19-21). This was the case twenty-four years after Abram's walk of faith in not just believing *in* the Lord, but believing the Lord (Genesis chapters 12-17). **And therefore** it **was imputed to him for righteousness.** Paul says, was it not "written for his sake alone, that it was imputed to him; **but for us also,** to whom it **shall be imputed, if we believe on him that raised up Jesus our Lord from the dead**; who was delivered for our offenses, and was raised again for our justification (Romans 4:23, 25). **"Therefore (in light of) being justified by faith,** we **have peace** with God through our Lord Jesus Christ: By whom also we have **access** by faith **into this grace** wherein **we stand,** and **rejoice** in hope of the **glory (righteousness)** of God" (Romans 5:1, 2).

Abram believed in the Lord and it was accounted him for righteousness, but the scriptures reveal though he may have believed in the Lord, he did not in the beginning emphatically, completely believe him. Genesis 15:8 records Abram's lack of complete faith in the promises of God, when Abram said, **"Lord God, whereby shall I know that I shall inherit it?"** Mankind's faith in believing in the Lord does not constitute faith in believing the Lord, and in Abram's case it was exemplified when he asked for **a sign of its future fulfillment** (Genesis 15:8). Yes, his faith in **believing in** the Lord accounted him for righteousness. But his **believing the Lord** would be tested over the next twenty-four years of Abram's walk of "faith to faith" (Romans 1:17) until he believed the Lord. He **believed in** the Lord and he was allowed to wait through his own stumbling until **Abraham believed God,** even though his timely faith in the beginning was counted to him for righteousness.

Scripture reveals **believing in the Lord does not constitute believing the Lord,** and this was Abram's condition in the beginning of his walk of faith. Paul in Romans chapter four traces his timely experience through to when Abraham believed the Lord and was fully persuaded that what God promised, the seed Isaac, he was able to perform (Romans 4:21). See how faith wrought with his works, and by works, was faith made perfect (James 2:21, 22), a direct answer to Genesis 17:1? Paul does not give us this information in any way criticizing the patriarchs of old. Abraham's faith in the beginning was characterized by believing in the Lord, and traced to the time he truly **believed the Lord.** Abraham's walk of faith is the same that takes place in the life of every believer. Even when he came to the place of faith when he **believed the lord,** was his faith tested? Of course it was. "And it came to pass **after these things that God did test Abraham,** and said unto him, Abraham: and he said, Behold, here I am. And he said, **Take now thy son, thy only son Isaac,** whom thou loves, and get thee into the land of Moriah; and **offer him there for a burnt offering** upon one of the mountains which I will tell thee of (Genesis 22:1, 2). James says, "Was not Abraham our father justified by works, when he had offered Isaac his son upon the altar?" (James 2:21).

As Abraham was tested in his day in **righteousness by faith into justification by faith** in Christ, so it will be again just before Jesus comes for this final generation (**Revelation 3:10**). Paul says, "For therein is the righteousness of God revealed **from faith to faith**" (Romans 1:17). And as Abraham was tested from "faith to faith" in his lifetime, so shall every believer be tested from "faith to faith" in the imputed righteousness of Christ just before Jesus comes in the clouds of heaven. Be sure, friends, this applies to you and me.

Many apply Romans chapter four to account faith as the only point of salvation necessary for acceptance with God. Peter says when we are studying Paul's writing to be very careful. "As also in all his epistles, speaking in them of these things; **in which are some things hard to be understood, which they that are unlearned and unstable**" in line upon line, precept upon precept (Isaiah 28:10), **"from faith to faith" (Romans 1:17)**, timeline upon timeline, twist and fail to compare, **"as they do also the other scriptures, to their own destruction"** (2 Peter 3:16). Christ's remnant people must at this crucial time understand what constitutes the true theme of righteousness by faith into justification by faith in Christ. It's **critical** and **deadly** to Christians who are in confusion. Paul says, "Who shall lay anything to the charge of God's elect? **It is God that justifies**" (Romans 8:33). Paul says, "But to him that works not, but **believeth on him that justifies the ungodly**, his faith is counted for righteousness" (Romans 4:5). Here we see the **critical emphasis on "but believeth on him that justifies the ungodly."** Abraham understood his condition before God, as was Job of the same mindset when he said, "I know it is so of a truth: but how should man be just (made right) with God? **If I justify myself**, mine **own mouth shall condemn me**: if I say, **I am perfect, it shall also prove me perverse"** (Job 1:2, 20). Here again we see Abraham, as well as Job, had to understand **"it is God that justifies."**

When Abram **believed in the Lord** and it was accounted him for righteousness, God, knowing the degree of faith in the beginning of Abram's walk from "**faith to faith**," gave him at that time the covenant sign signified by sacrificing (Genesis 15:5-18). Twenty-four years later, after he was grown in "faith to faith" (Romans 1:17), he emphatically **believed the Lord.** After knowing his blunder of producing an unauthorized child (Genesis 16:4), he was given by Jesus another covenant sign, called the sign of circumcision, his seal of imputed righteousness unto justification (Genesis 17:1-14; Romans 4:11; Romans 5:1). This is gospel order, God knowing what constitutes true heavenly justification unto life in His heavenly kingdom and working in the life of Abraham and in the life of every believer until this heavenly process of saving a man in undisputed righteousness is perfected. Paul said, "For **I am not ashamed of the gospel of Christ**: for it is the power of God to salvation to everyone that believeth; to the Jew first, and also to the Greek. **For therein (in the gospel)** is the righteousness of God revealed from **faith to faith**: as it is written, the just **(made right)** shall live by faith" (Romans 1:16, 17).

To you, my fellow reader, I do not want to be repetitious. However, when it comes to obtaining life-giving righteousness, the Bible is repetitious. So please let me say again, in Romans chapter four, Paul makes it exceptionally clear that although Abram "believed God and it was counted to him for righteousness," over twenty-four years had passed before he "received his new covenant sign of circumcision, a seal of the righteousness of the faith which he had yet being uncircumcised ... that righteousness might be imputed to them (who walk in the faith of Abraham) also." Circumcision was his generation's sign of present truth (2 Peter 1:12), his sign of obtaining precious faith (2 Peter 1:1) in the righteousness of Christ that leads to justification unto eternal life, and the right to be represented and accepted at judgment time in the heavenly sanctuary.

Circumcision was Abraham's seal of transferred righteousness, applied to his life's record in heaven's judicial judgment hall of justice. How can it be any more clear? Believe in the Lord Jesus Christ to be accounted with righteousness. Faith credits divine acceptable righteousness that no man can claim of himself (Romans 3:10). Accept God's seal of transfer, authorized in your generation by obeying it, and then and only then can one be imputed, clothed with life-giving righteousness to stand justified in the judgment hour (Revelation 6:17; 2 Corinthians 5:10; Daniel 7:9, 10,13, 14; Acts 17:31; Revelation 14:7). Paul says this process sealed the faith of Abraham in justification unto life, then Abraham became the "father of circumcision to them who are not of the circumcision only, but who also walk in the steps of that faith of our father Abraham, which he had being yet uncircumcised" (Romans 4:12).

Our heavenly Father will only justify man through the atonement produced by the life, death, and resurrection of Jesus Christ. Adam's sin nullified everything the principles of God's eternal code of conduct upholds in one's right to life. The adversary of souls knows this; he was the very first one in heaven to step out of justification by faith and give up heaven's bill of rights, the right of life-giving righteousness, and by his unequivocal lies he deceived one-third of God's holy angels into doing the same thing (Revelation 12:4). This greatest intellectual mind ever fashioned is an example to us all, that exalting intellect, power, education, and position over gospel order will not be tolerated in heaven. And the great apostle John says that just before Jesus comes again the great red dragon beast of Revelation 12:3, 13:1, and 17:3 will set up his own perversion of the gospel and deceive the whole world as to our legal, forensic right to justification unto life (Revelation 12:9).

Scripture uses names and expressions, beginning with Jesus, the cross, the gospel, faith, grace, blood sacrifice, circumcision, and baptism to convey to us the underlying critical issues and principles of God's orderly conduct in everything done respectively for the salvation of man under a divine timeline. Today, as well as in the past, many a believer has used a single Bible verse or expression as a single expression, constituting all they need for salvation. Please, friends, this is not and cannot be; many a believer is being misled by this unscriptural method of expressing salvation. The most widely used and misunderstood scriptural expression used today by believers and most religious leaders to define salivation is, "For by grace are ye saved through faith; and that not of yourselves: it is the gift of God (Ephesians 2:8).

The word grace today as well as in the past is terribly misapplied. Paul said, "Now to him that works is the reward not **reckoned of grace**, but of debt" (Romans 4:5). All our works in Christ are reckoned of grace. Grace is more than divine influence upon the heart and the reflection thereof. **Grace is divine judicial favor with God** applied through **righteousness by faith into justification by faith** in Christ. The great apostle Paul said, "But where sin abounded, grace did much more abound" (Romans 5:20). So what is he talking about when he uses the word grace? Paul also said, "That as sin hath reigned to death, even so **might grace reign (rule) through righteousness** to eternal life by Jesus Christ our Lord" (**Romans 5:21**). **Grace reigns or rules** in the life of the believer through the life-giving righteousness of Christ. **Grace does not reign over sin in one's life outside of the life-giving righteousness of Christ** (Romans 5:21). And that is biblical truth.

The Bible is clear; sin truly abounds or thrives in you and me. If grace does not abound over and above sin in the life of the believer, grace has no power to rule or reign over sin. Scripture says, "Noah found grace in the eyes of the Lord" (Genesis 6:8). Did grace reign in Noah's day? Grace was there. How did grace reign or rule in Noah's life? Only through the righteousness of Christ had grace any power over sin in the life of Noah. And how did Noah appropriate this righteousness so grace would abound and have the right to rule in his life? First, he also had to believe in the Lord, and it was accounted **to him for righteousness.** Then, "Noah built an altar unto the Lord; and took of every clean beast, and of every clean fowl, and offered burnt offerings on the altar" (Genesis 8:20). **By faith** Noah believed and obeyed gospel order in his day, the faith delivered to the saints through the gospel message and sign given to him by his forefathers. That is why the "Lord said unto Noah, Come thou and thy entire house into the ark; **for thee have I seen righteous before me in this generation**" (Genesis 7:1).

Paul, in his expression in Galatians 1:6, associates grace with the gospel of Christ. He also associated grace with righteousness when he said, "I do not frustrate the **grace of God**: for if **righteousness** come by the law, then Christ is dead in vain" (Galatians 2:21). In Ephesians 2:8 he says, "**For by grace** are ye saved through faith; and that not of yourselves: **it is the gift of God.**" Scripture defines **grace as a gift of righteousness**, a gift Jesus gives to us produced by his life, death, and resurrection, the righteousness God needs to save us. "For if by one man's offense **death reigned (ruled) by one;** much more **they which receive** abundance of grace and of **the gift of righteousness shall reign (or rule) in life by one**, Jesus Christ" (Romans 5:17). We receive abundance of grace and have a right to live under grace only through gospel order of **righteousness by faith into justification by faith** in Christ.

Faith is never legal faith outside of the righteousness of Christ (2 Peter 1:1, 2). Scripture testifies that the righteousness of Christ entitles us to the blessings of the covenants God so afforded man under divine grace through gospel order. We are no more saved by the grace of God in this generation without the imputed righteousness of Christ outside of gospel order, than was any generation in the past. The concept that the Old Testament believer was under law and the New Testament believer under grace is a fabrication of men. Grace is mentioned forty times in the Old Testament scriptures. I believe the religious school of thought in Jesus' day (Matthew 16:6) has a direct parallel to the two religious mind-sets of Catholicism and Protestantism that are being presented from our Christian institutions today. We are no less in a dispensation of grace than was Adam after he sinned and received an imputed robe of Christ's righteousness (Genesis 3:21; Isaiah 61:10).

Paul says, "Therefore **(in light of) being justified by faith, we have peace with God through our Lord Jesus Christ:** By whom also **we have access** by faith **into this grace wherein we stand**, and rejoice in hope of the glory of God" (Romans 5:1-5). **No righteousness** means we are without the right to God's grace. **No grace** means **no standing** (Revelation 6:17). **No standing** means **no hope** in receiving a literal crown of righteousness at the second coming of Christ (2 Timothy 4:8).

Friends, the **"thou shall not" (Genesis 2:17)** given to Adam is the same "thou shall not" given to Abraham, the same "thou shall not" that applies to every man today. The gospel preached to Adam after the fall is no different than the gospel preached to Abraham, and is the same gospel God uses to save everyone in every generation. The grace that God favored man with in the Old Testament is the same grace God favors man with in the New. The law of God is no different today than it was in the past. The Father of all heaven demands, "Thou shall not" be without the gospel of life-giving righteousness of Jesus Christ, which affords every man the grace to judicially present themselves and their commandment keeping before God (1 John 2:4).

Scripture testifies do not think to attempt to present yourself before God outside of the gospel of grace (Galatians 1:6). Do not think to attempt to present yourself before God without the necessary grace that reigns through the life-giving righteousness of Christ (Romans 5:21; 2 Peter 1:1). Scripture is clear, because of man's sinful condition after the fall, any attempt to offer any such representation in heaven would be considered immorally blasphemous. Scripture says, "I call heaven and earth to record this day against you, that I have set before you life and death, blessing and cursing: therefore choose life, that both thou and thy seed may live" (Deuteronomy 30:19). Abraham was the father of faith, the scriptures say, "Because that Abraham obeyed my voice, and kept my charge, my commandments, my statutes, and my laws (Genesis 26:5).

The world is so educated today that common sense has no more reasoning power than in the days of Jesus. Just as when holy angels in heaven decided they were so educated in the things of God that common sense could not keep them from rebelling, they "left their own habitation" (Jude 6) in heaven and are now reserved on this dark, dirty planet (Revelation 12:12) for judgment with all of us who choose to foolishly misapply the scriptures to our own destruction (2 Peter 3:16). Friends, now is the time to search the scriptures to find out for ourselves these wonderful hidden truths so precious to souls in a time when the religious school of our day parallels the schools of religious education in Jesus' day. "Then said Jesus to those Jews **(commandment-keepers of his day)** which believed on him, **If ye continue in my word, then** are ye my disciples indeed; And **ye shall know the truth, and the truth (of the gospel of Christ [Ephesians 1:13; Colossians 1:5]) shall make you free**" (John 8:31, 32).

After the fall of man shortly after creation, Jesus clothed Adam with the sign of sacrifice, a seal of the imputed righteousness He needed to save man from his deadly fall (Genesis 3:21). For one thousand and five hundred years, Jesus worked through heaven's providence to save a freshly created world from being eternally lost. After the flood and a time for man to show again his rebellious nature, God called Abram to separate from his descendants, to make of him a nation among future nations, to establish His governing principles on this fallen planet (Genesis 12:1, 2; Galatians 3:8).

Although Abraham was a man of faith, the scriptures reveal that because of his sinfulness, his faith faltered just like ours does. And in the process of the time and the era of Abraham's life, God was revealing to the universe the nature of what sin is and can do as it increases in intensity in the nature of man (Ephesians 3:9, 10). It was because of Abraham's failure in breaking the first covenant contract with Jesus (Genesis 15:18; 16:4), and the now established condition of the human family in a greater degree of sinfulness, that Jesus introduced the new sign of salvation. The seal of circumcision is a sign of faith, a seal of imputed righteousness to the next two millennia of earth's inhabitants (Romans 4:11). This new sign of faith, a new seal of imputed righteousness, was instituted so that they too might of their own free will chose to appropriate the right to life in God's glorious kingdom of everlasting righteousness (Romans 14:17).

⌒ *Chapter Seven* ⌒
Israel, Clothed with the Sun

"Ａnd I say to you, that many shall come from the east and the west, and shall sit down with Abraham, and Isaac, and Jacob, in the kingdom of heaven" (Matthew 8:11). Three men were called, anointed, and appointed to be fathers of a nation created among the nations of the world as representatives of gospel order among men. **Abraham** represents the **father of unrelenting faith**, which without, no man will see God (Hebrews 11:6). **Isaac** is a symbol of God's planning and **overseeing the born again experience** in one's life, which without, no man will see God (John 3:5; John 6:44). And **Jacob** was a **man who wrestled with God** and would not let go until he received the promised blessing (Genesis 32:27), which also without, no man will see God (Revelation 3:21). These three men symbolize three areas of development we all individually must pass through in our lifetime of character development. Accordingly, out of the loins of **Abraham, Isaac,** and **Jacob** would come **twelve sons,** patriarchs creating a nation among nations representing God's kingdom under divine governing principles of life. **These three men, fathers in gospel order, were seeds in the birth of a nation**.

As with every individual, the nation of Israel when it became an established nation among nations was authorized under divine credentials. Israel's birth was of faith, a birth of God's planning and design, a birth of wrestling with God and overcoming in a fallen world of developing nations among men. Critical in our understanding is the revelation of nations from the descendants of Noah to our time in the discernment of last-day events. Nations did not exist prior to the Babel incident of Genesis eleven. Although many nations would come and go, the scriptures reveal seven specific nations from the time of Abraham that the adversary of souls would use as dominating powers in time to oppress directly and indirectly those who would be represented as the Israel of God.

Prior to the birth of Israel, descendants from the families of Noah were developing into multitudes, kindred's, tongues, peoples, and nations. Seven of these nations are represented by seven specific characteristics of power symbolized in the scriptures as dragon or beast heads in Revelation 12:3; 13:1; and 17:3. These seven specific nations under satanic deception from Abraham's day are defined as nations or "beast that **was**, and **is not** and **yet is**" in Revelation 17:8. They would have birth, and **was** means they reign in power for a time. **Is not** represents the lost of controlling power. **Yet is** (or yet continue to exist) until the second coming of Christ (Daniel 7:12). "And there appeared another wonder in heaven; and **behold a great red dragon, having seven heads** and **ten horns**, and **seven crowns upon his heads**" (Revelation 12:3). John defines these seven heads as mountains, kings, and kingdoms as they rose as powerful nations in their time of conflict with God's people down through time (Revelation 17:9, 10). All were predicted to unite together in the end time to become an eighth power on the earth (Revelation 17:11), to eventually oppress or stamp the residue (**or remnant)** people of God (Daniel 7:7, 17) just before Jesus comes, igniting the battle of Armageddon (Revelation 12:17; Revelation 16:16).

Israel was called of God out of the loins of three representative men, as God's nation among nations, that men might be drawn to the only true God and His representative principles of life. Israel's primary ideal as a nation was to draw (John 12:32) all of humanity through the gospel of Christ, to be **reconciled to God** through the merits of our risen Lord. Paul says, "Now then we are ambassadors for Christ, as though God did beseech you by us: we pray you in Christ's stead, **be ye reconciled to God**" (2 Corinthians 5:20). "For it pleased the Father that in him (in Christ) should all fullness dwell; And, **having made peace through the blood of his cross,** by him **to reconcile all things to himself**; by him, I say, whether they be **things in earth, or things in heaven**. And you, that were sometime **alienated and enemies in your mind** by wicked works, yet **now hath he reconciled in the body of** his flesh through death, to **present you holy and unblameable and unreproveable** in his sight" (Colossians 1:19-22).

Scripture records that out of the loins of Abraham and Isaac, two sons would emerge (Genesis 25:21-23). In the process of time, the first born, Esau, would relinquish his birthright and the promised blessing of direct ancestry to the ancestral line leading to the birth of Christ. Although much is revealed in the struggles and conflicts between Jacob and Esau, the end results portray the characters these two men developed and the choices they made in their lifetime that sealed their eternal destiny. Although called to fill important positions among God's people, these two men demonstrated critical choices early in life that had great influences on the choices they made in later years.

Esau's sin of selling his birthright for a morsel of food, and Jacob's involvement in stealing the promised blessing from his brother by deceiving his father, separated a family called of God for a lifetime. It was after his flight from his homeland and twenty years of education in exile from the presence of his family (Genesis 28-31) that Jacob is told by Jesus to "return to the land of thy kindred" (Genesis 31:13). This, although obedient to his divine calling, was frightful for Jacob. Scripture says just before Jacob is about to meet his brother, believing Esau wants to take his life, he separates himself from the presence of his family (Genesis 32:23, 24). In Peniel (Genesis 32:30), in a night of anguish and fear, wrestles with Jesus for deliverance from the hands of his brother and the sins of his past.

There, in heartfelt repentance for past offenses, and a plea by faith in the promises of God with endurance and perseverance, Jacob obtained the reward, **"power with God"** and with men (Genesis 32:28). There, Jacob received **power with God that appropriates for man the righteousness of Christ,** and the peace with God we all need, the two foremost primary merits under gospel order that God needs in order to save man. There, Jacob understood the **"gospel of peace** (Romans 10:15); there, he understood "Therefore **being justified by faith, we have peace with God** through our Lord Jesus Christ" (Romans 5:1). There, he appropriated **"feet shod with the preparation of the gospel of peace"** (Ephesians 6:15). Remember, friends, the **first merit** of the gospel of Christ is imputed **righteousness,** which affords us peace with God (Romans 1:16, 17) in order that we may obtain the indwelling gift of the influencing power of the **Holy Spirit, justifying for us the right of receiving the atonement and the forgiveness of sins** (John 20:19-23). All was accomplished in perfect divine order. Oh, how wonderful is the orderly process and work of our heavenly Father in His perfect plan for the salvation of man.

It is critical to understand the process of reconciliation and authorization in the ambassadorship status of Jacob when he became Israel (Genesis 32:28), characterized in the statements of that day's experience between Jacob and Jesus. After his name is changed from Jacob to Israel, this humble servant of gospel order was clothed with divine righteousness, as a nation authorized with divine judicial authority for the salvation of the nations around him. After Jacob receives the divine blessing of God, he calls the name of the place where his experience happened **Peniel,** a name in Hebrew associated with the expression "the **face of God." "For I have seen God (Jesus) face to face and my life is preserved"** (Genesis 32:30). Peniel is a memorial of the time and place of Jacobs's direct encounter with Jesus, and the accomplishment of his born again experience.

After Jacob makes this statement (Genesis 32:30), the scriptures describe the weather conditions and then the physical condition of Jacob after his experience (Genesis 32:32). "And as he passed over Penuel, **the sun rose upon him,** and he halted upon his thigh" (Genesis 32:31). His physical condition was made known, yes, but why the weather? Why is this statement "**the sun rose upon him**" emphasized here? The word sun in the scriptures has a distinct and definite meaning in the Old Testament symbolism. In Genesis 37:9, 10, the sun, moon, and stars are symbols of family authority. **Sun=father, moon=mother, stars=older brothers,** as interpreted to Joseph by his father, Jacob, after Joseph told him of his dream that the sun, moon, and stars were bowing down to him. This was a representation of a future literal event.

The word **sun** is a **symbol for righteousness** in the Old and New Testaments. As the sun is the greater light in the heavens and has the superior effect on other planets, even so, Malachi 4:2 says, "But unto you that **fear my name** shall the **Sun of righteousness** arise with healing in his wings." In Revelation 12:1, John sees a "woman clothed with the sun," a fitting symbol of imputed righteousness given to the New Testament Christians. **On the day that Jacob became Israel, "the sun of righteousness rose on him as a nation with official credentials of imputed righteousness** and authority, as a nation with direct responsibility from heaven's judicial authorities to seek reconciliation for all men in every nation that would arise in this fallen world. From the time Jacob became Israel, to the first coming of Christ, Israel was a prefigured, Christ-centered, theocratic nation among nations, for the salvation of nations (Galatians 3:8).

To be Israel or an Israelite from the time of Jacob to the first coming of Christ meant every citizen had to be clothed with the life-giving righteousness of God. But that did not mean that every child born and circumcised of the seed of Abraham took it to heart and took the necessary steps in the calling of God. Paul said, "Brethren, my heart's desire and prayer to God for Israel is that they might be saved. For I bear them record that they have zeal for God, but not according to knowledge. For they being **ignorant of God's righteousness**, and going about to establish their own righteousness, **have not submitted themselves** to the righteousness of God" (Romans 10:1-3).

To be Israel or an Israelite means to be clothed with divine righteousness, clothed with the righteousness of Christ, clothed under the heading of **righteousness by faith into justification by faith** of Christ, having appropriated a divine bill of rights as citizens of Christ's heavenly kingdom through gospel order. Did not Jesus say, "And what nation is there so great, that hath statutes and judgments so righteous as all this law, which I set before you this day? **Only take heed to thyself, and keep thy soul diligently,** lest thou forget the things which thine eyes have seen, and lest they **depart**

from thy heart all the days of thy life: but teach them thy sons and thy sons' sons" (Deuteronomy 4:8, 9). Did not the God of heaven give to Israel all these principles so that they might understand gospel order? There would come a day when Jesus would say to the nation of Israel, "Therefore I say to you, The kingdom of God shall be taken from you, and given to a people bringing forth the fruits of it" (Matthew 21:43).

Literal Israel's failure in their calling from the time of Jacob to the first coming of Christ resulted in the calling of the first century New Testament Christians. It was the crucifixion of Christ that sealed the final rejection of the Jews as a literal nation and a representative people to the nations of the world. Jesus said, "Behold, your house is left unto you desolate" (Matthew 23:38). Desolate of righteousness, void of heaven's bill of rights and authority as God's nation among nations, now no longer called a nation under the divine credentials and guidance of the Holy Spirit. Paul says, "For they are not all Israel, which are of Israel" (Romans 9:6). And those principles apply today to every individual that fails to call upon the name of the Lord in life-giving righteousness.

The same principle applies to the word **Jew**, a synonym for the word **Judah**. The first time the word Jew is used in the scriptures is found in 2 Kings 16:6. It became a synonym for the house of Judah, tribe of Judah, land of Judah, king of Judah, when the twelve tribes of Jacob became divided over the controversy of who should be king in 975 B.C. Israel became the house of Israel, when ten tribes revolted in the north and chose their own king (1 Kings 12:1-20). The house of Judah was made up of two tribes of Jacob, Judah, and Benjamin, of which the word Jew became a synonym for the people residing in the southern part of the promised land. The words Judah and Jew have great symbolism. To be a **Jew** meant to be a **commandment keeper**, a **lawgiver, and commandment keeper from the heart**.

Paul said, "For he is not a Jew, which is one outwardly; neither is that circumcision, which is outward in the flesh: **But he is a Jew, which is one inwardly; and circumcision is that of the heart**, in the spirit, and not in the letter; whose praise is not of men, but of God (Romans 2:28, 29). In the blessing Jacob gave to his twelve sons before his death, to Judah his fourth son, he said, "The **scepter** shall not depart from Judah, nor **a lawgiver** from between his feet, until **Shiloh (symbolic name for a ruler from Judah, or Jesus)** comes; and unto him shall the gathering of the people be (Genesis 49:10). The word Judah or Jew means lawgiver, commandment keeper, or revealer of the principles of God's eternal code of conduct defined in Exodus 20:1-17 as the Ten Commandments. King David said, "**Judah is my lawgiver**" (Psalm 60:7). The **greatest Jew**, the **greatest commandment**

keeper, the **greatest lawgiver** ever to exemplify the moral code of righteousness, was none other than the **Lord Jesus Christ.**

The words Israel and Jew have great symbolic representations together. Divided they may represent a literal nation today in great conflict, and a nationality of people scattered throughout the world, but the spiritual application of these two words together have great spiritual value and represent the people who "**keep the commandments of God and (keep) the faith of Jesus**" (Revelation 14:12). The adversary of souls knows this, that division among God's people in any generation will lead to apostasy and ruin. He purposed to divide literal Israel from the beginning, and by the ninth century B.C. he succeeded. Dividing Israel and Judah is no different today than dividing the law and the gospel. **Israel** means to be **clothed with the sun** (Malachi 4:2), and is a symbol to every Christian who from the heart **believes in the Lord Jesus Christ** by faith, and it is accounted to him or her for life-giving righteousness (Romans 4:3).

A **Jew is a law giver**, a commandment keeper from the heart, a symbol of those who knowingly keep all the commandments of God (1 John 2:3, 4). Israel is a biblical symbolic expression of the law and the gospel combined. John says "Here is the patience of the saints: here are they, (**symbolic Jews**) that keep the commandments of God, and have the faith of Jesus, (**symbolic Israelites**) those clothed with the life-giving righteousness of Christ (Revelation 14:12). Only those Israelites, Christians clothed with heaven's bill of righteousness, which keep the commandment of God, will have a right to the tree of life, and enter in through the gates of the city when Jesus comes the second time (Revelation 22:14). All must pass this test of character exemplified by Jesus before He comes again (Revelation 3:10). All who **believe in the Lord** (Genesis 15:6) will have to **believe the Lord** (Hebrews 4:3) completely by the time Jesus comes again. This will happen again just before Jesus comes, bringing the true test of faith in our day as it was exemplified by the law and the prophets (Romans 3:21; Revelation 3:10). Jesus said, "**If ye keep my commandments, ye shall abide in my love;** even as I **have kept** my Father's commandments, and **abide in his love**" (John 15:10).

Jacob was authorized, and called Israel (Genesis 32:28) a nation clothed with the armor of God. With a divine bill of rights, having a breastplate of righteousness, his feet shod with the gospel of peace, having a shield of faith, with the helmet of salvation and the sword of the spirit, went forth to quench the fiery darts of the wicked (Ephesians 6:11-18). Now in a world beginning to be populated with nations, disconnected from righteousness, our wonderful savior would not have just a scattered group here and there, but a nation among nations for the salvation of nations. After Jacob became Israel he was able to meet his brother Esau with peace in his heart, knowing the gospel of peace is the power of God unto salvation to everyone that believeth (Ephesians 6:15; Romans 1:16).

From the time Jacob became Israel to the time Jacob entered Egypt, over thirty years of trial and conflict would take place in the life of Jacob and his twelve sons. Thirty-three years of educating Israel and preparing them to enter the first future dragon power of Revelations 12:3 in the line of nations was to be evangelized in the early days of Israel. **Egypt** is the **first dragon head**, nation mentioned in the scriptures as prepared by God through the experience of Joseph (Genesis 37-45), for the initial purpose of saving that nation in righteousness. And the scripture, **foreseeing that God would justify the heathen through faith** preached before the gospel to Abraham, saying, "In thee shall all nations be blessed" (Galatians 3:8).

As Abram was called, he was driven into Egypt by a famine in the land (Genesis 12:10). In order to evangelize Pharaoh and his people, Israel, who was Jacob, and his twelve sons, were also prepared of God and driven to Egypt (Genesis 42:1-3) to accomplish what **Abraham failed to do by his blunder (Genesis 12:18, 19)**. The nation of Israel would for a time occupy land in Egypt, that the Egyptian people could attain to the understanding of life without the righteousness of God is a life under satanic deception, leading to national death. Scripture says that for four hundred years Israel stayed in Egypt under a harsh people, until they eventually brought them into complete bondage (Acts.7:6). "Now there arose up a new king over Egypt, which knew not Joseph … Therefore they did set over them taskmasters to afflict them with their burdens" (Exodus 1:8-11). After the death of Joseph, Egypt would forget her calling in righteousness and retain the phrase "sons of man." The scriptures say, "Set thy face against Pharaoh king of Egypt, and prophesy against him, and against all Egypt: Speak, and say, Thus says the Lord GOD; Behold, I am against thee, Pharaoh king of Egypt, **the great dragon** that lieth in the midst of his rivers, which hath said, My river is mine own, and I have made it for myself" (Ezekiel 29:2, 3).

Foretelling and understanding critical issues in past and future events in the development of men and nations, in the outline of prophecy, is vital in the study of God's Word to the appointed people of God in our day. When Abram was told of his inheritance of land and seed in this world of sin, he was also foretold of events in time that would happen to God's people. "And he said unto Abram, Know of a surety that **thy seed shall be a stranger in a land that is not theirs**, and shall serve them; and **they shall afflict them four hundred years** (Genesis 15:13). Egypt became the first great dragon head in the oppression of God's people. It was not a prophecy, because God demanded its fulfillment. It was foretold in the light of the choices of both the people representing God's righteousness and the choices of Egypt and its leaders. Remember, Abram was in the beginning of his calling, because "of a famine in the land" (Genesis 12:10), led to Egypt by the conditions of his day. There he blundered as a representative of the righteousness of God, and the first endeavor by Jesus to evangelize Egypt as a nation took a detour.

Although prophecy foretold that Egypt would someday choose to reject her calling to righteousness, literal Israel, as a nation, for over seventeen hundred years, made many a blunder in the representation of the principles of God's kingdom in their witness to surrounding nations. Israel's fate would lie in the integral faithfulness in representing to the nations around her, her true calling in righteousness. Although God has had a people representing Him in every generation, it has been their blunders in time that has also fulfilled prophetic events among nations.

Israel holds much responsibility in the actions of individuals and nations that have resulted in the terrible choices they have made in the time of their calling to righteousness. Egypt, Assyria, Babylon, Media and Persia, Greece, Rome, these specific nations revealed in scripture, along with many other nations and peoples, have had their allotted time in direct contact with the people of God. These nations will, in the judgment hour message of Daniel seven and Revelation fourteen, have to answer for their failure in answering the call to appropriate as a nation the life-giving righteousness of Christ (Acts 17:31; Luke 10:12-14).

Egypt, the first biblical nation called to righteousness by God through the nation of Israel, was foreseen as afflicting Israel for "**four hundred years**" (Genesis 15:13). This was the time allotted her in her calling to gospel righteousness. Although the children of Israel weren't perfect, and made grave mistakes in their representation of God's governing principles, Egypt, because of her willful and prolonged longevity of oppression, did after her allotted time completely disconnected herself from being under the covering of Christ's righteousness. Imperative in every generation is the educating and training of leaders of God's people in gospel order. As it was in the days of Jesus in the training and educating of his disciples, so it was in the training and discipline of another of the great leaders of the children of Israel.

Moses was a man called and educated by God from his birth, for the primary purpose of delivering Israel from Egyptian bondage after Egypt's allotted time of her calling. Moses' life and training in the courts of

Pharaoh, through his exile in the land of Midian, is a testimony to all that everything we go through here is an education in leading us to life-giving righteousness. Moses was born in his generation to represent Jesus as a deliverer of God's people from bondage to a nation who, years earlier, was greatly blessed by heaven's mercy in revealing to them the character of God and the principles of life. As future leaders of Egypt chose to reject the ways of salvation, Jesus had no other choice after their allotted time to deliver his representative people from Egyptian bondage (Exodus 12:41).

Although Moses was informed of the plan of salvation, no man is forced to accept his calling because scripture reveals ones destiny. Scripture says, "**By faith Moses, when he was come to years, refused** to be called the son of Pharaoh's daughter; **Choosing rather to suffer affliction with the people of God,** than to enjoy the pleasures of sin for a season" (Hebrews 11:25). All of mankind has a calling in righteousness to become **sons and daughters of God** (1 Timothy 2:4). Each has a place in time and responsibility in gospel order to obtain a born again experience (John 3:5-7). But it is left up to each one of us whether or not we will choose to accept our destiny in Christ our righteousness. Moses was no different than anyone of us when it comes to appropriating the righteousness of Christ. This experience is conveyed to us at the calling of Moses by the Lord to deliver Israel from Egyptian bondage. Friends, I am not saying any of these things to degrade, criticize, or condemn any of God's representatives as to their mistakes in their respective calling in righteousness. All our failures may far exceed in great number any that I mention in this study to convey to you the principles of gospel order in Moses' calling.

"And the Lord said unto Moses in Midian, **Go, return into Egypt:** for all the men are dead which sought thy life, and **Moses took his wife and his sons**, and set them upon an ass, and he returned to the land of Egypt: and Moses took the rod (scepter) of God in his hand" (Exodus 4:19, 20) ... And Jesus said to Moses, "And thou shall say unto Pharaoh, Thus saith the Lord, Israel is my son, even my firstborn: And I say unto thee, Let my son go, that he may serve me: and if thou refuse to let him go, behold, I will slay thy son, even thy firstborn" (Exodus 4:22, 23). As these verses are expressed in the directing of Moses in the work appointed him, it is well for all of us to understand the **fate of anyone,** no matter how high the calling, who mistakenly or willfully **fails** the **mandatory steps** in obedience to gospel order.

After Moses separates from the presence of God, the scriptures say, "**And it came to pass by the way in the inn, that the Lord met him, and sought to kill him**" (Exodus 4:24). Whether it was willful disobedience or forgetfulness on the part of Moses we are not told, but this critical error in judgment by Moses at that time, of not circumcising his son, could have cost him his life. Circumcision was the sign of accounted righteousness into imputed righteousness in Moses' day. Moses' wife, Zipporah, had just had a son. Mandatory was the responsibility of Moses to "**circumcise the flesh of your foreskin; and it shall be a token of the covenant** betwixt me and you. **And he that is eight days old shall be circumcised among you**, that righteousness might be imputed unto them also (Romans 4:11), every man child in your generations" (Genesis 17:11, 12). It was through the intercession of Zipporah, Moses' wife, that Moses learned of his failure in performing the right of circumcision and spared him from losing his life and his calling among Israel.

"**Then Zipporah took a sharp stone, and cut off the foreskin of her son,** and cast it at his feet. She said surely a bloody husband art thou to me. So he let him go: then she said a bloody husband thou art" (Exodus 4:25, 26). She was signifying that Moses failed to perform the right of circumcision that could have caused their rejection and death. Again, as in every generation, appointed leaders are warned as to their responsibility in the first rights in gospel order. Can you imagine what it will be like when Jesus comes, when professed Christian leaders and their congregations find themselves without a wedding garment (Revelation 16:15), without the imputed righteousness of Christ, without a bill of rights in God's heavenly kingdom? As well as Abraham, Moses was quickly reminded of his duty in gospel order. **In order for Moses to be employed in God's service, he had to obey the sign of circumcision for his son, a seal of the imputed righteousness of the faith** which he must receive and perform in order that he too might be a father like Abraham. He would be a father of all them that believe, though they be not circumcised; that righteousness might be imputed to them also (Romans 4:11).

The people of God from the time of Abraham practiced the right of circumcision; this individual right was afforded them as the people of God with unalienable rights to divine privileges under the principles of gospel order. **Circumcision was the underlying foundation of instituting the right of transfer of accounted righteousness (Romans 4:3) into imputed righteousness (Romans 4:11) from Abraham through the Exodus, through the wilderness wandering of the Hebrews to the day before Joshua (Joshua 5:2-5) led Israel to entered the promised land mandatory to the first coming of Christ.** It was obligatory from the time of Abraham's covenant with God (Genesis 17:9-14) after his failure to wait for the promised seed, and it would remain in force until the first coming of Jesus Christ (Colossians 2:9-14).

Friends, it's critical for every gospel minister to understand: **It is not our work to deal with the specific sins of men until we first deal with the explicit sin that has put him in this condition, his present state of unrighteousness**. Jesus said, "Go ye into all the world, and **preach the gospel** to every creature" (Mark 16:15). He that believes must take the necessary steps in his generation in obtaining the imputed righteousness of Christ, righteousness first accounted by faith, righteousness then imputed by believing, by obeying the sign presented as the present seal of truth of the gospel in their generation (1 Peter 4:17; 2 Peter 1:1, 10-12).

At Creation, after sin entered the world, present truth for Adam in imputed righteousness was sacrifice. From the time of Abraham, present truth in imputed righteousness was circumcision leading up to the first coming of Christ. Man may take specific steps in putting away many bad habits of sinfulness, but the decree of unrighteousness (Romans 3:10) has only one remedy. It's by beholding "the Lamb of God, which **takes away the sin** of the world (John 1:29), and obedience to the gospel of Christ (2 Thessalonians 1:7, 8), and this applies to every generation.

When Jacob became Israel, a nation among nations was clothed with divine credentials of righteousness and responsibility for the primary purpose of revealing to the nations of this fallen world the principles of God's universal government. Their calling was to reveal to this fallen world the statutes, judgments, principles, and laws of divine universal order for the redemption of this world, that all may be drawn to Christ's redemptive activity and his life-giving principles. For over seventeen hundred years, from the birth of Israel as a nation to the crucifixion of Christ, Jesus did all he could do for those whom He had chosen to represent Him in the third and fourth millennia of earth's history. The next chapter will reveal Israel's actions and fate in rejecting and crucifying the Lord of righteousness.

ᖰ Chapter Eight ᖰ
Gospel Order and Israel's Last Call to Righteousness (A.D. 27)

For hundreds of years Jesus bore long with the nation of Israel. They were given heaven's blessing in the principles of God's kingdom. Circumcision was given to them to impress upon each individual the mandatory principles of gospel order, in what the God of the universe needs to save a fallen world from total annihilation. They failed to take it to heart in their understanding of their moral condition as fallen beings before God. Proud and boisterous, Jesus warned them, "And now, Israel, what doth the Lord thy **God require of thee,** but **to fear the Lord thy God,** to walk in all his ways, and to love him, and to serve the Lord thy God with all thy heart and with all thy soul, **To keep the commandments of the Lord,** and his statutes, which I command thee this day for thy good. Behold the heaven and the heaven of heavens is the Lord's, the earth also, with all that therein is. Only the Lord had a delight in thy fathers to love them, and he chose their seed after them, even you above all people, as it is this day. **Circumcise therefore the foreskin of your heart,** and be no more stiff-necked" (Deuteronomy 10:16).

During the seventy-year Babylonian captivity (Daniel 9:2; Jeremiah 25:11), because of their rebellion and unbelief in past responsibilities, Jesus, through the prophecy of Daniel nine, gave Israel the final warning as to her standing as a people clothed in life-giving righteousness. Daniel says, "Seventy weeks are **determined upon thy people** and upon thy Holy city, to finish the transgression, and to **make an end of sins,** and to make **reconciliation for iniquity,** and to **bring in everlasting righteousness,** and to **seal up the vision and prophecy,** and to **anoint the most Holy**" (Daniel 9:24). In the future, after the decree to restore Israel again as an independent nation (Ezra 7:12-28) with full self-governing control, seventy weeks of time prophecy would be allotted to Israel as probationary time by the majesty of heaven to make her calling and election sure (2 Peter 1:10).

Critical in understanding time prophecy is the concept of understanding the day/year/time principle the scriptures use to calculate time in prophecies. In the past, God used the day/year principles to educate His people to comprehending His mindset in prophecy. When the Israelites failed to believe the testimony of Caleb and Joshua about the land the twelve spies were sent to evaluate as a land suitable to occupy, they were denied access to its territory because of their rebellion and unbelief. A prophetic timeframe was given them in a day/year prophetic timeline of interpretation. "After the number of the days, in which ye searched the land, *even* **forty days, each day for a year**, shall ye bear your iniquities, *even* **forty years**, and ye shall know my breach of promise (Numbers 14:34). For forty years Israel wandered in the wilderness for its direct rebellion and apostasy of unbelief in a time of direct communication with their Lord and deliverer Jesus Christ.

Again in Ezekiel is the same prophetic time principle applied. "And when thou hast accomplished them, lie again on thy right side, and thou shall bear the iniquity of the house of Judah forty days: **I have appointed thee each day for a year** (Ezekiel 4:6). Also, in Daniel chapter four, Nebuchadnezzar is warned not to exalt himself in his power and majesty as the king of Babylon. But when his pride overpowered him, a voice from heaven decreed a seven day/year timeframe (Daniel 4:32-34) of discipline to chastise him for his **willful** neglect of obeying the council of God given him by the prophet Daniel (Daniel 4:19-27). To Israel as a nation, 490 years would be allotted to the remnant nation of Israel to take a decided stand in the principles of God's kingdom or lose their calling as the Israel of God.

Beginning at the command given in Daniel 9:25 to restore and rebuild Jerusalem from 457 B.C. (Ezra 7:12-26), to the anointing of Jesus at the baptism of John (Matthew 3:13), 483 years of the 490 years prophecy towards Israel was literally fulfilled. When Jesus was anointed as the Lamb of God who takes away the sin and unrighteousness of the world (John 1:29), Israel had only seven years left of prophetic probationary time "to finish the transgression, and to **make an end of sins**, and to make **reconciliation for iniquity**, and to **bring in everlasting righteousness**, and to **seal up the vision and prophecy,** and to **anoint the most Holy**" (Daniel 9:24).

This they failed to do, and seven years later at the stoning of Steven in A.D. 34 (Acts 7:1-60), the prophetic prophecy of 490 days/years would be completely fulfilled and literal Israel as a nation did *willfully separate from the privilege of being under the covering of Christ life-giving righteousness.* Then the gospel would go to the gentiles (Acts 13:45, 46) and the New Testament Christian Church would have the authority and responsibility of giving the gospel message to the entire world (Revelation 12:1, 2).

Foretold to Israel in Malachi 4:5 was the promise to send Elijah the prophet before the coming of the great and dreadful day of the Lord. Elijah was the forerunner, a prophet among all prophets, on the scene to announce Jesus the Lamb of God who takes away **the sin** (unrighteousness) of the world (John 1:29). Terrible was the condition of Israel at the first coming of Christ. Confusion, turmoil, and a time of spiritual darkness was in the midst of Jerusalem, a city called by Zechariah "the city of truth" (Zechariah 8:3). This terrible time of darkness among the people of God would only be rivaled by the condition of the 21st Century Christians and the world just before the second coming of Christ. The depth of darkness and condition of that ungrateful, unprepared generation is penetratingly depicted by the representation of unknown men at the birth of Christ seeking to see and worship their Lord. What emphasis was revealed by Matthew regarding the birth of Christ? Unknown men, wise men coming from the East, knew more about the prophecies of the first coming of Christ than the two religious academic institutions of Jesus' day (Matthew 2:1-7).

Was it not wise men from the East that announced the first coming of Christ when the church of his day was in darkness (Luke 2:79; 2 Corinthians 4:4, 5)? And does not the God of life-giving righteousness have a parallel of these men in place today, wise men (Daniel 12:3) "out of the east and out of the north" (Daniel 11:44)? They are prepared to announce the second coming of Christ in light of the darkness that covers the earth and the "gross darkness" of the Christians who are in spiritual darkness to the" truth of the gospel" message for today (Isaiah 60:1-3; Revelation 14:6, 7).

And where were the theologians and religious leaders when John the Baptist announced that Jesus is the Lamb that takes away the sin of the world (John 1:29)? How critical is the emphasis of the mindset of the Pharisees and the Sadducees in that critical era. For years controversy, contention, and hostility for power, position, and authority developed terrible dissension between these two mindsets of religion. Only at the first coming of Christ would a provisional unity emerge among these two religious rivals in the denunciation of Christ. At the baptism of Christ, John the Baptist, that great forerunner of Christ, does not hesitate to direct the identity of those responsible for the mindset of spiritual darkness of the people of God in Jesus' day. John was the first prophet to use the symbol of the **serpent** to emphasize the character and immoral fiber of the religious leaders who manipulated the scriptures to maintain their own power and position (Matthew 3:7). He also uses the phrase "**axe** laid to the root of the trees" (Matthew 3:10), denouncing the cunning character of these appointed spiritual leaders of the people, whose unethical methods where not according to gospel order. They were soon to be axed or **cut off** from their fatal deception. And Jesus, also at the end of His ministry, confirmed this unscrupulous, cunning snakelike mindset of most of the ministry existing in His day.

Therefore, He said, "You are witnesses to yourselves, that ye are the children of them who killed the prophets. Fill you up then the measure of your fathers. **Ye serpents, ye generation of vipers,** how can ye escape the damnation of hell" (Matthew 23:31-33). This confirmed their mindsets regarding Christ's crucifixion and death. The book of Revelation reveals in symbols (Revelation 12:14-17) the mindset of dragonlike civil leaders and serpentlike religious leaders working together in the last days (Revelation 16:13, 14). They will be preparing the world under satanic deception (Revelation 12:9) to rival the condition of the civil and religious leaders controlling the people of God in Jesus' day.

Jesus said of John the Baptist, "For I say to you, among those that are born of women there is not a greater prophet than John the Baptist" (Luke 7:28). John the Baptist was a prophet sent of God to foretell events that would transpire in his day that also parallel the very issues to take place in this final generation. Malachi.4:5 is a duel prophecy of Elijah, announcing the last call to righteousness in literal Israel existing in Jesus' day, and spiritual Israel existing in our day. This parallel prophecy of the last call to righteousness is to be given to the 21st Century Christians and the people of the world just before Jesus comes the second time. What happened in Jerusalem two thousand years ago will happen again on a universal scale. The warnings Jesus gave to Jerusalem were symbols of the final events to take place just prior to His second coming. The rejection of Christ by the false teachers of his day was just a **mole hill** of conspiracy compared to the **mountain of false teachers** presiding over the people in our day, crying peace and safety when true peace is only obtained through gospel order (Ephesians 6:15; 1 Thessalonians 5:1-3). Jesus said, "For many shall come in my name saying I am Christ (*I am Christian*) and shall deceive many (Matthew 24:4, 5).

The Lord is coming to execute judgment upon all who obey not the gospel of Christ (2 Thessalonians 1:7, 8; Jude 15). He is coming "to execute judgment upon all and to convince all (**Christians**) that are ungodly" *in the present state of unrighteousness (Romans 1:18).* All their *ungodly deeds (done in violation of the law of righteousness (Romans 9:31),* they have committed outside of the *"law of faith"* (Romans 3:27). Jesus illustrated *"obedience of faith"* (Romans 16:26) unto justification by faith (Hebrews 5:8, 9), "leaving us an example, that ye should follow in his steps" (1 Peter 2:21). The "law of righteousness" that witnesses through the "law of faith" is the one subject that is not half understood by the people of God.

These two primary principles (*laws*) of gospel order, exemplified in the plan of salvation by Jesus, will determine at Christ's second coming the Christian's right to eternal life in the kingdom of God (Matthew 6:33).

How critical it is for Christians in this generation to understand that faith is defined by the apostle Paul as the foremost principle, or *law* (Romans 3:27), in one's salvation. It was the foremost message Jesus gave to Israel at the beginning of His ministry. In Jesus' first and primary statement, "*Repent ye and believe the gospel*" (Mark 1:15), Jesus confirmed and established the primary principle, rule, and law in the establishment of the right to life for the fallen inhabitants of Planet Earth. If the "*law of faith*" (Romans 3:27) is not believed (Mark 1:15; 1 Corinthians 15:2), received (1 Corinthians 15:1), and obeyed (Romans 16:26), the "*law of righteousness*" (Romans 9:31) has no judicial right to establish the justification by faith (Romans 5:1) salvation process in the life of the Christian believer than it had to save the people of God in Jesus' day.

It was the mission of John not only to announce the "law of faith" in the "Lamb of God who takes away the sin of the world" (John 1:29), but also to announce the principle subject of his mission. **He was to announce the "law of righteousness" in the atonement process that brings in or establishes the believer in justification unto life.** This was the bill of rights Jesus produced for man's mandatory right of salvation in the kingdom of God. John the Baptist, a prophet among prophets, came to announce **the "who" of salvation, Jesus** (John 1:29), and the **"what" of salvation, the gospel produced by Christ** (Mark 1:15; Romans 1:16, 17) for the righteous restoration of the human family. Luke says, "And he came into all the country about Jordan, preaching the baptism of repentance for the remission of sins (Luke 3:3), "**to make an end of sins**," prophesied in Daniel 9:24. Please understand that outside of the "law of faith," the apostle Paul says even the food we eat is sanctioned as sin (Romans 14:23).

It was the central mission of John the Baptist to announce especially the first phase of Jesus' mission, which was to produce a perfect moral life without committing one sin mentally, morally, physically, spiritually, socially, every second, every minute, every hour of every day of his whole human life. Jesus produced for us the bill of rights Adam took from us at the fall of the human family (Genesis 3:11). This insight was made clear when Jesus said, "For John **came to you in the way of righteousness**, and ye believed him not: but the publicans and the harlots believed him: and ye, when ye had seen it, repented not afterward, that ye might believe him" (Matthew 21:32). John's mission was to announce the righteousness of Christ by pointing men "to the Lamb of God that takes away the sin (unrighteousness) of the world" (John 1:29) and laying "the axe to the root of the tree" (Luke 3:9). Trees in the scriptures are symbols for men (Mark 8:24). An axe is a symbol of "cutting off" (Genesis 17:14) the heart that is not right with God. Any and all in Jesus' day that would not believe and obey the gospel presentation of that critical time was to be cut off from the right of justification unto life (John 8:24; 15:22).

After Jesus' temptation in the wilderness, the first statement He made announced the last call to righteousness to Israel as a nation. "Saying, the **time is fulfilled**, and **the kingdom of God is at hand** repent ye, and **believe the gospel**" (Mark 1:15). The time prophecy of Daniel 9:25, 483 years of time for literal Israel, is fulfilled, the kingdom of God is at hand, the righteousness of God is at hand, take delivery of the kingdom of God, for the **kingdom of God is** ..."**righteousness**, and **peace**, and **joy** in the **Holy Spirit**" (Romans 14:17). **Repent** and **believe** the gospel (Mark 1:15). Repent and receive the gospel (1 Corinthians 15:1). Repent and obey (1 Peter 4:17) the **gospel of righteousness by faith into justification by faith** of Christ unto life. Or be cut off from the "**law of faith**" (Romans 3:27), the "**law of righteousness**" (Romans 9:31), "**the law of the Spirit of life**" (Romans 8:2) and the kingdom of God.

To repent and receive the righteousness of Christ is the first step in obeying the gospel of Christ. To repent and receive peace with God is the second step in the gospel of Christ. And to repent and receive the Holy Spirit, the indwelling power of God, is the critical third merit of the gospel of Christ. For over seventeen hundred years, Israel was clothed with the Sun of righteousness (Genesis 32:31; Malachi 4:2). This nation clothed with the righteousness of Christ, with the garments of salvation (Isaiah 61:10), was at its final critical hour, for the personified kingdom of God, Jesus Christ the righteous, was literally standing in their presence.

Although under the umbrella of righteousness by faith, signified individually by the ordinance of circumcision, their belief, acceptance, and obedience to gospel order totally depended on their belief in the "faith of the operation of God" through the transfer from circumcision to baptism (Colossians 2:10-14). Circumcision, the **sign of imputed righteousness of Christ** given to Abraham, had accomplished its timeline in the plan of salvation. It was a sign of being sealed in heaven's bill of rights, Christ's robe of divine righteousness afforded to Israel through its forefather, Abraham.

During the first coming of Jesus, Israel would lose its divine judicial authority at the sealing of Jesus (John 6:27), at the baptism of Christ. Jesus said, "**If I had not come and spoken to them, they had not had sin: but now they have no cloak (covering) for their sin**" (John 15:22).

The umbrella of righteousness by faith would now come under a new divine judicial heading. Remember, Abraham had received circumcision as a **sign**, a **seal** of the **imputed righteousness of Christ**. It was his sign of faith, his seal of imputed righteousness (see Romans 4:11) to be handed down to his future generations for over seventeen hundred years. And now at the first coming of Christ its divine meaning and purpose would be replaced with the ordinance of baptism (John 8:24; 15:22; Romans 6:3, 4; Colossians 2:10-14).

It's critically important to understand the sealing of Abram by the covenant sign of sacrifice (Genesis 15:9-18) was replaced twenty-four years after, in his walk of faith, by the covenant sign of circumcision (Genesis 17:10, 11). At the **first** coming of Christ the sign of circumcision was replaced by the sign of baptism in the **sealing of Jesus** as a man for man. Jesus said, "Labor not for the meat which perishes, but for that meat which endures to everlasting life, which the Son of man shall give to you: **for him hath God the Father sealed**" (John 6:27). The sealing of Jesus took place when Jesus came from His home in Galilee to the river Jordan to be baptized of John the Baptist. John said to Jesus when he saw Him, "I'm the one that needs to be baptized of you." And Jesus answered him, "Permit it to be so now: **for thus it becomes us to fulfill all righteousness.**" Then John permitted Jesus (Matthew 3:14, 15). Jesus at his baptism took the necessary steps in gospel order, in God's orderly plan of saving man. Jesus the man produced as a man every demand in the code of conduct, the law of God, the ten commandments placed on man because of Adam's sin.

The last call to righteousness for literal Israel legally began at **the sealing of Jesus** (John 6:27) at His baptism into the imputed righteousness of God. If Jesus had to produce in every critical phase the fine work necessary for the salvation of man, how can any sincere Christian say the law of God defined as the Ten Commandments, the divine code of conduct that governs life in the universe, were changed or were done away at the cross? Many at judgment time (2 Corinthians 5:10) will find out too late that **"the law of the Lord is perfect, converting the soul"** (Psalm 19:7).

How vital was the baptism of Jesus? It sealed Jesus as a man in the beginning of His ministry in the finite work of reconciling man to God. It magnifies the law of God (Isaiah 42:21), the code of conduct, the principles defining the character of our heavenly Father's divine being. The baptism of Christ became from Jesus day the Christian's sign (Romans 4:11) of obedience to the *"law of faith"* (Romans 1:5; Romans 3:27), his **seal** of obedience to the *"law of righteousness"* by faith (Romans 4:11; 9:31) . That places the Christian under the judicial heading or covering of "justification by faith"

(Romans 5:1) with the right to be indwelled with the "**law of the Spirit of life in Christ Jesus**" (Romans 8:2 as a citizen of the kingdom of God (Matthew 6:33). Righteousness and **holiness, holiness and righteousness** (Revelation 22:11), is the only standard of character allowed to stand in God's divine presence. It is the **only** standard of life allowed to exist in the universal kingdom of God. Jesus had to, in the beginning of His ministry as a man, take the first judicial steps in divine "righteousness unto holiness," heaven's divine bill of rights demands (Romans 6:19; Ephesians 4:24).

Again, how critical was Christ's baptism? Listen to the statement made by our heavenly Father at this critical hour of Jesus' baptism. "And lo, a voice from heaven, saying, **this is my beloved Son, in whom I am well pleased**" (Matthew 3:17). In this precious statement our gracious heavenly Father has declared to every son and daughter of Adam, who follows in the footsteps of Christ, the glorious words, "Thou art my beloved son, thou art my beloved daughter." This is **a divine, official declaration of ownership**, in righteousness, in whom the great I Am says, "I am well pleased" (Matthew 3:17; Psalm 2:7). This precious fatherly statement must be understood and taken to heart, in light of humanity having been unscrupulously taken captive by Satan, the author of unrighteousness, shortly after our creation (2 Timothy 2:26).

"And Jesus, when **he was baptized**, went up immediately out of the water: and lo, the heavens were opened to him, and he saw **the Spirit of God descending like a dove, and lighting upon him**" (Matthew 3:16). The merits of the atonement are everything to us. How critically important it is to understanding their value and orderly application in the life of Jesus. Right after Jesus was baptized to fulfill imputed righteousness for man, He was instantly endorsed by the Father and enclosed with the Holy Spirit. This principle application in the endorsement of our heavenly Father and enclosure of the Holy Spirit is critical to every born again son and daughter of God following in the footprints of Christ (1 Peter 2:21). Remember, Paul said the kingdom of God is "**righteousness** and **peace** and **joy in the Holy Ghost**" (Romans 14:17). Jesus said, "Seek ye first the kingdom of God and his righteousness" (Matthew 6:33). This divine order of gospel righteousness, peace, and Holy Spirit appropriation is exemplified in many parts of the scriptures.

When Jesus appeared to His disciples after His resurrection and showed them the marks of His righteous atonement, the first thing He says to them is, "**Peace** be unto you" (John 20:19). Scripture identifies **true peace** beginning first as peace **with God the Father** (Ephesians 2:14, Philippians 1:2), and **heavenly peace** is obtained through the **gospel of** peace (Romans 10:15; Ephesians 6:16). The apostle James also says, "And the **fruit** of **righteousness** is sown **in peace** of them that make peace" (James 3:18). This peace is first made with the Father of heaven and earth. After the disciples experienced this heavenly peace, Jesus said, "As my Father has sent me, even so send I you." "Receive you the Holy Spirit" (John 19:22). All in perfect order, Jesus appears, shows them the marks of His atonement, the marks of having appropriated heavenly judicial life-giving righteousness, and then announces God's peace with them and with man. He then announces to them the **endorsement of the Father** and **encloses them with the indwelling of the Holy Spirit**. All in **divine order** of reception, **righteousness**, then **peace**, then joy in the **Holy Spirit**" (Romans 14:17).

The baptism of Jesus is a symbol of the Son of God as the Son of Man, appropriating the **righteousness** of God, making **peace** with God the Father (Colossians 1:20), and then being endorsed, enclosed, and completely indwelled by the **Holy Spirit** (Ephesians 1:13). Paul said, "Therefore being justified by faith, **we have peace with God** through our Lord Jesus Christ: By whom also we have access **by faith into this grace wherein we stand**, and **rejoice** in hope of the glory of God. And not only so, but we glory in tribulations also: knowing that tribulation worked patience; and patience, experience; and experience, hope: And hope makes not ashamed; **because the love of God is shed abroad in our hearts by the Holy Spirit**," which is given to those that obey God (Acts 5:32; Romans 5:1-5).

When Jacob wrestled with Jesus and was overcome, he was made secure in the indwelling power of the Holy Spirit and was assured, "power with God and with men" (Genesis 32:28; 1 Thessalonians 1:5). "Now the God of hope **fill you with all joy and peace** in believing, that ye may abound in hope, **through the power of the Holy Spirit**" (Romans 15:13). The same judicial order of salvation is afforded to all men in every generation. The Holy Spirit given to the born again Christian through gospel order is not just in a drawing process, but resides in the heart of each individual to maintain a daily guidance and instruction in righteousness. The indwelling of the Holy Spirit in the life of every born again individual is critical for God to finish the good work begun in the individual (Philippians 1:6). By replacing impure thoughts, perverse sentiments, and rebellious actions with holy thoughts, heavenly affections, and Christ like actions, every believer is afforded the righteousness of Christ.

Jesus said, "Except a man be born of water and the Spirit he cannot enter into the kingdom of God, You must be born again" (John 3:5-7). Jesus took the first steps as a man for man in the born again experience when

He exemplified the steps one must take to appropriate the righteousness of God and have the right to be indwelled by the Holy Spirit of God. We were all born into the human family, of water in our mother's womb, in a nature of unrighteousness, under a decree of unrighteousness, suffering, and death (John 5:3-7; Romans 3:10).

We had no choice in the method and condition of our birth. But the born again experience Jesus speaks about is **not a baby** experience. It is at the **age of accountability** our heavenly Father draws us to Jesus (John 6:44) by the converting power of the Holy Spirit to appropriate the life-giving-righteousness of Christ. Our heavenly Father demands the imputed righteousness of Christ in order for us to be indwelled by the Holy Spirit in order to make us in character like our wonderful Lord and Savior, Jesus Christ.

This experience is initiated first by our heavenly Father (John 6:44), but is not experienced until the individual **chooses** of their **own free will** to take the necessary steps by obeying the gospel in his generation. **Adam** and all the sons of God (Genesis 6:2) in his day **obeyed** the gospel by taking the necessary steps of gospel order by **sacrificing**. Two millennia later, **circumcision** was introduced to **Abraham** as a **sign of obedience,** the seal in his born again experience. At the first coming of Christ, **Jesus made it clear** that if you want to be born again, **get in the water** of your own free will or stay in the human condition, which means "there is none righteous, no not one" (Romans 3:10).

At the baptism of Christ, gospel order was exemplified by the cooperative revelation of the Father, Son, and Holy Spirit (Matthew 3:16, 17), All working in harmony for the salvation of man. These steps in righteousness were commissioned per the directions of Jesus in the gospel commission given to His disciples (Matthew 28:19, 20). The baptism of Jesus represents being baptized into the life, death, and resurrection of Christ (Romans 5:10; 6:4) by accepting heaven's bill of rights and all the merits appropriated by the atonement of Christ (Romans 5:11). Being baptized into the life of Christ appropriates life-giving righteousness. Baptism into the death of Christ signifies appropriating a death certificate with our name on it (Galatians 2:20). And finally, being baptized into the resurrection of Christ signifies accepting Jesus as our advocate, our heavenly lawyer in heaven's judicial judgment hall of morality and justice (1 John 2:1; Hebrews 8:1-3).

Gospel order in every generation speaks to us collectively of the different aspects presented in the gospel message of the atonement. The **gospel of sacrifice** in Adam's day says to us the wages of sin is death and the soul that sins must **die** (Ezekiel 18:4, 20). Life is in the **blood**, and Jesus, the son of God and the son of man, had to shed His precious blood in order to save His creation. The **gospel of circumcision** given in Abraham's day says when it comes to any type of works of the flesh of any **man** in obtaining justification unto life, God has **cut off** any and all of man's attempts in any way to justify his immoral condition (Galatians 3:11).

Man is cut off because he is bankrupt of any merit, or the possibility of having anything to produce or obtain in any degree any molecule of legal forensic righteousness to merit life-giving righteousness. **Righteousness by faith into justification by faith** is obtained **by faith** in obedience to the gospel message of each millennium of earth's history in the battle over life-giving righteousness. And the **gospel of baptism** points to Jesus and to **Jesus alone** as the only justifiable atonement acceptable to God for the restoration of man. Produced by Jesus' righteous life, death, and resurrection as restitution for the unwarranted and unprovoked disgraceful sin of the world (John 1:29).

The reception and indwelling of the HOLY SPIRIT cannot be maintained unless Christ is continually believed, accepted (John 3:36), and obeyed (Hebrews 5:9). The merits of the gospel of Christ cannot be continually maintained unless the gospel is continually (Galatians 2:5) believed (Mark 1:15), accepted, received (1 Corinthians 15:1), and obeyed (2 Thessalonians 1:7, 8; 2 Peter 2:21). Gospel order is defined in scripture first by a man believing, receiving, accepting, and obeying the Lord Jesus Christ. Gospel order is secondly defined in scripture by a man believing, receiving, accepting, and obeying the "truth of the gospel" of his generation. By appropriating the sign of faith, the seal of imputed righteousness heralded to every generation by God's chosen.

At the baptism of Jesus the righteousness of God was forever judiciously stamped and accredited to humanity by Jesus Christ, the savior of the world. Paul says, "For as many as have been baptized into Christ have put on Christ" (Galatians 3:27). Putting on the imputed righteousness of Christ affords man peace with God. "And as many as walk according to this rule peace be on them, and mercy, and upon the Israel of God" (Galatians 6:16). Gospel order calls first for **righteousness**, then **peace**, and then as Jesus was endorsed and enclosed by the **Holy Spirit,** so is the believer and doer of gospel order. How critical it is for the minister of the gospel to **biblically understand** these **three governing principles** of gospel order. **Righteousness** with God, affords **peace** with God, into the right of being indwelled by the **Holy Spirit** of God in the heart of the believer.

What an **uninspired, unsanctified** gospel message is being given to the Christian world in our day. Christians are believing in an instant gospel, claiming a born again experience by just believing in the Lord Jesus Christ. Claiming the right of **righteousness by faith into justification by faith** of Christ unto eternal life by faith in Christ alone. **Never** in any part of scripture is this type of immediate salvation conveyed. **Abraham believed God in the gospel covenant promise** of gospel order of his day. "And being fully persuaded that, what he had promised, he (Jesus) was able also to perform, **land and seed** (Genesis 15:5; 17:9). And therefore it was counted to him for righteousness" (Romans 4:21-22). "And he **received the sign** of circumcision **a seal** of the righteousness of the faith (Romans 4:11). "Even so faith, if it has not works, is dead being alone" (James 2:17). Did Paul say to his prison keeper after he asked, "What must I do to be saved?" to just believe (Acts 16:30)? No, Paul said, believe on the Lord Jesus Christ, and you **shall be saved**, not believe and you are saved. **No one** is justified by faith outside of gospel order. Scripture says the jailer "took them the same hour of the night, and washed their stripes and **was baptized**" (Acts 16:33). The Holy Spirit does not completely indwell in any man or woman outside of believing, accepting, and obeying the truth of the gospel of Christ in any generation.

When Jesus obeyed, as a man for man, his own gospel message in his generation, he was completely indwelled **as a man for man** by the Holy Spirit of promise (Ephesians 1:13). When the multitude believed the gospel message of Peter and the apostles they were baptized, and then and only then did they receive the gift of the Holy Spirit (Acts 2:38). Believe, receive, obey, baptize, and indwelled was the gospel order of reception in Jesus' day. When Saul was converted and baptized he was filled with the Holy Spirit (Acts 9:17, 18). Before that he persecuted the Christians (Ephesians 3:6). Millions upon millions today have accepted unscriptural fabrications of faith never authorized in scripture.

Many a Christian today uses phases of salvation conveyed to them by ministers of unrighteousness (2 Corinthians 11:13-15), fabricated to work on their feelings for Christianity in order to satisfy some cherished desire. **No man can willfully offer up to God praises and thanksgiving without the sweet savor of the imputed righteousness of Christ through gospel order**. Many today who are **"hungering and thirsting** for righteousness" (Matthew 5:6) are searching to understand these wonderful truths necessary for a true heart conversation to Christ, in order to stand at His second coming (Revelation 6:17). There are many wonderful truths in scripture, but the one truth necessary for the salvation of man has been hidden beneath the rubbish of error and weighted down by creeds, powerless outside of the "truth of the gospel," to justify and sanctify the believer.

If Jesus were here today he would rebuke the ministry and the schools of our day with the same denunciation of the leaders of his day. Although we are living today in a **self**-deceived, **self**-righteous, **self**-complacent generation of believers, there is no excuse for the gospel minister not to "Cry aloud, spare not, lift up thy voice like a trumpet, and show my people their transgression and the house of Jacob their sins" (Isaiah 58:1). **John the Baptist was a messenger of righteousness (Matthew 21:32)** entrusted to speak the words of truth to his generation. Constrained by the Holy Spirit and stimulated by holy zeal, he entered upon the performance of his duty without coldly calculating the consequences of his speaking the words the Lord gave him.

If he were preaching the truth of the gospel in this generation he would find himself, his house, his message made the subject of criticism by the majority of Christian believers. His manners, life, circumstances, and everything and anything about him would be inspected and commented upon. But more so his call to righteousness would be especially picked to pieces, refuted, rejected as the voice of another spirit. John was a man sent of God with indomitable faith and courage, a heart made strong by constant communion with God. Where is John the Baptist today?

We are living now in that generation "**when they will not endure sound doctrine**; but after their own lusts shall they heap to themselves teachers, having itching ears" (2 Timothy 4:3). Ministers who please their congregation with just enough Christianity to keep them in a stupor, men who love to be commended in illicit admiration unwarranted by scripture (Psalm 146:3, 4). Now is the time, Paul says, "Preach the word; be instant in season, out of season; reprove, rebuke, exhort with all longsuffering and doctrine" (2 Timothy 4:2). Preach, Paul said, whether they will hear or forbear. **No** righteous justification means **no** salvation. **No** believing, accepting, and obeying the truth of the gospel in your generation means **no** salvation (2 Thessalonians 1:7, 8).

From the beginning, from Abel down through every generation, the minister of truth has been refuted, hated, criticized, condemned, and killed for the truth as it is in Jesus. Paul said watch thou in all things, endure afflictions, do the work of an evangelist, make full proof of thy ministry (2 Timothy 4:5). Many today are preaching a **soft** Jesus, a **soft** gospel to **soft** congregations and church members who want to be **pampered in unscriptural righteousness**. Friend, God is not soft on sin. If you think He is just take a scriptural look at the cross and what Jesus had to go through to redeem us (1 Corinthians 6:20; 1 Peter 1:18, 19). The true minister cannot afford at the cost of precious souls to flatter or yield to the desire to please anyone or any congregation to avoid criticism.

The gospel minister has not the time to study self-interest of his own or the saints, but desires to open before the people the glory of "the truth of the gospel" that will hasten the second coming of Christ (2 Peter 3:12). The ministry is God's ordained, appointed means of reaching and instructing the people in gospel truth. Paul said, "How shall they preach, except they be sent? As it is written, **how beautiful are the feet of them that preach the gospel of peace, and bring glad tidings of good things**" (Romans 10:15). How many today who claim to have beautiful feet are walking the walk and talking the talk?

Christianity in this generation claims having the indwelling power of the Holy Spirit. **Everything** and **anything** is looked upon as a sign of his reception. **Miracles, slaying in the spirit, prophets** and **prophecy, tongues, miracle water**, and **hand cloths** are all claimed as signs of the indwelling power of the Holy Spirit in many a Christian. John the revelator tells us, "For they are the spirits of demons, working miracles, which go forth to the kings of the earth and of the whole world, to gather them to the battle of that great day of God Almighty" (Revelation 16:14). **Signs and wonders** were **never taught** by Jesus as a sign of the indwelling power of the Holy Spirit. Scripture teaches the reception of receiving the indwelling of the Holy Spirit is according to gospel order. Paul said, "In whom ye also trusted, **after that ye heard the word of truth**, the **gospel of your salvation**: in whom also **after that ye believed**, ye were **sealed with that Holy Spirit of promise**" (Ephesians 1:13).

The sealing of the Holy Spirit in the ministry of Jesus as a man for man came at his baptism according to gospel order. Paul said, "Now he which **established us, with you in Christ**, and hath anointed us, is God, Who hath also **sealed us, (in divine righteousness)** and given the earnest of the Spirit in our hearts" (2 Corinthians 1:21, 22). **Established us with you in Christ** was Paul's work in establishing churches. "And as they went through the cities, they **delivered them the decrees for to keep**, that were **ordained of the apostles and elders which were at Jerusalem**. And so were the **churches established in the faith**, and increased in number daily" (Acts 16:4, 5).

Scriptures says, "Nevertheless the foundation of God stands sure, **having this seal**; The Lord knows them that are his. And, Let everyone that names the name of Christ depart from iniquity (2 Timothy 2:19). God has always had a sign, a seal identifying his people in divine imputed righteousness. **Abel** speaks to us today of his **excellent blood sacrifice**, his **sign and seal** of imputed righteousness (Hebrews 11:4). **Noah** was seen righteous before God in his day, because he **sacrificed** (Genesis 8:20) being sealed in the imputed righteousness of Christ.

On and on it goes, from **sacrifice to circumcision,** from Adam through to Abraham, Isaac, and Jacob, down through the history of Israel as a nation, and now at the first coming of Christ it is exemplified in perfect divine gospel order by the **baptism of Christ.** Only heaven knows how the adversary of souls has worked down through the ages to manipulate and hide these glorious truths necessary in the salvation of man. Just before Jesus comes again the final gospel sign and sealing message of God's imputed **righteousness of Christ** will be given again on a universal scale, and **then** and **only then** will the end come (Revelation 7:1-3; 14:6-12).

Jesus said to the leaders of his day, "**John came to you in the way of righteousness** and you believed him not" (Matthew 21:32). "And all the people that heard, and the publicans, **justified God, being baptized with the baptism of John.** But the Pharisees and lawyers **rejected the counsel of God** against themselves, being not baptized of him" (Luke 7:30). Rejecting being "buried with him in baptism, wherein also ye are risen with him through **the faith of the operation of God,** who hath raised him from the dead (Colossians 2:12). Rejecting Christ, refusing to comply with the present truth of gospel order in Jesus' day (2 Peter 1:12), the gospel of **righteousness by faith into justification by faith** in Christ, by being baptized disconnected literal Israel from life-giving righteousness (Matthew 21:43; 23:37, 38). A precursor to the 21st Century Christian Catholic Protestant Church and the world prior to the second coming of Christ.

⌒ *Chapter Nine* ⌒
The New Testament Church and the Mystery of Iniquity

"For the **mystery of iniquity doth already work:** only he who now letteth will let, until he be taken out of the way" (2 Thessalonians 2:7). Iniquity is man's condition before God, and is defined as one being in violation of God's moral code of conduct. In violation of heaven's bill of rights, the description of righteousness, the ten principles that govern life in God's universal kingdom demand as legal precedence. David said, "Behold I was sharpened in iniquity and in sin did my mother conceive me" (Psalm 51:5). To be in iniquity represents man in an illegal, immoral, unrighteous, depraved nature and character, destitute of life-giving righteousness. He is totally bankrupt of any value in God's universal kingdom. Unless he affords himself of heaven's bill of rights, God's gift of life-giving righteousness, he is unsafe to allow to eternally exist in God's universal kingdom and must eventually be eradicated from life.

The mystery of iniquity is an important phrase in scripture applying especially to last-day events. It is nothing new in our day, because the apostle Paul said the mystery of iniquity was already working in his day (2 Thessalonians 2:7). How prevalent is Paul's statement in that he was a major contributor in the work of the mystery of iniquity at the birth of the New Testament Christian Catholic Church. Scripture says of Paul, "concerning zeal persecuting the church," "made havoc of the church, entering into every house, and haling men and women **committed them to prison**" (Philippians 3:6; Acts 8:3). Has it not always been, especially since the days of Jesus, those representing the mystery of iniquity, those rejecting life-giving righteousness, persecuting, condemning, and jailing those who did not agree with them in Christ our righteousness? The church leaders of Jesus' day worked through civil power to control religious doctrine. As it was in the days of Jesus, so shall it be again just before he comes in the clouds of heaven. The mystery of iniquity at work in Jerusalem in Jesus' day was the birth of the union of church and state, which would haunt the righteous down through the last two millennia of earth's history and climax in a universal civil and religious confederate union just before Jesus comes again.

John says, "And I saw *three* unclean spirits like frogs come out of the mouth of the *Dragon*, the voice of civil government, out of the mouth of the *Beast*, and out of the mouth of the *False Prophet.*" John pictures three united, Bible-based areas in the world who just before Jesus comes again will be prepared by the "spirits of devils" to control the hearts and minds of the religious populace of the world, to influence and control the whole world to battle against the great day of God Almighty (Revelation 16:14). These three symbols of civil and religious unity find their origin at the time of the baptism of Christ. The dragon, primarily a symbol for the devil and Satan (Revelation 12:9), has a secondary biblical application in scripture to civil leaders in Old and New Testament applications.

The **first great** dragon power, found in scripture to have persecuted Israel as a nation, was Egypt. "Son of man, set thy face against Pharaoh King of Egypt, and prophesy against him, and against all Egypt. Speak and say, Thus says the Lord God; Behold I am against thee, **Pharaoh king of Egypt** the **great dragon** that lies in the midst of his rivers, which hath said, My river is mine own, and I have made it for myself" (Ezekiel 29:1, 2).

The **second power in scripture represented as a dragon** power to persecute Israel as a nation **was Babylon**. Scripture says, "**Nebuchadnezzar the king of Babylon** hath devoured me, he hath crushed me, he hath made me an empty vessel, he hath swallowed me up like **a dragon**, he hath filled his belly with my delicates, he hath cast me out" (Jeremiah 51:34). It was Babylon in the sixth century (605 B.C.) that completely shattered Jerusalem and cast Israel out as a self-governing nation for a time in the Middle East (Jeremiah 25:8, 9). And at the birth of Jesus the book of Revelation pictures another dragon called Rome, **the third representative dragon power** in scripture who, through **Herod the king,** at the time of the birth of Jesus "seek the young child to kill him" (Revelation 12:4; Matthew 2:1-3, 13). Friends, the word dragon in scripture has primary and secondary applications, first to Satan and second to specific nations, governments, and civil administrations that are or have come under the deception and complete control of the original dragon, Satan, who was cast out of heaven (Revelation 12:9). The mystery of iniquity born in Jesus' day consisted of the Roman empire, the civil dragon voice of that era working with the two religious schools of ecclesiastical education in Jerusalem, directing the mindset of the people into creating and using a union of church and state in order to crucify the Son of Man (Matthew 27:20-22; John 19:14, 15).

The first attempt by Satan to produce the mystery of iniquity had its establishment when man attempted to build the tower of Babel recorded in Genesis11:1-9, shortly after the great flood of the second millennia of earth's history. Although Babel was detained at its birth in its attempt to control the world, it would see its first true characteristic at the time of Babylon in the days of Daniel the prophet. "Nebuchadnezzar the king, **the civil legislative leader** of that then known world empire, made an **image** of gold, its height sixty cubits, its breadth six cubits; he hath raised it up in the valley of Dura, in the province of Babylon" (Daniel 3:1). Here we see one of the primary biblical world civil leaders taking upon himself through his own personal authority the prerogative to be liberty of conscience for the peoples of that generation. A civil government implementing its religious beliefs to the ultimate conclusion of death upon anyone who opposed its diabolical confederacy of church and state (Daniel 3:1-6).

The biblical dragon power of Babylon (Jeremiah 51:34), with its legislating **power to command and demand worship,** about six hundred years before the first coming of Christ, made an **image** on the plains of Dura (Daniel 3:1). An image that parallels the last dragon head of the seven-headed beast of Revelation 17:3. This seventh dragon head (the United States of America [Revelation 13:11; 17:3-10]) will give life to an "**image** to the beast" (Revelation 13:14, 15), the Protestant churches of the United States, within the confines of its judicial authority (Revelation 13:15). And join hands with Revelation 13:1-10, the beast out of the sea, known by past scholars as the Roman Catholic Church, into legislating the one religious doctrine that the Papacy **(Sunday worship)** claims as **her mark** of ecclesiastical authority in religious doctrine.

Revelation 13:11-18 pictures the future deadly civil beast out of the earth, the United States of America. Just before Jesus comes, unites a world confederacy of church and state to crucify the final everlasting gospel message of Christ's life-giving-righteousness (Revelation 14:6-12). By honoring this long-time religious civil controlling beast power of Catholicism, which for 1,260 years controlled Europe's populace with its deadly confederate union of church and state. When this prophecy is fulfilled (Revelation 13:11-17), the earth will completely disconnect from the privilege of appropriating the life-giving righteousness of Christ and earth, our planet, will come to its end.

Revelation 13:18
The revelation and progression of the number 666. As it was in the beginning, as it was in the days of Babylon, as in the days of Jesus, so shall it be just before Jesus comes again.

As it is in defining scripture according to Bible interpretation of "line upon line, precept upon precept" (Isaiah 28:10), 6 is the numerical number of man as he was created on the six day (Genesis 2:24-31).

666 is the symbolic number of "a man" (Revelation 13:18) who believes he rules in the place of God. In Ezra 2:13, an Israelite named Adonikam has six hundred sixty and six descendants, who would rule in his place or position as father or leader after he died. Adonikam is a word beginning with Adoni, meaning to rule, (the sovereign, *human* or *divine)* representative leader, as Christ was the principal leader, author of the Christian faith. How undeniably have men replacing others in past positions of authority, in religious and political seats of authority, taken upon themselves *the place of religious sovereign, or rulers in the place of God; civil* and religious leaders in their progression of time, taking upon themselves *increasing excessive judicial rights* and power to oppress and kill millions who did not and would not compromise their faith. Did not Jesus say, "That whosoever killeth you will think that he doeth God service" (John 16:1, 2)?

In Babylon's day, Nebuchadnezzar the king sets up an image representing two sixes. "Nebuchadnezzar the king made an image of gold, whose height *was* threescore **(60)** cubits, *and* the breadth thereof six **(6)** cubits: he set it up in the plain of Dura, in the province of Babylon (Daniel 3:1). **Two sixes represents Nebuchadnezzar**, one man's mind controlling Babylon's system of government, and Nebuchadnezzar, one man's mind initiating and controlling his ideal of religious worship, the civil controlling the religious to the ultimate conclusion of death.

In Jesus' day there were *three* manmade, **man-appointed,** antagonistic antichrist forces in Jerusalem. Consisting of the two academic schools of ecclesiastical education controlled by the *Pharisees* and the *Sadducees* under the rule, direction, and consent of *one man,* the High priest (Matthew 26:63-65). The appointed spiritual leader of that critical era; uniting with the *dragon's voice of Rome* to crucify the Son of God (Matthew 16:6; Mark 8:15; Luke 20:19, 20; Matthew 27:1, 2; 27:24).

In the last days a parallel of these three antichrist forces will soon be in power again (1 Corinthians 10:11). Representing the final world powers that believe they have the right to sit and rule Christianity in the place of God. These *three* present-day, self-appointed, sovereign Christian forces are revealed in Revelation thirteen as three sixes. *The beast out of the sea-6* (Revelation 13:1), the *beast out of the earth-6* (Revelation 13:11), and *the image of the beast-6* (Revelation 13:14, 15); they are *presently working together, soon to unite,* to control the world through Christian sovereignty.

The Bible predicts just before Jesus returns the *beast out of the earth*, the **United States**, will give life to *the image of the beast* (**Apostate Protestantism**) in honor and reverence to the beast out of the sea (**Catholicism**). *The antichrist system, revealed to the world during the Protestant reformation of the sixteenth century, that exalted "the man of sin, the son of perdition."* **"Who opposeth and exaulteth himself above all that is called God, or that is worshipped; so that he as God sitteth in the temple of God, shewing himself that he is God (2 Thessalonians 2:3, 4);** The spiritual leader, sovereign of the Papacy that initiated the horrors of the dark ages in Europe, soon to be again in this final generation the exalted spiritual leader, **sovereign of three sixes (666) in the place of God,** head *of* the Christian world.

Soon to unite to legislate the *mark* (Sunday worship [Revelation 13:16]) of unbiblical Christian suppression. Misleading the civil and religious world in exalting and legislating the Mystery of Iniquity into establishing MYSTERY BABYLON THE GREAT upon the earth (Revelation 17:5). So powerful will the deception be that Islam and Judaism seated in the Middle East will cooperate and concede to this final fatal deception. Which both the Papacy and Islam, who love church and state affiliation, had their birth in the sixth and seventh century A.D. with the mindset to enforce their doctrinal beliefs by civil and religious authority. All this will be accomplished by the deceptive power of "spirits of devils working miracles" (Revelation 16:14), deceiving the whole world (Revelation 12:9) into controlling its populace **in the last hours of earth's history,** resulting in the battle of the great day of God Almighty (Revelation 16:14).

The book of Revelation pictures and defines different aspects of the **Great Red Dragon Beast** power defined in Revelation 12:3; 13:1, and 17:3. In Revelation 12:3, this Dragon beast has seven heads, on each head is a **crown,** and on the seven **heads** are ten horns. This Great Red Dragon beast illuminates God's description of the power of Satan, controlling the minds of man in church or state administrative forms. Kingdoms from the time of the birth of Israel as a nation in producing seven empires in the earth, oppressing and persecuting God's people to the time of Christ's second coming; Seven heads or seven kingdoms with ten legislative horns of administrative power. These seven heads began with the biblical kingdom of Egypt at the time when Jacob became Israel (Genesis 32:27), and ends with the final head as being the United States of America, a topic we will discuss in future chapters.

In Revelation 13:1 this seven-headed ten-horned Dragon Beast is again revealed, but this time this seven-headed power **is called a beast.** It has seven heads and ten horns. But this time the **crowns** are not on the heads but focused on the ten **horns,** revealing a time prophecy relating to the fall of the old civil Roman Empire which had its birth in 168 B.C. and fell as a civil power in A.D. 476, a prophecy which also corresponds with Daniel seven. Although civil Rome, the sixth head of the seven-headed dragon beast, ceases to be a world civil empire after A.D. 476, Rome takes on a new prospective. It raises its ugly head again in A.D. 538 as an ecclesiastical or religious controlling power and influence in the earth by its religious "**little horn**" (Daniel 7:8) of power in Europe, called the Papacy, from A.D. 538 to A.D. 1798

A now new religious "**little horn**" (Daniel 7:8, 20, 21) power on the earth which will again receive power for just one prophetic hour, just before the second coming of Christ (Revelation 17:3, 12). It's the prophecy of Daniel seven that reveals the rise and time frame of the duel power of (**civil and religious)** Rome as it raises its ugly two-horned head in the earth from 168 B.C. to the second coming of Christ. In Daniel seven, four beast powers or governmental heads are revealed in earth's history (Daniel 7:3) from the time of Babylon in 605 B.C. to the second coming of Christ. Outlined to give us understanding about four of the seven heads of the seven-headed Dragon Beast of Revelation 12:3; 13:1; and Revelation 17:3.

After the rise and fall of old Babylon from 605 B.C. to 538 B.C. (Daniel 7:4), the duel power of the Medes and Persians takes control of the then-known world from 538 B.C. to 331 B.C. (Daniel 7:5). Following the reign of Medes and Persians, Greece takes control of the then-known biblical world from 331 B.C. to 168 B.C. (Daniel 7:6). And after the reign of Greece, Daniel sees in "night visions, and behold a fourth **beast**, dreadful and terrible, and strong exceedingly; and it had great **iron teeth**: it devoured and brake in pieces, and stamped the residue (remnant) with the feet of it: and it was **diverse (different)** from all the beasts that *were* before it; and it had **ten horns**" (Daniel 7:7).

After Greece fulfilled her allotted time as a controlling power in Europe and the Middle East (Daniel 11:1-4), the next and most earth-shattering power to rise on the earth was **Rome**. Rome began her reign in 168 B.C. and reigned as a civil power on the earth until A.D. 476 When the old civil Roman Empire collapsed, Europe broke into **ten divisions of independent nations**; these nations or divisions of nations have been defined as England, France, Spain, Germany, Italy, Switzerland, Portugal, the Heruli, the Vandals, and the Ostrogoths. Three of these ten horns, according to Daniel 7:8, were to be "plucked up by the roots," which meant the Heruli, the Vandals, and the Ostrogoths ceased to exist shortly after the beginning of their endeavor to be established as nations in Europe. Daniel saw this incredible prophetic insight; the Heruli, (A.D. 493), the Vandals (A.D. 534), and the Ostrogoths (A.D. 538) were destroyed at the root of their origin before they could be fully established among the other seven nations in Europe (Daniel 7:8, 20).

Then in Daniel 7:8, Daniel sees a "little horn" "coming up among" the new civil horns developing in Europe, called by Daniel an all-important, critical "**little horn.**" Friends, it's important to understand horns represent the legislative and judicial controlling power of the seven-headed dragon beast of Revelation.12:3; 13:1; and 17:3. This "**little horn**" that rises up out of the ten horns after the three horns were uprooted in Europe was not another civil horn, but a **religious horn** known and revealed to the Christian world during the Protestant Reformation by the great preacher Martin Luther as the Papacy.

This newly born religious horn that rose out of the ten horns of the old Roman Empire is none other than the oppressive and persecuting horn of the New Testament Christian Catholic Church (Daniel 7:8, 11; 14-45), which apostatized from the doctrines of Christ in the second century A.D. and is now after A.D. 476 in complete apostasy. Shortly after A.D. 476, after civil Rome is eradicated. She, the apostate New Testament Christian Catholic Church, takes hold of the newly formed seven civil government horns, newly born in Europe, in order to enforce her religious doctrines on the then-known world. This new religious horned beast head of Rome is identified in scripture as the sixth head of the seven-headed beast of Revelation 12:3 and 13:1; 17:3, 10; and Daniel 7:7-25. This sixth head follows the oppressive power of the first five biblical heads of Egypt, Assyria, Babylon, Media and Persia, and Greece, who once *"was, is not, but yet is"* (Revelation 17:8), or are still in existence when religious Rome takes full control of the new European populace after A.D. 538

What makes the sixth head of Rome "**diverse**" (**different**) in Dan.7:7, 23 is that she rose up as a civil head with a civil horn of authority from 168 B.C. to A.D. 476 and metamorphosed into a religious head controlled by the religious little horn power of the Papacy after A.D. 538 For forty-two prophetic months (Revelation 13:5), or for 1,260 years of prophetic time in Europe, from A.D. 538 to 1798, Rome, the sixth head of the seven-headed Dragon beast of Revelation 12:3; 13:1; and 17:3 with its "**little horn**" of religious power revealed in Daniel 7:8, 20-25; and Revelation 13:1-10, took hold of the seven newly formed nations of authority in Europe from A.D. 538, and by the European civil power afforded her, Catholicism oppressed and persecuted any who opposed her religious beliefs.

She will again, just before Jesus comes, not just be in control of Europe's populace, but be in complete control of all civil and religious authority in the earth. This scripture truly predicts her power will be great and determined (Daniel 8:23-27), backed by the world, and escorted by the seventh horn head beast of the United States, the last head of Revelation's seven-headed dragon beast (Revelation 13:11; 16:13; 17:10). But rest assured, friends, scripture says when she, the Papacy, has reached her goal of earthly civil and religious control, she has only one prophetic hour (Revelation 17:12) of complete religious and civil oppression before Jesus comes again and shuts her down forever.

It's important to understand that in Nebuchadnezzar's day, civil government took the seat of authority over religious faith (Daniel 3:1-7). This principle of civil government in the seat of power over the religions of the world existed for hundreds of years, down through to the first coming of Christ. After the death of Jesus, scripture foresees and predicts through the prophecies of Daniel, the apostle Paul and John the revelator, the ultimate collapse of the truth of the gospel of the New Testament Church. Which by the fourth century A.D., the New Testament Christian Church had entirely lost the comprehensive "truth of the gospel of Christ" (Colossians 1:5; Revelation 2:18-29).

Before the close of the fifth century A.D., warring factions within and outside of her territorial empire have completely eradicated the civil government of Rome. In that metamorphosis of time between A.D. 476 and A.D. 538, the Roman Christian Catholic Church, claiming the name and title of Christ, and because of massive changes in the governments of Europe, the Papacy fornicates with civil leaders of that critical era (Revelation 17:1, 2). Because the empire of civil Rome is now extinct, the Christian people in Europe want a central figure to oversee their dominion. In the year A.D. 538 the civil governments of the new world order in Europe established among themselves a new independent **little horn of authority** called the Papacy, at that time no longer called the Christian Catholic Universal Church but titled the Roman Catholic or Universal Church.

How prophetic the New Testament Church, apostatizing in time, hundreds of years of time, then taking the seat of Christian sovereignty in the European continent, oppressing those who would not sanction her dogma of the Christian faith. A prophetic union of church and state predicted to have a biblical timeline of power for 1,260 years of religious and civil intolerance (Luke 21:24; Revelation 11:2, 3; 12:6, 14; Revelation 13:5; Daniel 7:25; 12:7). History testifies how terrible was this union of church and state that resulted in the death of millions by civil-backed, unscriptural Christian doctrine for over twelve hundred years of Catholic Church history. Scripture pictures and predicts this terrible confederacy of death will raise its ugly head again on a universal scale, just before Jesus comes the second time.

Prior to the first coming of Jesus, the **two ecclesiastical schools** of the **Pharisees** and **Sadducees** initiated a structure in Jerusalem having its roots in Babylonian and Grecian "philosophy and vain deceit, after the tradition of men, after the rudiments of the world, and not after Christ" (Colossians 2:8). Both of these two religious academic institutions contended with each other for power to control every aspect of religious and civil life when Israel was under its covenant with God. Not able to agree and unite because of their differences, contention and confusion permeated the ministry and the people under their hypercritical management. At the ministry of John the Baptist (Matthew 4:5-10), a subtle union emerged among the Pharisees and Sadducees (Matthew 22:34) in the revelation of the one in whom they would find a common ground of antagonism. The mystery of iniquity (2 Thessalonians 2:7), already working in Jesus' day, consisted of the two religious schools of the Pharisees and Sadducees uniting together with civil Rome, saying, "We have no king but Caesar" (John 19:15).

Listen to the words of Jesus describing to his disciples the characteristic of those who would oppose gospel order. "Then Jesus said to them, **Take heed and beware of the leaven of the Pharisees and of the Sadducees**" (Matthew 16:6). Of course, the disciples did not at that time discern and understand that their religious leaders would do anything unbiblical, a mindset that still exists today, but Jesus warned them of the unscriptural union of church and state. "Take heed and beware of the teachings of the Pharisees and of the Sadducees. They shall put you out of the synagogues (churches): yes, the time cometh, that **whoever kills you will think that he doeth God's service**" (Matthew 16:6; John 16:2).

Again Jesus warns them of the mystery of iniquity at work in his day. "And he charged them, saying, **take heed, beware of the leaven of the Pharisees, (church) and of the teaching of Herod (state)**" (Mark 8:15). Church and state was the central focus in Jesus' day in the mind of Satan to be used for the sole purpose of controlling the minds of the people into the crucifixion and death of Jesus. Beware, he said, of the leaven (the teaching) of the Pharisees, those powerful religious leaders he called serpents (Matthew 23:32, 33), "which is hypocrisy, for there is nothing covered, that shall not be revealed; neither hid, that shall not be known" (Luke 12:2). Be careful, my Christian friend, if you think that you can participate in anything that looks Christian when the state is allowed to partake in any Christian activity.

It's amazing and a wonder as the modern world **reads, sees,** and **hears** of the terrible atrocities of churches and state religions created and organized down through the centuries that members will continue to flock to these same organizations. Ecclesiastical powers that have the same mindset today of religious intolerance without inquiring and studying their doctrines, activities and history in world affairs. Many condemn the faith of the Pharisees and Sadducees and what they did, knowing Christ rejected them, but continue to flock to these religious establishments today, which have the same mindset and religious background of intolerance. Most Christians today have no idea of the hidden canon codes of many of the churches or denominations they attend. Let the Christian denominations today have the power the state afforded the church in Jesus' day, or the state power afforded the **Roman Catholic Church in the dark ages,** and they will then see and understand too late the very destructive nature of this biblically forbidden union.

Just before Jesus comes again, scripture foretells the dragon voice of the United States, with its legislative and judicial authority (Revelation 17:13), will because of the two united voices of **Catholicism** and **Protestantism,** unite within her governmental confines; a union of civil and religious antagonism in opposition to its two biblical horns of **civil** and **religious** constitutional rights afforded her by her constitutional liberty (Revelation 13:11). This union soon to materialize in our country will oppress and **crucify** the **final gospel message of righteousness by faith unto justification by faith into the imputed righteousness of Christ** (Revelation 14:6-12). Friends, in the near, near future our country will civilly, religiously, judicially deny all within its confines the right of civil and religious liberties. All will be compelled to worship in this country, and eventually the world, a religious doctrine manufactured according to the few Christian leaders who ascribe to their own unbiblical doctrines. This future threefold union in the United States, with the Roman Catholic Church united with American Protestant Churches within our governmental confines, after it establishes its united confederacy of church and state in our country, will lead a global confederacy that will more than rival any civil and religious persecution of any past generation (Revelation 13:1-18). A confederacy the Papacy held in Europe for over twelve hundred years.

Soon "MYSTERY BABYLON THE GREAT" ([Revelation 17:5] **the title given to this last generation of Planet Earth**) will give sway to "**THE MOTHER (the Roman Catholic Church) OF HARLOTS (the Protestant Churches of the United States),** AND **ABOMINATIONS OF THE EARTH**." In order to overshadow and unite with the **Islamic governments**

of the Middle East influenced by the overwhelming power of the United States (Revelation 13:11-18). Which will again rise up for a short time (Revelation 17:10) the ugly head of Satan, to battle God's Remnant Church (Joel 2:32: Revelation 12:17) as the world sets up **Sunday worship,** igniting the final battle of Armageddon (Revelation 16:16).

Not long after Jesus' statements (Luke 20:9-18) "the chief priests **(the church leaders)** and the scribes the same hour sought to lay hands on him; and they feared the people: for they perceived that he had spoken this parable against them. And they watched him, and sent forth **spies, which should pretend themselves just men** that they might take hold of his words, so they might deliver him to the power and authority of the governor **(state)**" (Luke 20:19, 20). Friends, the mystery of iniquity today needs to be understood in the light of the specific events that occurred in Jesus' day. The word iniquity in the New Testament has two specific meanings. **Iniquity** in some specific verses in scripture is defined as **legal injustice.** Legal injustice is the characteristic of any church or state legalizing unethical principles unjustified under God's code of conduct that governs His universal kingdom.

In 2 Timothy 2:19, Paul says, "Nevertheless the foundation of God stands sure, **having this seal,** The Lord knows them that are his. And, Let everyone that names the name of Christ **depart from iniquity**." Here Paul emphasizes the critical character of those who have the seal of Christ's imputed righteousness obtained through gospel order (Romans 4:11, Revelation 7:1-3) to depart from iniquity or legal injustice.

To depart from iniquity and from legal injustice represents when a church or state establishes laws contrary to Bible principles. The true Christian does not comply with any such church or state legislation (Acts 5:29). The church or state may authorize divorce for any reason, but the church has only one legal condition for divorce. The state may sanction drinking, gambling, abortion, etc, but the Christian will avoid any illegal authorized church/state injustice. When Judas sold Jesus to the Jews for thirty pieces of silver, Peter said he purchased a field with the reward of **iniquity** (Acts 1:15-18), a reward based on church authorized **legal injustice.** Again, Peter told Simon the sorcerer after he tried to buy the power of the Holy Spirit that he was in the bond of iniquity, in bondage to the acts of legal injustice (Acts 8:22, 23). A practice the New Testament Church would now no longer tolerate for a time after its birth.

Paul said to the Corinthian church, "Rejoice not in iniquity, but rejoice in the truth" (1 Corinthians 13:6). Rejoice not in using the legalized unjust legislation of your era for any reason, for what may be legal on earth is not always legal under heaven's Judicial Legislative Authority. And James said, "The tongue is a fire, a world of iniquity, a powerful tool under the principle of freedom of speech, used in a legalized unjust way to cause injury, iniquity, and death. Iniquity, legal injustice, oh, how terrible it is used today by church and state officials to work out issues and circumstances to arrange their own unscriptural agendas. But the mystery of iniquity Paul spoke about in 2 Thessalonians 2:7 has a different definition.

It is in 2 Thessalonians 2:7 that the word iniquity finds its biblical cry to this generation living just prior to the second coming of Christ. Iniquity defined in this verse is critical to our understanding in the light of the final world union of Church and State confederacy, soon to be fully materialized just before Jesus comes. *Iniquity in this verse applies and means to be in violation of the law and the gospel of life-giving righteousness.* Soon to be heralded to the worldwide apostate Christian churches when they unit with state legislation in violation of the law of life-giving righteousness. It is critical for all Christians to understand and comply with God's eternal code of conduct; that unless one has appropriated heaven's bill of rights, Christ's life-giving righteousness, through gospel order, this final generation of Christians will be classified in the judgment as one in iniquity (Matthew 7:21, 22), or in violation of the gospel of **righteousness by faith into justification by faith.** *The mystery of iniquity is selling a gospel message today that has no legal precedent in heaven's judgment hall of judicial order* (Daniel 7:9; Acts 17:31; Hebrews 8:1, 2; and Revelation 14:6, 7).

There is a difference in God's eyes between being in iniquity, in violation of Christ's life-giving righteousness, the sin Adam placed on us when he violated the law of righteousness (Genesis 3:6; Psalm 51:5; Romans 9:31), and practicing iniquity called legal injustice. Adam had no idea what he was doing when he ate the forbidden fruit (Genesis 3:6). The world and the church are practicing legal injustice, iniquity because the church or state justifies unethical practices. **Iniquity defined as legal injustice** can be confessed and forgiven (1 John 1:9). But iniquity, violation of the law, one continuing to reside in violation of life-giving righteousness or the "law of righteousness" through gospel order, cannot and will not be tolerated in the judgment hour of Revelation 14:7. There is a big difference between *confessing your sins and confessing your condition.* The only remedy for confessing and redeeming our condition is in obeying the "truth of the gospel" of Christ.

Paul says, "If we sin willfully *after that we have received* the knowledge of the truth, **(the truth of the everlasting gospel of Christ's life-giving righteousness (Revelation 14:6-7),** there remains no more sacrifice for sins, but a certain fearful looking for of judgment and fiery indignation, which shall devour the adversaries" (Hebrews 10:26, 27). Christians who are in iniquity **when Jesus comes again,** in violation of Christ's life-giving righteousness, **in violation of "to the law and the testimony"** (Isaiah 8:20), are outside of the commonwealth of the rights of the children of God and **cannot** and **will not** be allowed to live in God's eternal kingdom. We have to be obeying the everlasting gospel message of Revelation 14:6-12 when Jesus comes the second time in order to be sealed (Rev. 7:1-3) in **righteousness by faith into justification by faith** of Christ and have in our possession heaven's bill of rights in order to be eternally saved.

We must all have a sign, a sealed biblical covenant contract (**Isaiah 24:5; John 3:33**) endorsed by God the Father in order to stand through the final conflict of oppression just before Jesus comes in order to pass into heaven's bliss. Friends, any **man, woman,** or **child** who wants to stand in righteousness (Revelation 6:17) at the second coming of Christ must understand these issues in gospel order, afforded especially to this final generation through Christ's Remnant Church (Joel 2:32; Revelation 12:17). The gospel message from the day Jesus introduced it to Adam was a life-and-death message, a life-and-death issue. No justification by faith means no eternal life, and no heaven unless the righteous robe of Jesus' perfect bill of rights covers us, appropriated through gospel order.

This definition of iniquity, to be in violation of the law of life-giving righteousness (Matthew 7:23) is depicted by Jesus in many verses of scripture. Jesus said, "Not every one that says to me, Lord, Lord, shall enter into the kingdom of heaven; but he that doeth the will of my Father who is in heaven. Many will say to me in that day, Lord, Lord, have we not prophesied in thy name? And in thy name have cast out demons? And in thy name done many wonderful works" (Matthew 7:21, 22)?

Here we see scripture emphasizing the wonderful works of many a Christian, feeding the hungry, clothing the naked, calling upon the name of the Lord, prophesying and even casting out devils. All believing one day they will enter heaven's abode and forever reign in Jesus' heavenly kingdom. But the whole emphasis of these three critical verses is, "**And then will I profess to them, I never knew you: depart from me, ye that work iniquity,** ye that work in violation of the law, ye that work outside of Christ life-giving righteousness (Matthew 7:23). Friends, these Christians will be lost, they have been deceived into believing another Jesus, another gospel, another spirit (2 Corinthians 4:4; 2 Corinthians 11:4). And they will be forever rejected from heaven's abode because they have chosen not **"to seek ye first the kingdom of God and His righteousness"** (Matthew 6:33).

No works of the flesh are acceptable in God's universal kingdom outside of heaven's bill of rights (Philippians 3:4). How critical it is for Christians to understand this heavenly principle of life. All the good we do outside of gospel order, outside of Christ's life-giving righteousness appropriated by believing, accepting, receiving, and obeying Christ and the gospel He produced, will negate any and all of man's good works on this planet. Paul said, "Be not deceived, **God is not mocked**, for whatsoever a man sows, that he shall also reap" (Galatians 6:7). Whatsoever a man sows under the umbrella of Christ's life-giving righteousness will receive an eternal righteous reward. Whatsoever a man sows outside of Christ's life-giving righteousness will receive an eternal sentence of unjust or unjustified in heaven's judgment hall (Revelation 22:11) and be separated from God eternally (Ezekiel 18:4); For he that sows to the unrighteousness of his flesh cannot biblically sow to the righteousness of Christ and the indwelling power of the Holy Spirit.

In Matthew 13:41, Jesus said, "The Son of man shall send forth his angels, and they shall gather out of his kingdom all things that offend, and **them who do iniquity**." To be doing iniquity applies not only to good people, but to church-going Christians doing good things outside or *"short of the glory of God"* (Romans 3:23), short of Christ's life-giving righteousness. David said, *"The heavens declare his righteousness, and all the people see his glory" (Psalm 97:6). God's glory is his righteousness (Philippians 1:11),* which without no man can see God and live. In Jesus' parable of the wheat and the tares (Matthew 13:36-41), Jesus makes it dreadfully clear that the seed of gospel truth of accredited imputed righteousness will be more than rivaled just before Jesus comes by the seed of the Mystery of Iniquity. The apostate 21st Century Christian Churches clothed with civil authority.

The Mystery of Iniquity (2 Thessalonians 2:7) is the mystery of being deceived in thinking and believing all Christians are saved in Christ's righteousness, when truly the majorities are still in iniquity, still in violation of heaven's bill of rights placed on us by Adam's willful sin (1 Timothy 2:14). In Revelation 12:9 the great dragon, Satan, will through the dragon powers of civil government, uniting and working through the serpent powers of the Christian Churches, deceive the whole world (Revelation 12:9) in rejecting heaven's Bill of Life-giving righteousness. Our bill of rights, the same bill of rights he rejected in heaven (1 John 3:8; Jude 7; 2 Peter 2:4) and lost the right to heaven's blessing. Jesus said when all this is said and done, and the holy angels are done separating the wheat from the tares, "there shall be *wailing and gnashing of teeth"* (Matthew 13:42).

This Christian wailing and gnashing of teeth is pictured and characterized in the final events of Revelation 17:15, 16 and Jeremiah 8:19, 20. John the revelator pictures in Revelation 17:12, ten horns of power which support the whore of Babylon (Revelation 17:3-5) with their legislative and judicial authority (Revelation 17:13). A whore in scripture is a church that fornicates with state government (Revelation 17:1, 2). The 21st Century Christian Churches are now organizing a universal union of Christian churches soon to be supported by the kings of the earth (Revelation 17:1, 2).

When it's too late, these **Ten Horns of power** (Revelation 17:16), *five in the Middle East, three in Europe,* and *two in the United States,* shall hate the whore, the 21st Century United Christian Catholic Protestant Churches. Seated, as defined by Daniel, *"through his policy also he shall cause **(Church) craft** to prosper in his hand"* (Daniel 8:25) upon the seven-horn-headed beast of Revelation 12:3 and 17:3. The scarlet-colored beast having seven heads, made up of seven biblical defined empires that have since the time of the birth of Israel as a nation opposed the truth of the gospel. These **ten horns of civil and religious authority** (Revelation 17:9-13) **on the seven heads,** when it's too late for anyone to be saved, shall in the end turn and make the 21st Century Christian Catholic Protestant Churches desolate of church members, uncover her apostasy, eat her flesh, and burn her with fire (Revelation 17:16). Millions of deceived Christians in fury at their religious leaders and teachers.

Why? Because they have prevented them from believing, receiving, accepting, and obeying the final gospel message heralded to this final world by Christ's Remnant Church (Revelation 12:17; 14:6-12). Uniting, opposing, and condemning those who are **justified** (Romans 5:1) by the Everlasting Gospel message of Revelation 14:6-12 to death (Revelation 13:15). **Good Christian people** deceived into believing and worshiping the religious civil beast powers of Revelation 13:1-18. The religious beast out of the sea, Catholicism (Revelation 13:1-10), along with the civil beast out of the earth, the United States of America (Revelation 13:11). Who legislates within its territorial empire the religious authority of the image of the beast, Protestantism (Revelation 13:11-16). And initiate in the world the mark (Sunday worship) of the beast, Catholicism's unscriptural day of religious authority.

In Matthew 23:26-28, Jesus said of the Church leaders of his day, indeed **appear beautiful outward**, but are **within full of dead men's bones,** and of all **uncleanness,** Thus you also **outwardly appear righteous** to men, but within ye are **full of hypocrisy and iniquity**, in violation of God's moral code of righteous conduct. Men standing in highly respected religious positions of authority, ministers and priests full of degrading atrocities, church-covered iniquities open to world view (Luke 12:3). More so now in the twentieth and twenty-first centuries like never before known. Yet many pass by these atrocities because ministers, priests, and denominations **outwardly appear righteous,** denominations and men void of the truth of the everlasting gospel and the understanding of how to convey the gospel of life-giving righteousness to a world of gross darkness and death (Isaiah 60:1-3). Jesus said, "Finish up then the measure of your fathers. Ye serpents, ye generation of vipers **(church leaders and teachers),** how can ye escape the damnation of hell" (Matthew 23:33).

When the United States legislates the one united principle doctrine of the 21st Century Christian Churches (Sunday worship), the measure of God's forbearance will then have been filled up in heaven's judicial hall of Justice and then God's full and final display of "this gospel of the kingdom shall be preached in all the world, for a witness unto all nations; and then shall the end come" (Matthew 24:14). It's coming, friends, it's coming faster than anyone can anticipate. Christians in this country may believe they can infringe their doctrinal Christian beliefs through government legislation, but the adversary of souls well knows this amalgamation of ambassadorship status (2 Corinthians 5:20) will lead Christianity into its fatal fall in world apostasy (2 Thessalonians 2:10-12).

Christ **never asserted** his **doctrinal rights** upon state government to be legalized, and **never taught** his disciples any such rights. You will never read in scripture Christians **demanding Caesar for Christian rights**. Jesus said, "My kingdom is not of this world" (John 18:36). "Therefore give to Cesar the things (secular, civil duties) which are Cesar's, and to God the things (sacred) which are God's" (Luke 20:25). **A Christian** is an **ambassador**, a representative of God's governing principles in **ambassadorship status only**, with no legal say in and of any government to afford legislated faith. The **church** and the **home** is the **religious embassy** of **Christian sovereignty**.

Iniquity defined that destroys true Christian Agape love placed in the heart of the newly born again believer by Christ our righteousness

In Matthew 24:12, Jesus said, "And because **iniquity abounds**, the love of many *will* wax cold." When the lack of understanding and applying what the apostle Paul calls "the truth of the gospel" (Galatians 2:5, 14; Colossians 1:5), the love so necessary for the believer to possess and maintain will "*wax* cold" (Matthew 24:12). Has not this prophetic gospel prophecy again found its way in the heart of those who God has called through "the testimony of Jesus" (Revelation 12:17) to give the last gospel call to this misguided Christian world (Revelation 14:6-12)?

Has the gospel defined by Paul as "*my gospel*" (Romans 2:16, 16:25; 2 Timothy 2:8), the gospel he says, "*I preach among the gentiles*" (Galatians 2:2), been perverted and changed to "another gospel" (Galatians 1:6, 7) or even to say into many gospels? Has the agape love defined and lived by Jesus, the apostles after their Pentecostal experience, waxed cold among us? How many will deny this truth that the love of many has waxed cold?

It's evident today, the Christian agape love so experienced by Christ and the apostles is now scarcely to be found. In almost all Christian Churches the first love of believing and receiving Christ as their personal Savior and Lord is wanting. Above all this heavenly divine agape love so promised to Christ Remnant Church through gospel order (Joel 2:32; Revelation 12:17), the biblical vestige of the "**woman clothed with the sun** (Revelation 12:1), is wanting because of its ministers' and members' refusal to council together as to what constitutes the "**truth of the gospel**" of Christ. In what the gospel is, says, and what the gospel of Christ does for the individual believer. Christ's Remnant Church, clothed with heaven's judicial authority, has the duty and responsibility to preach the last gospel sign, the final sealing (Romans 4:11) message to this dying world. Counseled about iniquity and the specific iniquity to be revealed to this last generation just before Jesus comes (2 Thessalonians 2:7, 8).

Christ's Remnant is God's end-time Church, with the final end time "*everlasting gospel*" message defined as the everlasting gospel of **righteousness by faith that leads to justification by faith** in Christ in the judgment hour message designated for this final generation (Revelation 14:6-12). His last-day church critically called, anointed, appointed, still after 162 years terribly wanting of the early and latter rain messages of Joel 2:23 in paralleling the early rain Pentecost power bestowed on the New Testament Church at its birth (Acts 1:8; 2:1-3). To the all-critical latter rain Pentecost "great power" (Revelation 18:1) to be bestowed on Christ's latter-day Remnant Church (Joel 2:32; Revelation 12:17).

Is it not inevitable? Will Jesus bestow upon His Remnant Church agape love and the Pentecostal power they so need if the corporate church will not in one gospel tone "speak the same thing" (*the everlasting gospel*) in order to be "perfectly joined together in the same mind and the same judgment" (1 Corinthians 1:10). "For the hour of his judgment is come" (Revelation 14:7) speaks to us collectively the final "everlasting gospel" message (Revelation 14:6) for this final generation. Will we not believe the *early rain* message of *righteousness by faith* given to the early Christian Church (A.D. 31), repeated to the nineteenth century Seventh-day Adventist Church that through the early rain message of *righteousness by faith* (Revelation 14:6, 7) she may contemplate and herald the *latter rain* message of *Justification by faith (Revelation 14:9-11)*.

The world is dying *under a decree of unrighteousness* (Romans 3:10). And God cannot and **will not** empower a people to give the "loud voice" of *Justification by faith* of the *third angel* of Revelation 14:9-11 when many, if not most, are in serious doubt of what constitutes the "loud voice" of the *first angel* gospel message (Matthew 24:14) of *righteousness by faith* commissioned in Revelation 14:6, 7. How many have become lethargic, dormant because of their resistance of the specific gospel light and truth defined by the apostle Paul as the "*power of God*" center in Christ, the cross and the gospel (1 Corinthians 1:18, 24; Romans 1:16). Which would make the Remnant at this present crisis time, called in Revelation 14:7, "the hour of his judgment," *teachers of righteousness in Christ* (Daniel 12:3; Joel 2:23; Romans 1:17).

Joel 2:23 is very specific in its instructions of receiving the early rain (teacher of righteousness) into receiving the latter rain (teacher of righteousness or righteousness unto justification by faith). It must be understood that this concept of receiving the early and latter rain is an individual as well as a corporate experience. Specifically defined in the everlasting gospel message of Revelation 14 to be heralded "to earth's final generation (Matthew 24:14). The early rain in the born again (John 3:5-7) experience today is a righteousness by faith first angel message of line upon line, precept upon precept, defined biblically for this final generation in the two specific verses of Revelation 14:6, 7. That also defines clearly the second angel's message (Revelation 14:8), revealing the condition of the Christian Churches who have rejected the "judgment hour" righteousness by faith message of the first angel given during the eighteen thirties and forties Advent movement. Which directly leads into the latter rain third angel test message (Revelation 3:10; Revelation 14:9-12) of Justification by faith. A parallel walk in the gospel steps of that gospel faith of our father Abraham from "faith to faith (Romans 1:16, 17, 4:11, 12; 5:1).

If an individual will not believe and accept the early rain gospel message of righteousness by faith presented at the time of their calling (John 6:44) to Christ and his righteousness, it will be nearly impossible for them to pass the latter rain test (Revelation 13:10) of Justification by faith (James 2:21) defined in Revelation 14:9-12. This application also applies

to Christ's Remnant Church that must be at the coming of Christ biblically sealed in righteousness by faith into Justification by faith. How many
are confused by the misinterpretation of how the final sign, seal gospel
covenant (Romans 4:11; Isaiah 24:5; 56:1-8; Revelation 14:6, 7) of imputed
righteousness should be conveyed to this final generation into Justification
by faith. The everlasting gospel message of Revelation 14:6, 7 is a righteousness *by faith sign question* that leads to a *justification by faith seal* prior to
the second coming of Christ.

How many in the Remnant are confused as to why their communities do not respond to evangelism? Will God draw and open the hearts
of faith to communities **when Church doctrine** has more focus on manmade salvation than the *"truth of the gospel of Christ"* (Galatians 2:5,
14; Colossians 1:5; Ephesians 1:13) which must first be cemented in the
hearts of the believer. The gospel from Genesis to Revelation has always
had a signed, sealed everlasting covenant contract under heaven's judicial
authority (2 Timothy 2:19). Centered in Christ our life-giving righteousness, which must be presented to every man, woman, and child on this
planet before the final winds of strife are let entirely loose on Planet Earth
(Revelation 7:1-3). God's Remnant Church (Revelation 12:17), also called
in scripture **Laodicea** (Revelation 3:14-22), is defined by Christ as a lukewarm church, neither cold nor hot. Counseled with the specific warning
as to its calling to "**open the door**" of faith (Revelation 3:20; Acts 14:27) in
order to believe, accept, and present to the world.

1. *The first angel's message of righteousness
by faith (Revelation 14:6-7)*

**2. *The second angel's message revealing the Christian Churches
" is fallen, is fallen" and are presently uniting together for the
final global confederacy of church and state (Revelation 14:8).***

**3. *The third angel's message is justification by faith. In
contemplation of the world churches soon to legislate the
"mark of the beast" (Revelation 13:16, 17; 14:9-11).***

For years, Jesus has been pleading with His "church of Laodicea
(Revelation 3:14-18) to believe and accept the final everlasting gospel message founded on Divine, Creative, Redemptive Authority. Produced and
instituted by Jesus the living Christ, the "beginning of the creation of God"
(Revelation 3:14). To contemplate their condition of neither being *cold*, as

Job defines cold as one being without a garment, naked, as Adam was in the beginning after he lost his "robe of righteousness," his garment of salvation (Job 24:7; Isaiah 61:10). Or *hot* (*fervent*), a commandment keeper, "mighty in the scriptures" *"fervent* (hot) in the spirit" "instructed in the way of the Lord" "speaking the things of the Lord (Acts 18:24, 25).

Brethren, why should iniquity, being void of Christ's life-giving righteousness, continue to testify in the membership of Laodicea, Christ's Remnant body of believers waiting for the second coming of Christ? Why? Because many, if not most, have chosen not to be fully grounded in understanding what constitutes the "loud voice" of the first angel of Revelation 14:6, 7. The critical "saying" of the second angel (Revelation 14:8). And finally the "loud voice" of the third angel (Revelation 14:9-11). It's time to heed the counsel and demand of Heaven's judicial authorities and open our eyes to our spiritual condition as a body of believers in Christ our righteousness. This condition makes us at the present time of **upcoming calamity** a lukewarm Remnant Church, cold as though bitten with frostbite (Revelation 3:16). How long, brethren, will we be in doubt of our sign sealing gospel message.

How long will we be in confusion, causing many to leave our churches because iniquity abounds (Matthew 24:12). Will we continue to wait until the prophetic "shaking" (Hebrews 12:26, 27; Isaiah 13:11-13) removes those *"cold"* among us. Those who continuously refuse to put on the wedding garment of Christ our righteousness (Revelation 19:7, 8). Those who have chosen to continue to *"walk in the shame of thy nakedness" lest he walk naked, and they* (in the judgment hour) *see his shame" (Revelation 3:18, 16:15).* From those who have sealed their standing (Ephesians 6:13; Revelation 6:19) in Christ our righteousness unto Justification of the Spirit (1 Timothy 3:16) in this generation's signed, sealed covenant contract (Hebrews 10:15-25) as Jesus was sealed in his (John 6:27). Soon God will have no choice but at "such a time as this" (Esther 4:14) to finish the work and cut it short in righteousness by separating the wheat (precious grain) from the tares (unbelieving blots of iniquity) (Matthew 13:39, 40). Oh, the terrible dread that is soon to come upon the Christian world.

Jesus is saying, "**How long shall I see the standard,**" the sign sealed banner pole of the Remnant Church, the token, sign, flag of her message (Revelation 14:6, 7), dead in the wind? How long shall we see the standard of life hidden beneath the rubbish of error? How long shall we *hear the sound of the 7th trumpet of Revelation 10:7 in entertainment tones as a substitute for the seventh trumpet blast of warning to a fallen world?* How long will the Laodicea's voice of the seventh angel (Revelation 10:7) blow the warning gospel message of the seventh trumpet in a lukewarm, muffled, lethargic sound (Jeremiah 4:21, 22)? How long, brethren, how long?

Year after year, Jesus has been saying, "**My people** *are* **foolish**, they have not known me; they *are* sottish (play) children, and they have none understanding: these *are* wise to do evil, but to do good they have no knowledge (Jeremiah 4:22) how to present life-giving righteousness to an unjust world. The world and the Christian church are in bondage to the "**sin unto death**" (1 John 5:16), and the majority of the members of the Remnant Church have no knowledge of how to explain or how to give from the Bible and the Bible alone life for them that do not know they are in bondage to the sin unto death (1 John 5:16).

Friends, this is not criticism or condemnation, this is the reality, the condition of Christ's Church presiding under heavenly Judicial Authority in this generation. John said, "These things have I written to you that **believe on the name of the Son of God**; that ye may **know that ye have eternal life**, and that ye **may believe** on the **name** (**understand and know**) of the Son of God from a converted, born again Christian heart (1 John 5:13). Because iniquity abounds, Jesus said, **the love of many has waxed cold** (Matthew 24:12). Iniquity in this context is a gospel issue, and because of confusion in gospel order among the membership of God's last day church, the agape love afforded to us by Jesus through gospel order is negated. Agape love is a divine Godly power which can only be bestowed in an ongoing foundation only if its members **biblically continue** in **the truth of the gospel** message of Christ (Galatians 2:5).

When gospel righteousness, gospel order (Romans 14:17; John 20:19-23) is not completely, biblically taught (Hebrews 5:12), preached (Mark 16:15; Matthew 28:19), understood, supported, obeyed (Mark 16:16), and maintained through biblical principles of present gospel truth, when it is not fully understood by the people entering the Remnant Church, then heaven is hampered from bestowing ongoing agape love in the hearts of the Christ's Remnant believers. It is then its members are hampered from the power they so need to retain, maintain and represent Christ from a converted heart. Agape love has no God-given judicial heavenly right to abound in the heart of the believer of any Church unless the truth of the gospel continues to be believed, accepted, and obeyed in a sign sealing covenant given especially to Christ's Remnant Church (Revelation 12:17; Isaiah 56:1-6).

Is it not scriptural? Did not Jesus say, "For without me you can do nothing" (John 15:5)? Isn't it incredible how men, ministers, church members preach love, the love of Jesus, and how we should love one another as Jesus loves his church? Is it not also truly biblical that the love necessary for **true agape love** to dwell in the hearts of church members is only available through gospel order? Man is completely void of any such love; it's not possible for me to agape love anyone unless heavenly agape love is bestowed on me and in me by the indwelling power of the Holy Spirit. The love manifested in the Last Day Christian Remnant Church is a travesty to heaven's inhabitants. Heavenly agape love can never dwell in the church or in the heart of any member until first we accept the fact that the human heart "is **deceitful above all things**, and **desperately wicked**: who can know it?" (Jeremiah 17:9). Second, we **choose** to believe, accept, and obey the everlasting gospel message for this generation (Revelation 14:6-12; Isaiah 56:1-8). Third, we **ask** and **pray** on a continual basis. Jesus said, "Ask and it shall be given you seek and you shall find, knock and it shall be opened unto you" (Matthew 7:7; Luke 11:9).

Friend, how can any church member manifest and maintain true Christ like agape love in the church without believing and maintaining the latter rain message necessary (Revelation 14:6-12; 18:1) for the indwelling agape power of the Holy Spirit. Agape love so manifested by Jesus and the Apostles at Pentecost can only be maintained by the indwelling power of the Holy Spirit, and the indwelling power of the Holy Spirit can only be maintained if one continues in the truth of the everlasting gospel message authorized in heaven today (Galatians 2:5; Revelation 14:6, 7). **Righteousness by faith unto Justification by faith in Christ has always had a sign of faith; a seal of imputed righteousness from Genesis to Revelation (John 3:33; Romans 4:11; 2 Timothy 2:19).**

In Abraham's day, circumcision (Romans 4:11) was his sign of imputed righteousness that led to his seal of imputed Justification by faith (Romans 5:1) when he passed the test (Genesis 22:1, 2), "when he had offered Isaac his son upon an altar of sacrifice (James 2:21). Of which circumcision was transferred in the days of Jesus to baptism "through the faith of the operation of God" (Colossians 2:12). Not all remnant believers understand God has a biblical gospel sign, seal in this final generation, called the seventh-day Sabbath. It's a mystery to many because of controversy among the ministry and the membership for the obvious reason that they will not study the issue together. "**That ye all speak the same thing and that ye be perfectly joined together in the same mind and in the same judgment**" (1 Corinthians 1:10) as to what the present judgment truth of the gospel (2 Peter 1:12) represents as biblical salvation in the 21st Century (Romans 1:16, 17; Revelation 7:1-3; 10:7; 14:6, 7).

Jesus has a sign-sealing message all its members must corporately understand and obey as a gospel issue before it can be anything else. If we truly believe the voice of the true witness to the church of the Laodicea (Revelation 3:14-22) and believe the gospel latter rain (Revelation 14:9-11, 18:1) message to be given to this final generation, then and only then will we receive the latter rain power of Revelation 18:1, essential to stand through the last days as witnesses of Christ's life-giving righteousness (Revelation 3:19, 20).

When this unity in everlasting gospel order is manifested in the last days of remnant time, when Christ's end time Remnant Church makes herself ready (Revelation 19:7) by biblically cutting off iniquity and biblically clothing herself with the Son of life-giving righteousness (Revelation 19:8) through gospel order. Then and only then will she receive the **Pentecostal power** she needs to stand as the "Remnant" in righteousness in the last days (Revelation 18:1).

When this characteristic is fully materialized in Jesus' Remnant body, she will stand in the "day of darkness and of gloominess, a day of clouds and of thick darkness, as the morning spread upon the mountains: **a great people and a strong; there hath not been ever the like, neither shall be any more after it, even to the years of many generations**. A fire devours before them; and behind them a flame burns: the **(heavenly)** land *is* as the **Garden of Eden before them**, and behind them **(the earth) a desolate wilderness**; yea, and nothing shall escape them (Joel 2:2, 3).

When this total faith is completely manifested among God's remnant people she will be globally accosted by the deceptive power of the Mystery of Iniquity (2 Thessalonians 2:7). Which at that time has become **MYSTERY BABYLON THE GREAT, THE MOTHER OF HARLOTS AND ABOMINATIONS OF THE EARTH** (Revelation 17:5) in a worldwide confederacy of church and state legislation. Scripture says when these things are all in place, when the Mystery of Iniquity (2 Thessalonians 2:3-7), the mystery of holding Christians in violation of Christ's life-giving-righteousness, he the man of sin, the son of perdition (Daniel 11:44; 2 Thessalonians 2:3) will rise up in complete enmity towards Christ's Remnant Church, in a fury that heaven has never before seen.

Therefore, says Daniel, "therefore he **(the Vicar of Christ, the sovereign head of the 21st Century Christian Catholic Protestant Church, will unite with the future Protestant union of church and state in America)** shall go forth with great fury to destroy and utterly to make **(sweep)** away many" (Daniel 11:44). "And he **(the world-wide appointed head of the woman, the 21st Century Christian Catholic Protestant Churches) that will sit on the seven-headed beast of unjustified earthly powers (Revelation 17:1-3) which has set up his Mark (Sunday worship) of false Christian doctrine**

in the Christian Church since the sixth century) shall plant the tabernacles of his palace (the mark of the seat of his religious authority in
Catholicism [Revelation 14:9; 16:2]) between the seas, (the peoples of the
earth) [Revelation 17:15]) and especially in the glorious holy mountain."

"But tidings (the everlasting gospel of Revelation 14:6-12) out of the
east and out of the north (the three angels' message of Revelation.14:6-12
that originated out of the Northeast corner of the United States in the
eighteen thirties and forties), shall trouble him" (Daniel 11:44). "Yet he
(the man of sin, the son of perdition" (2 Thessalonians 2:3), the sovereign head of the Mystery of Iniquity) shall come to his end, and none (of
the Christian world presiding in the earth in the end) shall help (protect) him" (Daniel 11:45).

Ministers, ministries, and denominations under the heading of the
Mystery of Iniquity are deceiving many a Christian in this generation.
Keeping the Christian believer in the bonds of iniquity, in violation of life-
giving righteousness, righteousness they so need to have the legal right to
stand in justification in the day of Christ. When Jesus finally stands up in
heaven's judgment hall of justice (Daniel 12:1), man's probation on Planet
Earth is over, then Jesus pronounces the final fate of every man, woman,
and child living on Planet Earth. Saying, "He that is unjust (unjustified
for life), let him be unjust (unjustified) still: and he which is filthy, let
him (who has filthy Christian works of unrighteousness [Isaiah 64:6])
be filthy still: and he that is righteous, (has appropriated gospel justification) let him be righteous still: and he that is holy, (whose mind is under
complete authority and controlling influence of the indwelling power
of the Holy Spirit [Isaiah 30:21]) let him be holy still" (Revelation 22:11).

Friend, Jesus is about to come and it is critical, Jesus said, "He that
overcomes the same shall be clothed in white raiment; and I will not blot
out his name out of the book of life, but I will confess his name before
my Father, and before his angels" (Revelation 3:5). Unless we are clothed
in the white raiment of Christ's life-giving righteousness through gospel order, Jesus cannot and will not present our name before our heavenly
Father in heaven's tribunal for eternal redemption unto eternal life. He then
has no other choice but to blot out our names from the Lamb's book of Life
(Revelation 21:27) and then the sinner, still in iniquity because of Adams
sin, still under the decree of unrighteousness (Romans 3:10) after this is
pronounced guilty; Justified only to be completely eradicated from eternal
life. Please let this not be our fate in the judgment hour message that's been
going on in the heavenly Sanctuary for over 160 years (Daniel 7:9-14; 2
Corinthians 5:10; Hebrews 8:1-3; Revelation 14:6, 7).

⌒ *Chapter Ten* ⌒
Islam, 9/11, Mystery, Babylon the Great, & the Final Scenario of Apostasy

"**A**nd upon her forehead was a name written, **MYSTERY, BABYLON THE GREAT, THE MOTHER OF HARLOTS AND ABOMINATIONS OF THE EARTH**" (Revelation 17:5). Mystery Babylon, the trinity of apostasy presently being set up in the earth will soon, according to Bible prophesy, fulfill its final destiny in world affairs. **Mystery, Babylon the Great,** is what the inhabitants of the world will be deceived into becoming just before Jesus comes again in righteousness (Revelation 19:11). It's the Mystery of Iniquity (2 Thessalonians 2:7) so long misunderstood that produces Mystery, Babylon the Great, the title and name given to this final generation of earth's inhabitants as they unite in a global union of church and state. Mystery Babylon has a **Mother,** *the Roman Catholic Universal Church*; has daughters, or **Harlots,** the *Protestant Churches of the United States and the world.* Now in complete apostasy, once antagonistic to the mother, but presently has returned to her side. These two present Christian schools of ecclesiastical influences are presently uniting underhandedly with the **Abominations of the Earth** (Deuteronomy 18:9-14), the *nations central to the Middle East* that will shortly support MYSTERY BABYLON'S united, religious, concealed agenda of *false worship.*

This whole system of religious apostasy is the subject of Revelation 9 through 19, along with the prophecies of the book of Daniel in chapters 1 through 12, revealing the mysterious puzzle pieces concerning the apostate affairs of men. These mysteries unknown through past ages have though prophetic interpretations become a complete picture. The apostle Paul was not speculating when he said, "Now all these things happened to them for examples: and they are written for our admonition, **upon whom the ends of the world are come.** For whatsoever things were written aforetime were written for our learning, that we through patience and comfort of the scriptures might have hope" (Romans 15:4; 1 Corinthians 10:11). Daniel and Revelation, the two most important prophetic books in scripture, are crying with information depicting the critical events presently taking place on Planet Earth.

Critical is the final warning given to God's Remnant Church in the sixteenth chapter of Revelation. In this chapter, in the fifteenth verse, Jesus says, "Behold, I come as a thief. Blessed is he **that watches**, and keeps his garments, lest he walk naked, and they see his shame" (Revelation 16:15). If the Bible had illuminating flashing lights they would be flashing now with an intensity never before seen in history (Luke 21:36). I am coming, Jesus says, **"blessed is he who watches."** Watches what? The **Trinity of Apostasy**, the **Mystery of Iniquity** (Revelation 16:13), **the three world leading civil and religious powers** symbolized first by the **Dragon voice of the United States,** secondly by the beast power of **Roman Catholicism seated in Europe,** and lastly by the **false prophet system of Apostate Protestantism.** Presently being **worked by the deceptive "spirit of devils,** "working miracles, which go forth to the kings of the earth and of the whole world, **to gather them to the battle of that great day of God Almighty"** (Revelation 16:14).

"**Watches what?**" The works of the **Dragon, Beast,** and **False Prophet (Revelation 16:13)** symbols of the three last-day Christian, controlling religious and civil powers of the earth. Influenced by "spirits of devils" preparing this present generation in the time when the presentation of the final gospel message (Revelation 14:6-12) of **righteousness by faith into justification by faith** in Christ is being presented to the world. The only Robe of Righteousness available for the sin of the world (**John 1:29**). Presently being offered to every man, woman, and child on Planet Earth. A garment of pure, unadulterated righteousness to cover this final generation presently living in the present judgment hour message of Daniel 7:1-14; 8:14; Acts 17:31; and Revelation 14:6-12. The only garment heaven will accept to cover the naked condition of unrighteousness placed on man by Adam's sin shortly after the creation of Planet Earth. A covering of Christ's righteousness so that the shame of man's nakedness (unrighteousness [Revelation 3:18; 16:15]) does not appear in heaven's Judicial Hall of Justice in the judgment hour presently taking place in heaven's heavenly Sanctuary (Hebrews 8:1-5).

More so these three powers the **Dragon, Beast,** and **False Prophet** are working in the **three biblical areas** God has used in past ages as central locations to reveal the governing principles of his Kingdom. These **three areas** are the **United States, Europe,** and the **Middle East.** In the third and fourth millennia of earth's history, the area known as the Middle East was the first location God used (Galatians 3:8) to reveal to developing nations after the great flood his life-governing principles in a centralized government called Israel. Israel's birth from the loins of Abraham, Isaac, and Jacob would still be the central location in the Middle East today if they had not rejected Jesus, the Lamb of God who takes away the sin (*the unrighteousness*) that condemns the world (John 1:29). Abraham at one time was a Babylonian, called out of the Ur of the Chaldees, the land of his birth, called out of Mesopotamia from an area defined as land between the rivers, the Euphrates and the Tigris. Called out of Nineveh of Assyria, out of Babylon. Names for the location in prophetic time of his relatives and descendants who eventually become antagonistic and oppressive to those who accepted God's governing ideology of His divine character and Kingdom.

The Middle East, for two thousand years after the call of Abraham, was the central location for the proclamation of the gospel to every nation, kindred, tongue, and people of that era. History and scripture records the one-time domineering nations of **Egypt** (Exodus 6:5). Then for a time **Assyria** (2 Chronicles 33:11)**,** then **Babylon** (Daniel 1:1), then **Media-Persia (Daniel 5:26-28), the first four heads of the seven-headed dragon beast of Revelation 12:3; 13:1; 17:3.** Along with all other tribes, peoples, and tongues that had their allotted time in history to appropriate life-giving righteousness.

These nations, or one-time governing bodies in the **Middle East** who rejected life-giving righteousness, will just before Jesus comes again unite with the Dragon voice of the United States (Revelation 13:11). The Beast power of the Roman Catholic Church (Revelation 13:1-10), along with her Protestant daughters, the "Image to the Beast." The now present-day apostate Protestant Churches of the United States (Revelation 13:15). In a world confederacy of Christian church and state legislation, revealing the one unscriptural Christian doctrinal tradition of **Sunday worship,** introduced to the world in the second century at the birth of the New Testament Christian Universal Church.

Today the **Middle East** is the present central focus of contention with the present biblical Dragon power of Revelation 13:11and 16:13, the United States of America. In order for the **Mystery of Iniquity** (2 Thessalonians 2:7) to elevate **Mystery Babylon the Great** (Revelation 17:5) to the pinnacle of control in the earth. The Middle East must be open to the powers that be in order for the devil, Satan, the adversary of souls, to unite the two most influential religions of the world with the civil governments of the world for the final battle over life-giving righteousness. **Egypt, Syria, Iraq,** and **Iran** represent the biblical seats of the fanatical arm of Islam's past oppressive descendants of Righteous Noah (Genesis 7:1).

Rebellious children characterized by the unruly nature of Ishmael (Genesis 16:11, 12). The undisciplined sons of Lot, Moab, and Ammon

(Daniel 11:41), and the profane fornicator Esau or Edom (Hebrews 12:16; Daniel 11:41). Who in their lifetime rejected life-giving righteousness and educated a mindset of religious hostility for generations; who for their own religious conviction since the birth of Islam in the seventh century A.D. will not tolerate without deadly consequences interference within their own confines of faith. Soon this area will as prophecy predicts be temporarily freed of religious intolerance. And Islam will cooperate with the Mystery of Iniquity into forming MYSTERY BABYLON THE GREAT (Revelation 17:5) in a union of Christian religious and civil universal oppressive control.

The next location used by God for the proclamation of the gospel essential for our study in understanding last day events is **Europe**. Because of Israel's rejection of the gospel with the crucifixion of Christ, prophecy did predict a time and name change for those who would promulgate the truth of the gospel (Isaiah 65:13-15). After the ascension of Christ, at the birth of the New Testament Christian Universal Church (Revelation 12:1, 2), the name Christian was established as the dominant title for those who would embrace the truth of the gospel (Acts 11:25, 26; 1 Peter 4:16). It is with divine emphasis scripture records and foretells prophetic events especially for this last generation (1 Corinthians 10:11).

For two thousand years the hearts and minds of the inhabitance of the Middle East were afforded all of heaven's wondrous blessing. And because of their rejection in their allotted time in prophecy of hearing the words of life that whole area of nations, tribes, and peoples eventually became an educated, antagonistic mindset of fighting factions against themselves and the biblical "truth of the gospel," fabricating their own mindset of righteousness and the governing principles of God's Kingdom. Eventually Asia (Acts 16:6, 7) would become an unsafe location, a **bottomless pit ([Revelation 9:1, 2] the seat of Islam)** of religious and civil antagonistic opposition to centralize the overseeing of the gospel of Jesus Christ.

After the destruction of Jerusalem in A.D. 70, a battle for central church authority and control began to emerge among the future leaders of Christ's Universal Church. After the death of the twelve apostles, within a few hundred years, four locations, **Jerusalem, Alexandria, Antioch,** and **Rome** emerged as centralized areas for different nationalities of people accepting the Christian faith. Because of the **falling away first (Galatians 5:4; 2 Thessalonians 2:3)** from "the **truth of the gospel" (Galatians 2:14)** by the middle of the second century A.D. (Revelation 2:4, 5) and because of many unscriptural elements entering the New Testament Christian Universal church, Rome by the fourth century A.D. became the center of all Christian doctrine.

So terrible was the pride and power of the New Testament Christian Church based in Rome that she, by the time Christianity became a popular sect of religious belief, and with her influence in the capital city of power of the then-known world. The New Testament Christian Church in Rome exalted herself as the central controlling Christian force *(sovereign)* in the earth. So terrible was the pride of the religious leaders in Rome between the second and sixth century. That even the name and title of the New Testament Christian universal Church (Acts 11:26; 1 Peter 4:16) was changed to the Roman Catholic *(universal)* Church, a name more focused on men than on Christ.

It's not understood when the universal name given to the Christian Church evolved into the Roman Catholic Church in the minds of the people of the world. But eventually the name change from Christian to Roman brought into the minds of men in future ages the seductive deception of men looking to **self-appointed men and churches** instead of the teaching of Christ's written word as the sole source of Christian doctrine. Heaven only knows how powerful and deceptive the satanic forces have over the minds of men since the fall of Adam. Men created in the image of God sold into bondage to principalities and power of darkness of this evil world (Ephesians 6:12). Deceiving, controlling, and blinding "the minds of them which believe not, lest the light of the glorious gospel of Christ, who is the image of God, should shine unto them" (2 Corinthians 4:4).

And so Europe was afforded to be the next area allotted by God for the proclamation of the gospel of Christ. A new location of developing nations, tongues, and peoples that would arise out of the fall of the old Roman Empire. New nations not so antagonistic to the gospel of Christ and the principles he exemplified to the preceding generations in the Middle East. It was through the missionary journeys of the apostles (Acts 28:16; 2 Timothy 1:7) that Rome was established with an early group of believers. For the sole purpose of expanding through future Europe the faith once delivered to the saint. But in time, hundreds of years of time, the pride of men again took control under the influence of the adversary of souls, and Rome became the central control of the Christian faith through the **scepter of civil governments,** instead of the **scepter of Christ our righteousness** (Hebrews 1:8). Jesus foresaw the fall of the Roman Catholic Church; he predicted an allotted time (Luke 21:24; Revelation 11:1-4) to this future Church of the Gentiles (Acts 13:46) after she would completely apostatize by taking full control of Europe's populace by the **deadly union of Church and State**. In A.D. 538 the new Roman Christian Catholic universal Church took up **the scepter of Christian doctrine under the scepter of** civil authority in Europe. Two scepters of authority over the conscience of men biblically predicted to last 1,260 years of religious and civil intolerance upon those who desired liberty of conscience.

For **1,260 years** the Christian Church of the Gentiles (Acts 9:15; 13:46; 18:6) from **A.D. 538 to 1798** (Luke 21:24; Revelation 11:2, 3; 12:6, 14; Revelation 13:5; Daniel 7:25; Daniel 12:7), under her new name, the Roman Catholic Church in Europe held millions captive under the umbrella of civil authority. Until the Napoleon war took the scepter of civil rights out of her hand (Revelation 13:3). Thus in February of 1798 the Catholic Church lost the power to legislate her doctrines though civil authority. Soon, friends, real soon **the Dragon power of the United States** (Revelation 13:11; 16:13) will, just before Jesus comes, through the seductive power of the Harlots of Protestant Christianity in America (Revelation 17:5), restore to the Roman Catholic Church in America and the world the unscriptural right of civil and religious legislation by legislating her ecclesiastical mark of religious authority or **Sunday worship**.

The **United States** will, in the near future, lead the world in making a universal confederacy with the religious system based in Rome. So long **heralded by the Protestant Reformation as the Antichrist** Church of the Dark Ages. A widow for the last two hundred years without a government to enforce her religious beliefs, soon (Revelation 18:7) to be no widow at all, soon for the last time the Christian Church will marry the state and sit in religious authority on the legislative civil kings of the earth (Revelation 17:1-3). Dictating what should be legislated as what day should be kept as a universal religious doctrine, **Sunday legislated worship**.

In the last four millennia of earth's history God has used two central locations in the earth, central locations established under heaven's providence to spread the good news of life-giving righteousness. In the third and fourth millennia of earth's history, the nation of Israel from its birth to the first coming of Christ held the scepter of church authority in the location known today as the Middle East. And it's with great sadness we study the history of the New Testament Christian Church in Europe for her allotted time in the last two millennia of earth's history. As she began with the scepter of Christ's righteousness for a short time in the Middle East, and then relocating in Europe, ending her civil and religious time frame as the Roman Catholic Church clothed with the scepter of civil authority. Two churches, two dual millennial time frames, two different locations on Planet Earth, Israel centralized in the Middle East, Roman Catholicism in Europe. Two different starts at different times and phases in earth history, both ending in apostasy as unions of church and state confederacies.

The **first**, established through the descendants of Abraham, Isaac, and Jacob. The **second,** called and established through the preaching and teaching of the apostles of Christ (Acts 13:45-47). Two areas in prophetic history of past powerful continents because of their **willful** rejection in time of life giving-righteousness. Now no longer safe havens at the beginning of the nineteenth century to be safe locations for the final centralization of the last sign sealed gospel covenant to be given to this final world generation (Isaiah 24:5; 56:1-6). Two areas in the world, the Middle East (Revelation 9:1, 2) and Europe (Revelation 17:8), now **two bottomless pits** of religious and civil antagonistic minds. Soon to unite in a final attempted suppression of Revelation 14:6-12, everlasting gospel message of life-giving righteousness.

It was the prophetic eye of Jesus that foretold the rising of the greatest nation ever to exist under the deceptive dominion of the prince of this world (Luke 4:5, 6). A nation that would rise up in an area of the world untouched for thousands of years by the religious and civil mindsets of past generations; An area where God would setup a nation **under two constitutional protective horns** of **religious** and **civil** legislative security or the separation of church and state. This nation, my friends, is none other than the **United States of America**. Just as the **Papacy suffered her deadly wound** in 1798 (Revelation 13:3) **by losing the power of the state** in Europe. The United States rose up out of prophetic providence after 1776 as the last area on Planet Earth (Revelation 13:11) where Jesus would, through the advent movement of the eighteen thirties and forties, set up a centralized center for the proclamation of the last gospel message to this fallen world.

For over two hundred years our nation has been a pillar for religious freedom and a witness to the areas that in the past have failed in heaven's fundamental principle of freedom of conscience in religion. An area predicted soon to repudiate its governing principles that have afforded her the covering of God's protective hand. Soon, according to Bible prophecy, the United States will relinquish the two governing horns (Revelation 13:11) of protection afforded the peoples of our country and the **two horns** of our **civil** and **religious** rights will become **two governing horns** of oppression. Legislated upon those who chose to believe and obey Revelation's final gospel message to the world, in light of their heavenly right under heaven's principle of freedom of conscience in religion.

On September 11, 2001, a terrible act of aggression, based on religious intolerance of a fanatical few in the Middle East, took place in an area called in scripture *"out of the east and out of the north"* (Daniel 11:44). A fitting biblical symbol of the United States where the great advent movement of the eighteen thirties and forties heralded the beginning of the last gospel call of Daniel 7:9-14 and Revelation 14:6-12. To be given to every nation, kindred, tongue, and people just before Jesus comes again. We are presently living in this prophetic time defined in the sixteenth chapter of Revelation as the time when five specific verses are flashing with intensity unparalleled in prophetic history (Revelation 16:12-16). John says, "And the sixth angel poured out his vial **upon the great river Euphrates**; and the **water thereof was dried up**, that the way of the **kings of the east** might **be prepared**" to give the final everlasting gospel message to the world (Revelation 10:7; 14:6-12; 16:12-16).

The Euphrates, since the time of Babylon 605 B.C., has been a biblical symbol for those waters, peoples (Revelation 17:15) who support a mindset of antagonism against any and all called by God to represent and convey **anything to do with Christ**. Friends, it's time to study and believe biblical history. When the Roman Catholic Church appropriated the civil hand of governments in Europe in A.D. 538 , a new religious system was being ordained in the Middle East to challenge any and all Christian Catholic influence and interference.

For over fifteen hundred years, **Islam and the Roman Catholic Church** has contended for civil and religious control over the peoples of the Middle East and Europe, at times taking and controlling some territories within each other's boundaries. **Two** religious systems: **Roman Catholicism** (Revelation 13:1-10) and **Islam** (Revelation 9:1-21), since the middle of the sixth and seventh century A.D., totally **set in their religious canon codes** to control the peoples of the world through their own mindset of religious and civil intolerance. Jesus said, "They shall put you out of the churches; yea, the time cometh, that whosoever kills you will think that he is doing God service" (John 16:2).

What Revelation 16:12 is saying at this present time is that the antagonistic mindset of those symbolized by the symbol Euphrates will be "**dried up.**" Until the militant destructive mindset of religious hostility is subdued for a time in the Middle East and the world, until the last gospel message of Revelation 14:6-12 is given to all believers. Including Arab believers that are willing to appropriate the life-giving righteousness of Christ. For centuries, scholars have studied and looked for specific events in the Middle East, outlining the events leading to the battle of the great day of God Almighty (Revelation 16:16).

A similar time of this "drying up" process of the great Arab river or Euphrates symbolized in Revelation 9:14-21 occurred over a century ago during the great advent movement of the eighteen thirties and forties. This whole outline of the rise of Islam with its cloud of error and terror seated in the Middle East is outlined in the **Trumpets of Revelation 8 and 9**. These trumpets in scripture are symbols of trouble and the sounds of war, but most importantly they are messages of warnings.

Especially are the trumpet sounds of the fifth and six trumpets; Trumpets revealing the history of conflict between Catholicism in Europe and Mohammedanism or Islam in the Middle East from A.D. 629 to August 11, 1840. Especially is the Sixth Trumpet critical in its insight to last-day events. These trumpets are critical in the outline of nations and religions in the books of Daniel and Revelation in understanding last-day events.

There are three systems of apostate religions in the book of Revelation. All symbolized in Revelation 1 through 19, whom in their time of power in the earth have apostatized from the teachings of the gospel of Christ. These are **Islam, Catholicism,** and **Apostate Protestantism**. Soon these three powerful religious systems will unite under one religious head (*Catholicism*). All working through the civil arm of earthly governments, as they unite to enforce religion on the world, willfully rejecting the last gospel message given by Jesus Christ to John the Revelator (Matthew 24:14; Revelation 14:6, 7).

The **first four of the seven trumpets** recorded in Revelation 8:6-13 define the fulfilled wars of the Goths, Vandals, Huns, and Heruli in the fifth century (A.D. 419-476). Which caused the breakup of the old Roman Civil Empire; all having an influence in dividing the Western seat of the Old Roman Empire into ten different kingdoms or governments by A.D. 476. It was at that time Civil Pagan Rome ceased to exist. By the middle of the sixth century, Rome had a complete transformation; a complete conversion from a civil power to, now beginning in A.D. 538, a new "**crafty**" (Daniel 8:25) Roman Catholic religious state, clothed with the cruel arm of civil authority, enforcing her religious doctrines in the affairs of men.

It's the Fifth Trumpet recorded in Revelation 9:1-12 that opens to view the rise of the Arab Mohammedanism Islamic creed in the seventh century (A.D. 629). This ecclesiastical power of the antagonistic contentious (Romans 2:8) descendants from the time of Noah, who rejected life-giving righteousness, would "**torment**" (Revelation 9:5) all Catholic influence in the Middle East and Europe. Especially was the prophetic time period of "**five months**" or **one hundred and fifty literal years** (Ezekiel 4:6; Numbers 14:34) of prophecy revealing a civil Arab king named Othman (Revelation 9:5). Who established and set up the Ottoman Empire in the Middle East in order to unite the Arab world to harass the eastern provinces of the Greek Empire under the legislated influence of Rome from July 27, 1299, until July 27, 1449. And complete the work outlined in the fifth trumpet of Revelation 9:5-12.

It was during the advent movement of the eighteen thirties and forties that the sixth trumpet came to its complete interpretation and revelation in the outline of time prophecy. In 1838, one of the leading ministers
preaching the Advent message in the United States published an exposition
on Revelation nine, predicting the final timeframe and biblical fall of the
Ottoman Empire that controlled the Middle East by an armed Islamic state.

This prophecy became a complete realization on August 11, 1840. Dr.
Josiah Litch took the prophetic position of time prophecy of Revelation 9:15
of "**an hour, a day, a month, and a year**," and boldly made public his views
that the Turkish Ottoman rule in the Middle East would end August 11,
1840. He published a "**year**," or 360 prophetic days, were 360 years in prophetic time; a **month**, or thirty days, as thirty years; one **day** as one year.
An "**hour** being a twenty-fourth part of a day, a symbol for 15 days, which
brought the total time of Revelation 9:15 or the sixth trumpet, pertaining to the Ottoman Empire, to 391 years, 15 days. He then added the 391
years and 15 days to the fifth trumpet (Revelation 9:10) concluding date of
July 27, 1449, and took the qualified position that on August 11, 1840, the
Ottoman Empire which restricted the Islamic world from Turkey to Egypt
would be subdued.

When public journals published the claims of Dr. Litch, thousands
upon thousands watched for the termination of the prophetic fall of the
Islamic Ottoman Empire. At its conclusion on August 11, 1840, when the
appointed time took place (Revelation 9:13-15), the nation of Turkey, the
seat of the Ottoman Empire, lost its oppressive control of the Arab world
because of its lack of protection from outside Arab nations. Turkey accepted for the first time protection from four Christian nations, that of
Russia, Prussia, Austria, and England. Christian powers Islam has long
hated as rival, impious powers. This prophetic insight was fulfilled as to its
allotted biblical time, and the Advent question in the United States in the
eighteen thirties and forties demonstrated to the religious world that the
Advent movement, the day/year time principle of Bible time prophecy, was
as sound as the throne of Christ and of great biblical magnitude.

At the time of its termination, thousands watched for the fulfillment of
the prophetic fall of the Ottoman Empire. At its conclusion on August 11,
1840, when the appointed prophecy was fulfilled, hundreds were converted to the Advent movement. Jesus said, "And this gospel of the kingdom
shall be preached in the entire world for a witness unto all nations; and
then shall the end come" (Matthew 24:14). And at that time, from August
11, 1840, the Middle East was temporarily open to the proclamation of the
advent of Christ (Revelation 1:7).

But just like many of God's anointed and appointed in the biblical past, the designated message given to the early Advent believers took a slow road of travel. And accordingly the Middle East, along with other nations, closed their boundaries to the everlasting gospel message of Revelation 14:6-12. And as we still see today, Islam will not tolerate Christianity within its territorial confines. But Jesus said, and this "**gospel of the kingdom will be preached in all the world for a witness to all nations and then shall the end come**" (Matthew 24:14).

What tells us today this drying up process that took place August 11, 1840, is again taking place in the Middle East? Are the three Bible-predicted present day influences of the **Dragon, Beast,** and **False Prophet** powers of Revelation 16:13 working mutually in the territorial seat of Islamic domination? These three dominating, influencing Christian organizations and powers are presently being influenced by "**spirits of devils**" (Revelation 16:14) to **unite** the "**kings of the earth,**" both civil and religious leaders of the world to prepare them for the battle of Armageddon. For years religious intolerance has been denounced by most of the world, and at this present time one of its foremost strongholds for religious aggression is gradually being "dried up" (Revelation 16:12) by Christian powers and influence. A parallel scenario that took place in the Middle East over 160 years ago that must be in place according to Bible prophecy in order for the final gospel message to go to the whole world (Matthew 24:14).

Scripture says,
"And the sixth angel poured out his vial upon the great river Euphrates
(a symbol for the arm of religious intolerance in the Middle East)
and the water (of aggression) thereof was dried up, that the way
of the kings of the east might be prepared" (Revelation 16:12).

"And I saw three unclean spirits like frogs *come* **out of the**
mouth of the Dragon, and out of the mouth of the Beast, and
out of the mouth of the False Prophet (Revelation 16:13).

DRAGON
"An unclean spirit like frogs is come out of the mouth" the
legislative and judicial powers of the **Dragon** (Revelation 16:13).
(The Civil voice of the United States of America*)*
To Presently
Dry up the religious antagonistic fanatical arm of
aggression centered in the Middle East

BEAST
"An unclean spirit like frogs is coming out of the
mouth of the **Beast**" (Revelation 16:13).
(The Roman Catholic Universal Church*)*

To Presently
*Unite the world under one religious head
(2 Thessalonians 2:3, 4; Revelation 13:3, 4).*

FALSE PROPHET
"An unclean spirit like frogs is come out of the mouth"
of the **False Prophet** (Revelation 16:13; 19:20)
(**Apostate Protestantism**).

To Presently
*Undermine and influence the Christian world to respect, honor,
and venerate the ecclesiastical MARK of Roman Catholicism
(SUNDAY WORSHIP). The first beast of Revelation 13:1-
10 and accept its mark or sign of its sovereign head who sits
and rules in the place of God (2 Thessalonians 2:3-6).*

IN ORDER
To unite a total world confederacy of Church and State
religious oppression against the final everlasting gospel
message of life-giving righteousness (Revelation 14:6-12).

MYSTERY, BABYLON THE GREAT, THE MOTHER
The Roman Catholic Church

OF HARLOTS
The Apostate Protestant Churches

AND THE ABOMINATION OF THE EARTH
The Islamic Nations Central to the Middle East

*Who are today presently being prepared by the Mystery of Iniquity, for
the final erosion of biblical gospel truth. My friends, are you being prepared?
There are only two ways one can be prepared. The future children of God by*

the Mystery of Godliness (1 Timothy 3:16), which has its foundation in the Mystery of the Gospel of Christ (Romans 1:16; Ephesians 6:19), or the children of men by MYSTERY BABYLON THE GREAT which has its foundation in the mystery of iniquity (2 Thessalonians 2:7).

How is it that the two religious Christian systems of Roman Catholicism and Protestantism, who have for over four hundred years detested each other, are presently joining hands in world and Middle East affairs? How is it that Islam, so terribly antagonistic towards Catholicism, has in the last few years allowed the head of the Roman Catholic Church for the first time to patronize its area with his presence? How is it that Judaism also has allowed the future head of the 21st Century Catholic and Protestant Church to also patronize its religious establishments? Is the religious world, according to Revelation 13:3; 17:8, **"wondering after the beast"?**

Do you think, friends, the religious contention between the United States and the arm of terrorism in Iraq, in Mesopotamia, the "land between the rivers" (Tigris and Euphrates) in the Middle East, is just a coincidence in minor world affairs? Do you think the so-called tolerance and unity taking place between Protestant denominations and Catholicism in our day, especially in the United States, when Communism has just a minor stronghold on world affairs, is just a happenstance? We are living now in the time when Bible prophecy is warning the world about its most major world-shattering biblical event just about to take place on Planet Earth, before most of the world's religious and political minds can catch the deception before it's too late.

We are living **now** when Revelation 16:12-16 is crying, screaming, through prophetic interpretation, that the **United States,** the **dragon voice** of Revelation 13:11; 16:13, is fulfilling her destiny as the final biblical world-leading, world-controlling power in the earth. Working with the ecclesiastical Beast power of **Roman Catholicism** (Revelation 13:1-10; 14:9; 15:2; 16:13 17:3; 19:20). The **ecclesiastical image of the beast** (Revelation 13:15), **false prophet system of Apostate Protestantism** of Revelation 16:13; 19:20, in order to unite the world in a final global apostasy. Civil governments, Catholics, Protestants, Muslims under one Christian scriptural mark (Revelation 13:16; 14:11) of global, civil, and religious rebellion. Eventually uniting and legislating on a global scale the mark of the beast (Revelation 13:3; 13:15; 14:11) **(Sunday worship),** in opposition to the one principle in God's Eternal Righteous Code of Conduct, the Seventh-day Sabbath (Exodus 20:8-11), and shatter the final everlasting gospel covenant contract afforded this last generation just before Jesus comes again (Isaiah 24:5).

Reader, the Great Red Dragon Beast of Revelation 12:3; 13:1; and 17:3 is about to be a complete prophetic fulfillment of prophecy. This seven-headed dragon beast is symbolized by seven scriptural world powers in time from the time of the birth of Israel as a nation (Genesis 32:27-32) to the second coming of Christ. Seven heads from the three world locations God has used as central areas to promulgate the gospel of Christ. Seven heads, strongholds for the present religious systems centralized in the Middle East, Europe, and the United States that will soon authorize universal church and state oppression in opposition to the last gospel message of life-giving righteousness.

We are presently seeing the marshaling of the nations of the world preparing the peoples of the world for the final conflict over life-giving righteousness. Those who participate in this final confederacy of apostasy, no matter how small their involvement, will find at the second coming of Christ they have broken their gospel covenant with God (Isaiah 24:5; 56:1-8). They will at the day of his coming be without hope and without life-giving righteousness **central to obtaining eternal life** (Revelation 6:17; Ephesians 6:14-19).

Revelation's Great Red Dragon Beast
Confederation Having Seven Biblical Heads Are

1.	2.	3.	4.	5.	6.	7.
Egypt	Assyria	Babylon	Medo-Persia	Greece	Rome	U.S.
Dragon		**Dragon**			**Dragon**	**Dragon**
Ezek. 29:2, 3		Jer. 51:34			Matt. 2:1-13	Rev. 13:11
Located		**Middle East**			**Europe**	**America**
		Islam			*Catholicism*	*Protestantism*

Having Ten Horns
Of
C---**Civil** and **R**---**Religious**
Legislative Horns of Authority

C	C	C	C	C	C	C R	C	R
1.	2.	3.	4.	5.	6.	7. 8.	9.	10.
Egypt	Assyria	Babylon		Medo-Persia		Greece	Rome	United States

Seven-Headed Dragon Beast of Global Oppression

United by Spirits of Devils (Revelation 16:13) Coming out of the Mouth of the

Dragon	Beast	False Prophet
United States	Catholicism	Apostate Protestantism

How can we understand these important symbols?
Study 2 Timothy 2:15 Every word. Matthew 4:4 Line upon line. Isaiah 28:9-10

The Kingdoms of this world are not the kingdoms of Christ. John 18:36

Seven-Headed Dragon Beast with Ten Horns Belong to Satan Luke 4:5, 6

Defining the Seven-headed Dragon Beast

Revelation 17:9 Mind which has wisdom.
Seven heads are Seven Mountains
Revelation 17:10 **Seven heads** are **Seven Mountains Kingdoms**
or Independent Governments, Nations on the Earth

Revelation 17:12 The 10 Horns are **Ten Kings** or
the governing power in or on the Heads

Revelation 17:10 five have fallen from Life-Giving Righteousness when John wrote the Book of Revelation

These five fallen kingdoms have rejected life-giving righteousness in their controlling lifetime and oppressed the people of God from the time of the birth of the nation of Israel. Genesis 32:28; 1732 B.C. Kings and Kingdoms of this world are under the deceptive control of Satan (**2 Timothy 2:24-26**).

Five Fallen from Life-giving Righteousness

1.	2.	3.	4.	5.
Egypt	Assyria	Babylon	Medo-Persia	Greece
1706 B.C. to 740 B.C.	605 B.C.	538 B.C.	331 B.C.	168 B.C.
Genesis 46:3	Daniel 1:1	Daniel 7:5	Daniel 7:6	Daniel 7:7

One Is.

6.

Civil Pagan Rome   **Religious Papal Rome**
168 B.C. to A.D. 476 A.D.   538 to 1798 to Second Coming
Daniel 11:14-28   Rev.13:1-10 Dan.11:31-45

**"The other has not yet come, and when he comes he
must continue a short space" (Revelation 17:10).
This power in the earth has the shortest lifetime span among the seven biblical heads**

7.
United States
1776 to Second Coming
Revelation 13:11-18

**Revelation 17:11: "And the beast that was, and is not, even
he is the eight, is of the seven, and goes to perdition."**

8.
Eight Powers in the Earth

**All Seven Heads Unite to make the Eighth
Power of oppression in the Earth**
Egypt Syria Iraq Iran Greece Rome United States
*"When the United States rules the world the
Catholic Church will rule the world,"*
Chicago Daily News, May 5, 1900

Ten Horns

Revelation 17:12: "And the **ten horns** which thou saw are **ten kings**, which have received no kingdom as yet; but receive **power as kings** one hour with the beast." The Ten horns are the legislative and judicial horns of the governing powers in the present-day seven-headed scarlet beast (Revelation 17:3) centered in the Middle East, Europe, and the United States, soon to govern the citizens living in these biblical, world-leading civil and religious areas of apostate gospel locations.

Horns
R---**Religious** C---**Civil**
Church State

C	C	C	C	C	C	C R	C	R
1.	2.	3.	4.	5.	6.	7. 8.	9.	10.
Egypt	Assyria	Babylon	Medo-Persia		Greece	Rome	United States	
Egypt	Syria	Iraq	Iran		Greece	Rome	United States	

————Middle East———— ——Europe—— ——America——
————Islam———— —Catholicism— —Protestantism—

Revelation 17:12
"And the **ten horns** which thou saw are **ten kings**, which have received no kingdom as yet; but **receive power** as kings **one hour** with the beast.

Revelation 17:13
"These **(Ten Horns)** have one *mind*,
(Church and State)
And shall give their *power* **(Police Force)**and *strength* **(Judicial Authority)** to the sovereign head of the 21st Century Christian Catholic Protestant Churches just before the second coming of Christ.

"But **receive power** as kings **one hour** with the beast" (Revelation 17:12).

One hour in prophecy is 15 days of prophetic history
Revelation 17:9
"The seven heads are seven mountains on which the woman sits."

She, the Woman
The 21ˢᵗ Century Christian Catholic Protestant Universal Church
Sits in
Full legislative and Judicial Control
On the Seven Biblical Apostate Heads of
Of

C	C	C	C	C	C	C R	C	R
1.	2.	3.	4.	5.	6.	7. 8.	9.	10.
Egypt	Assyria	Babylon	Medo-Persia		Greece	Rome	United States	
Egypt	**Syria**	**Iraq**	**Iran**		**Greece**	**Rome**	**United States**	

————Middle East————   ——Europe——   ——America——

————House of Islam————   —Catholicism—   —Protestantism—

—Beast from Bottomless Pit—   —Out of Sea—   —Out of Earth—

—Rev. 9:1-2—   —Rev 13:1-10—   —Rev. 13:11-18—

Friend, it's critical to understand how the Great Red Dragon Beast power of Revelation 12:1; 13:1; and 17:3 was before it came to pass completely foreseen by the prophetic eye of Jesus before the "foundation of the world" (Revelation 13:8). The fall of Satan from heaven, the plan of salvation, the affairs of men, everything we think, say, and do is known before it comes to pass and is known by the **all-knowing, all-powerful**, **ever-present God** of the universe. There is nothing said or done in God's universal kingdom, nothing thought of that has not been thought of before. The minds of men are either receivers for the thoughts of the righteous mind of the Holy Spirit of our life-giving God, or the influence and thoughts of the unrighteous, unscrupulous mindset of the adversary of souls (Revelation 12:9: 2 Timothy 2:26). Man may believe he has the ability to say, invent, produce, and think a thought of something new and creative of themselves. But scripture says there is **nothing new** under the sun (Ecclesiastes 1:9) that can be thought of, said, or done that has not been thought of, said, or done either by the God of the universe or by the adversary of souls.

We may believe what we want, but rest assured that Jesus the Omnipotent Lord God (Revelation 19:6) of the universe has reigned forever in the past and will forever rule in the everlasting future. He has promised and will deliver a pure universe in the future without sin and the unscrupulous thoughts of sin. There will come a day when the redeemed of this planet will never again have an evil thought, desire, or passions. There will come a day when only the pure, unadulterated Spirit of God will exist over all the created minds of the vast creation of the universe. There will never be again any evil thoughts, desires, or feelings among men. Scripture predicts there will come a day when never again will there be any suspicions, contentions, or controversy between any created beings in God's universal kingdom.

All will be in perfect harmony because of the glorious sacrifice of our Lord and savior, Jesus, the living Christ. Who gave himself that the universal kingdom of God the Father may throughout the entire future universe be under the comforting influence of the HOLY SPIRIT of God. Who, after earth's influence and reign of sin, has proven to man and the entire universe (Ephesians 3:10) that only the creative power of our Omnipotent God has the eternal right to rule, dwell, and influence all creation by his comforting Holy Spirit of Agape love.

Outside of our place in the universe there is peace and harmony throughout the universe. There are no hospitals, prisons, or law enforcement agencies. There are no struggles to make a living or worry about a place to live. Out there in God's vast universe there are no worries about any danger of anyone or any evil thing happening to anyone in heaven. There is no fear were God sits in righteousness over a universe that has chosen not to separate and deviate from the principles of God's life-giving influence and power of Jesus, the Creator of the universe. Yes, sin did originate in heaven; And because of Adam's **willful** choice to separate from the power and influence of the authority of Christ, the originator of sin, Satan, was allowed to possess and influence the only planet that allowed him to enter its confines with his sinful, unrighteous ways (Revelation 12:12, 13).

It's not difficult today to understand why God has allowed him to reveal to us and the universe what created beings would become outside of the influencing power and creative, righteous thoughts of the Creator of the universe. Satan and his cohorts for the last six thousand years have revealed to us and the universe what the whole heaven would be like if he or any created being took, or was given control to govern the universe. Scripture says after the cross, Satan and his cohorts lost all sympathy with the universe over his controversy with God and the heavenly principles that govern life in Jesus' universal kingdom. Scripture says after the cross (Revelation 12:10-12; John 12:31, 32) Satan was **"cast down"** into the earth, and his anger is now completely focused on those who would appropriate life through the life-giving merits of Jesus, the savior of man and the universe, from malignancy of sin.

The seven-headed dragon beast with its ten horns is about to become a complete power in the earth. When these ten horns on the seven-headed dragon beast receive power as kings, one hour with the beast

(Revelation 17:12). These ten horns, especially the first five horns represented on the first four heads of the house of Islam.

C	C	C	C
1.	2.	3.	4.
Egypt	Assyria	Babylon	Medo-Persia
Egypt	**Syria**	**Iraq**	**Iran**

—————Middle East—————
—————House of Islam—————

The leading influential powers represented in the Middle East, will unite with Mystery Babylon the Great in a world confederacy of church and state. Daniel says, **he "the man of sin," "shall plant (secure by unjust legislation)"** the tabernacles of his palace **(their universal, unbiblical day of worship that will be secured with the civil and religious powers of this planet).** Purposed and created by the 21st Century Catholic and Protestant Church, he, "the man of sin," will plant "between the seas," between the peoples of the earth (Revelation 17:15) **(Sunday worship),** his mark of authority in religious things. But not until it is planted in the "**glorious holy mountain**" will the end come (Daniel 11:45). Not until it is accepted and planted by Friday-keeping Muslims and Seventh-day Sabbath-keeping Jews will the end come. Legislated in old Jerusalem, on the old temple mound foundation of the earthly sanctuary, where today a Muslim mosque sits, so long ago given to Israel to foreshadow the redemptive activity of Christ in the Sanctuary in heaven.

Soon, friends, Catholics and Protestants in the United States will unite *because of political corruption.* Because of "men's hearts failing them for fear, and for looking after those things which are coming on the earth: for the powers of heaven shall be shaken" (Luke 21:26). When the United States, the last head of the seven-headed dragon beast of Revelation.17:3, whose "coming is after the working of Satan with all power and signs and lying wonders (2 Thessalonians 2:9), to unite the world in civil and religious legislation. Our country will "**cause all,** both small and great, rich and poor, free and bond, to receive a mark in their right hand, or in their foreheads (Revelation 13:16, 17; Exodus 13:9; Deuteronomy 6:8; 11:18). That no man might buy or sell, save he that had the mark **(Sunday worship)** or the name of the beast, or the number or mark of his name" (Revelation 13:16-18; 14; 14:11).

This mark of the 21st Century Christian Catholic Protestant Church **(Sunday worship)** will just before Jesus comes be easily accepted by the Christian and Protestant world. But what is outstanding about this future prophecy is the conversion. Of *"all, both small and great, rich and poor, free and bond, to receive a mark in their right hand, or in their foreheads."* Which includes Friday-keeping Islam, who for fifteen hundred years have hated the 7th Day-Sabbath-keeping Jews and the Sunday-keeping Christians. It is only through the error and terror of what's happening in the Middle East and the world, but more so by the influence and work of **"spirits of devils working miracles"** (Revelation 16:13, 14), that Islam will finally accept and legislate **Sunday worship** that will decide the final destiny of Islam and every soul presently living on this planet.

When Islam legislates the Mark of the Beast in the confines of its territory in the Middle East, on the old temple mound in Jerusalem, the world has only "one hour" (Revelation 17:12), or 15 days, of probationary time left before Michael stands up in the Heavenly Sanctuary (Daniel 12:1) and says, "He that is unjust, let him be unjust **(unjustified)** still: and he which is filthy, let him be filthy still: and he that is righteous, let him be righteous still: and he that is holy, let him be holy still" (Revelation 22:11). At that time probation closes, and every man, woman, and child's fate on this earth is sealed for eternity.

Reader, my heart trembles as I write for fear of what's coming upon the earth. The world has had time to learn and know the Mystery of Godliness (1 Timothy 3:16), the Mystery of the Gospel of Christ (Ephesians 6:19). Unless we are all biblically grounded in the Mystery of God before it is finished (Revelation 10:7), the mystery of iniquity will be our fate (2 Thessalonians 2:7). Paul says, "Now to him that is of power to **establish you according to my gospel,** and **the preaching of Jesus Christ**, according to the revelation of the **mystery,** which was kept secret since the world began. But **now is made manifest,** and **by the scriptures of the prophets**, according to the commandment of the everlasting God, **made known to all nations for the obedience of faith**" (Romans 16:25, 26). Paul also says, "And for me, that utterance may be given to me, that I may **open my mouth boldly**, to make known the **Mystery** of the **Gospel**" (Ephesians 6:19). This text applies to all gospel believing Christians who study (2 Timothy 2:15) to know and believe what the **mystery of the truth of the gospel of Christ biblically is** and speak it out of a converted heart.

In Revelation 16:12-16 the symbols of the final confederacy in the three areas in the earth where the gospel has had its greatest light is presently portrayed. In verse twelve, two symbols are depicted in two critical areas in the earth. **The first is "the great river Euphrates,"** a symbol of the peoples of the Middle East, who through the nation of Islam has oppressed anything to do with Christianity for the last fifteen hundred years. This area is soon to be temporarily "dried up" of its fanatical arm of terrorism until the soon mark of authority of the now 21st Century Christian Catholic Protestant Church (**Sunday worship**) is legislated in the world, on a universal scale.

The second symbol is a direct message to the "kings of the east," a fitting symbol to Christ's 21st Century Seventh-day Adventist Remnant Church. Who for over one hundred and sixty years in light of the judgment hour (Revelation 14:6, 7) has been foreordained through the testimony of Jesus (Revelation 12:17; 19:10) to announce the second coming of Christ. This present Advent Remnant Church parallels the "**kings of the east**" that announced the first coming of Jesus at his birth (Matthew 3:1, 2), when literal Israel was in complete spiritual darkness (Luke 1:79). These "**kings of the east**" represent the people from the location in the earth where the first and second angel's everlasting gospel message was first presented to the world during the great advent movement of the early eighteen forties. Out of the Northeast corner of the United States rose the loud cry of the first angel and second angel's messages of Revelation 14:6-8. "Saying with a loud voice, Fear God, and give glory to him; **for the hour of his judgment is come**: and worship him that made heaven, and earth, and the sea, and the fountains of waters."

In Daniel 11:44 this symbol "**out of the east and out of the north**" depicts the Remnant Church (Joel 2:32; Revelation 12:17) in the final conflict with the 21st Century Christian Catholic and Protestant Church when she sits in power on the scarlet-colored beast of Revelation 17:3 with full civil and religious legislative powers over the religious and civil world. These "**kings of the east**" with the final gospel "tidings out of the east and out of the north" (Daniel 11:44) will "trouble him" the man of sin, the son of perdition (**2 Thessalonians 2:3**); the leader of the near future 21st Century Catholic and Protestant Church in the final conflict over life-giving righteousness. When the apostate 21st Century Christian Catholic Protestant Churches confederate into a world union of legislated church and state, the final battle over life-giving righteousness will begin. When the 21st Century Christian Church legislates the mark of her united church and state unity (**Sunday Worship**) "between the seas" (Daniel 11:45), between the peoples of the world (Revelation 17:15). "**He**," the Vicar of Christ, whose religious name numbers 666 (Revelation 13:18) along with his supporters in church and state confederacy, shall come to "**his**" end, and none shall help "**him**" (Daniel 11:45).

This end is depicted in Daniel 11:45 when the woman, the 21st Century Christian Catholic Protestant Church, sits (Revelation 17:3) in full world legislative authority over Revelation's seven-headed beast. When the ten horns of Revelation 17:12 finally legislate Catholicism's mark of Christian authority (**Sunday Worship**). *When the Mark of the 21st Century Christian Catholic European beast and America's Protestant image to the Beast* (Revelation 13:9) sets up (**Sunday worship**) "**the mark**" of Catholicism declared authority (Revelation 14:11). And is finally accepted and legislated in Old Jerusalem, the area of decades of contention and controversy between Muslims, Jews, and Christians, probation soon ceases in heaven. "Michael stands up" (Daniel 12:1), and the "time of trouble" such as the world has never seen envelopes the earth, culminating in the seven last plagues and the second coming of Christ.

On September 11, 2001, the waters of the antagonistic arm of Islam symbolized in scripture as the Euphrates, or the Middle East, assaulted the United States of America. The last area called by God to beacon the final gospel message to this darken world (Revelation 14:6-12). As a result of this terrible attack, the **Dragon** voice of the **United States** (Revelation 13:11), along with the serpent religious Papal beast out of Europe (Revelation 12:14, 15; 13:1-10), united also with the apostate Protestant image of the beast (Revelation 13:15) in the United States and began its final predicted movements to subdue or "dry up" the mindset of intolerance of the oppressive arm of Islam towards Christianity.

This fulfillment of prophecy (Revelation 16:12-14) is a beacon illuminating the final critical cry to the whole world that "spirits of devils" are presently "**working miracles**" which go forth to the kings (**civil and religious leaders**) of the earth and the whole world, to gather them to the battle of that great day of God Almighty (Revelation 16:16). Especially to the anointed, appointed **21st Century Seventh-day Adventist Remnant Church** (Joel 2:32; Revelation 12:17) is this time in prophecy given. To quickly illuminate and council her to get herself ready for the conflict by putting on the wedding garment, the robe of Christ's life-giving righteousness (Revelation 19:7, 8). In order to give to the world the specific seventh trumpet sound of Revelation 10:7. The definite sound, **proclaiming in forensic detail the everlasting gospel message of Revelation14:6-12.** In order for everyone to hear and appropriate Christ's everlasting, life-giving merits; to establish all individuals in an everlasting gospel covenant (Isaiah 56:1-7), defined in the everlasting gospel message of Revelation 14:6, 7.

Believer, it's so important, so critical to this last generation, to look biblically and study scripture today like never before. Jesus is knocking at the door of faith (Revelation 3:20; Acts.14-27) with an intensity of agape love that can only be understood in the light of the only gospel message mentioned in the book of Revelation. It's truly critical to understand that no one can live in God's heavenly Kingdom without a bill of rights. Without Christ, our life-giving righteousness, without what the everlasting gospel of **righteousness by faith into justification by faith** in Christ is saying in a sign sealed covenant contract afforded this final generation (Isaiah 24:5). Heralding to everyone the privilege of living eternally with Jesus Christ, glorified eternally, universally (John 17:5), as sons and daughters of God; In order to stand in the divine presence of our glorious and gracious heavenly Father. My friends, it's time to look and live, for **God is truly a faithful and true witness** in human affairs (Revelation 3:14).

~ *Chapter Eleven* ~
The Hour of His Judgment Is Come

Jesus said, "And this gospel of the kingdom shall be preached in the entire world for a witness unto all nations and then shall the end come (Matthew 24:14). Two thousand years ago, Jesus sat with his disciples on the Mt. of Olives, mournful over the nation he had raised up in the Middle East among nations to represent gospel order and the principles that govern life in His universal Kingdom. Knowing fully at that time what would happen to literal Israel and their capital city because of their rejection of life-giving righteousness. His heart was set to impress his chosen down through the final two millennia of earth history, in the events leading down to the final gospel message to be given to this generation living just prior to the time of his second coming.

When asked by his disciples for a sign **(singular)** (Matthew 24:3) of his coming and the end of the world, Jesus was specific in his first council to his believers about the apostasy of the New Testament Christian Universal Church down though time and those who would cause its fall from grace (Galatians 4:4). The first thing Jesus emphasized was "**take heed that no man deceive you**" (Matthew 24:4). This statement is one of the most vital of all statements made by Jesus in his narration of future events leading down to the time of his second coming. His statement, "Take heed that no men deceive you," is also implied by the apostle Paul in his emphasis about the man of sin that was revealed to the Christian world in Europe by the great evangelist Martin Luther at the beginning of the Protestant Reformation (2 Thessalonians 2:6).

Paul also said, "**Let no man deceive you** by any means: for *that day shall not come,* except there come a falling away first, and that **man of sin be revealed**, the son of perdition (2 Thessalonians 2:3). Critical is the emphasis by both Jesus and the apostle Paul for God's people down through time, and especially in our generation the important principle that the great deception of the last days would come through the ministry constituting the Catholic and Protestant Churches presiding in the last days of earth's history. Jesus said, "**For many** will come in my name, saying, I am

Christ **(I am Christian);** and will deceive many" (Matthew 24:4). Critical is the instruction given by Jesus of many being deceived by men claiming the Christian faith; The apostle Paul in his statement, "Let no man deceive you," is directly pointing to the New Testament Christian Catholic Church from the time of the beginning of its **apostasy from the truth of the gospel** (Revelation 2:2-5) to its exalting a single man as the Vicar of God (Revelation 2:12-17) in A.D. 538 To its revelation at the time of the reformation by the early reformers in the 16th century as the antichrist system revealed in scripture (2 Thessalonians 2:3-9). And finally, just before Jesus comes again, giving acknowledgment to that one man again, as the head of the **21ˢᵗ Century Christian Catholic Protestant Churches**, a process in time leading from the first century A.D. to the second coming of Christ.

The last and most critical of all, "**Let no man deceive you**" (1 John 3:7), is given by the apostle John directly pointing to the critical issue facing this generation in the final great deception of the Mystery of Iniquity (2 Thessalonians 2:7), setting up and establishing MYSTERY BABYLON THE GREAT, THE MOTHER OF HARLOTS AND ABOMINATIONS OF THE EARTH (Revelation 17:5). John, the writer of five New Testament books, instructs us on the emphasis in the final deception most critical today in man deceiving man as the same critical issue today that faced every past generation; the importance of obtaining and doing righteousness in the light of the gospel of life-giving righteousness. He says, "He that does righteousness, is righteous, **even as he (Jesus as a man) is righteous**" (1 John 3:7; John 6:27).

Remember, Jesus appropriated the life-giving righteousness of God as a man for man by obeying the sign of faith, the seal of imputed righteousness when he was baptized by John in the Jordan at the beginning of his ministry in A.D. 27 (Matthew 3:13-17; John 6:27). Jesus as a man obeyed as a man (2 Peter 2:21, 22) the everlasting gospel sign, seal of his generation, in appropriating as a man the righteousness of God outlined in the gospel message of **righteousness by faith into justification by faith** by being baptized. **Baptism** was introduced in Jesus' day by John the Baptist as a sign of faith, a seal of imputed righteousness (Matthew 21:32; Luke 7:29, 30; 2 Peter 1:1), witnessing how Jesus as a man "does righteousness, and is righteous before God as a man according to gospel order. Revealing and establishing before God and the universe the phrase "**even as he is righteous**" was after the fall the complete duty of man to respond to the faith once delivered to the saints (Genesis 3:21; Isaiah 61:10). Obedience to the Gospel of Christ (Romans 1:16, 17; 2:8), obedience to the Gospel of **righteousness by faith into justification by faith** in Christ testifies, bears witness to "**he that does righteousness, is righteous, even as he (Christ) is righteous**" (1 John 3:7).

In these three critical statements, "**Let no man deceive you,**" Jesus, the apostle Paul, and John characterize the Mystery of Iniquity (2 Thessalonians 2:7), the now revealed mystery of man deceiving man by Christianity claiming righteousness outside of gospel order; Especially in oppressing the gospel message of life-giving righteousness in the apostate confederacy of the union of church and state. In 1 John 3:8 the apostle John is critical in stating the principle of life-giving righteousness and how the rebellion started in heaven and the issue in the fall of Satan and his angels. John says, "He that committed **sin (offense)** is of the devil; for the devil **(willfully)** sinned **(fell short of the mark, fell short of the glory of the life-giving righteousness of God)** from the beginning. For this purpose the Son of God was manifested, that he might destroy the works of the devil" (1 John 3:8).

It was Satan who first rejected life-giving righteousness and caused the rebellion, war that first took place in heaven (Revelation 12:7). It was Satan that deceived one-third of the angels that believed him and was cast down to the earth (Revelation 12:9) because Adam accepted his ministry of unrighteousness and death, through his **willful, deliberate** transgression of God's eternal code of "thou shalt not" (Genesis 2:17; 3:11; Exodus 20:1-17). And John, in the twelfth chapter of Revelation, says that the devil and Satan will deceive the whole world (Revelation 12:9). Characterized through the Dragon symbol or the voice of civil government, and by the serpent symbol characterized by the full and willful apostasy of the 21st Century Catholic Protestant Churches; Symbolized by Jesus as becoming religious vipers (Matthew 23:29-33; Revelation 12:14, 15) as were the religious leaders of his day. John, in his statements about the issues from the fall of Lucifer to the second coming, is strong in his emphasis on Jesus, "the Son of God was manifested, that he might destroy the works of the devil" (1 John 3:8), in deceiving all of humanity, particularly in rejecting the final gospel message to be given to the world in order to obtain life-giving righteousness (Revelation 14:6-12).

It's critical to understand the devil has **one primary goal**, to completely **separate man from God**; Or to separate him from what God needs central in the life of his creation, the full and complete application of the **purity of the righteousness of Christ** in the soul character of every created being. The adversary of souls knows that by "**philosophy and vain deceit**" (Colossians 2:8), by **manipulation of the scriptures** (2 Peter 3:15, 16), by the **traditions of men**, after the **rudiments of the world** (Colossians 2:8), and by all deceivableness of unrighteousness in them that perish; because **they received not the love of the truth (of the everlasting gospel of Christ (Revelation 14:6, 7),** that they might be saved (2 Thessalonians 2:8). He can and will bring most of humanity in these last days to believe the great final, fatal lie (2 Thessalonians 2:11). Claiming Christianity without gospel order into the imputed righteousness of Christ by which he will deceive the Christian world (Revelation 12:9).

The Bible gives no value attached to a mere profession of faith in Christ without gospel order. Let ministers and people remember that the "**truth of the gospel** only hardens if it does not save the candidate for heaven (Galatians 2:5-14; Ephesians 1:13; Colossians 1:5). There is no middle ground or fence-sitting when the "truth of the gospel is presented. Only agape love placed in the human heart that is shown by righteous works through the indwelling power of the Holy Spirit is counted genuine in God's eyes (James 2:17-23). God, in his Holy Word, has made us responsible for the light of the **truth of the gospel** message (Revelation 14:6-12) given to us in this generation to make us wise unto salvation (2 Timothy 3:15). Whatever is done through agape love from the influencing, indwelling power of the Holy Spirit through the gospel of Christ, however small, is accepted and rewarded of God, even for those who at this time have a limited amount of Gospel truth.

But let it be understood an everlasting gospel message is soon to encircle the earth (Revelation 14:6-12) and there will come a day when the true and sincere Christian, from the heart, "shall return, and discern between the righteous and the wicked, between him that serves God and him that serves him not" (Malachi 3:18); Between the real biblical "truth of the gospel" and the fabricated gospels being presented by the diverse Christian churches today, soon to be cut short in righteousness (Romans 9:28).

How critical it is for us to understand that the works of the devil will be destroyed here on Planet Earth along with his manmade, organized confederacy of civil governments, symbolized by the Dragon symbol, with the United States leading the dragon's voice under its judicial and legislative authority of government (Revelation 13:11). Along with the Beast power of Roman Catholicism (Revelation 13:1-10; 14:9) and the image of the beast power of Apostate Protestantism of Revelation 13:15; 14:9, and all those who choose to reject the final gospel invitation of appropriating Christ's life-giving righteousness or heaven's glorious bill of rights.

Scripture is clear about the destruction of sin, Satan, and his work of unrighteousness on planet Earth. Jude 1:6 says, "And the angels which kept not their first estate, but left their own habitation, he hath **reserved** in everlasting chains under darkness (**of this world [Ephesians 6:12]**) to the **judgment** of the great day. When Satan and his angels left their habitation because of their rebellion in unrighteousness, war began in heaven (Revelation 12:7), and he and his angels were "**cast out into the earth** (Revelation 12:9). And because of Adam's sin, they took possession of all the earth and its inhabitance in their work of destruction and death. It is here on Planet Earth that Peter says, "For if God spared not the angels that sinned, but cast *them* down to **hell (a planet called earth, where torment never ends as long as there's life)** and delivered *them* into **chains of darkness**, to be **reserved** to **judgment** (2 Peter 2:4).

Ezekiel also says that God will bring Satan and his cohorts to "**ashes upon the earth** in the sight of all them that behold thee. All they that know thee (**Satan**) among the people shall be astonished at thee, thou shall be a terror, and **never shall thou (Satan) be (exist) anymore**" (Ezekiel 28:18, 19). Peter says, "But the heavens **and the earth**, which are now, by the same word are kept in store, **reserved to fire** against the day of judgment and perdition of ungodly (**or unrighteous**) men … But the day of the Lord will come as a thief in the night; in the which the heavens shall pass away with a great noise, and the elements shall melt with fervent heat, **the earth also** and the works that are therein shall be burned up" (2 Peter 3:7-10; Isaiah 24:6). Justifying his statement, "What shall the end be of them that obey not the gospel of God?" (1 Peter 4:17; 2 Thessalonians 1:7-8).

It's here on Planet Earth that Satan and all that follow in his footsteps, who withhold as well as pervert the truth of the gospel of Christ (Romans 1:18; Galatians 1:7), will meet their final end; Peter says they were delivered into **chains of darkness**, to be **reserved** to **judgment.** Paul says, "As it is appointed to men once to die but after this the **judgment**" (Hebrews 9:27), so it is critical for us to **biblically** understand the last call to life-giving righteousness in the light of the everlasting gospel judgment hour message of Revelation 14:6-12. John says, "And I saw another angel fly in the midst of heaven, having the everlasting gospel to preach to them that dwell on the earth, and to every nation, and kindred, and tongue, and people, **Saying with a loud voice**, Fear God, and give glory to him; for **the hour of his judgment is come**" (Revelation 14:6, 7). This is a verse describing the beginning of the judgment recorded in the prophetic book of Daniel.

Daniel says, "I beheld till the thrones were cast down, and the Ancient of days did sit, whose garment *was* white as snow, and the hair of his head like the pure wool: his throne *was like* the fiery flame, *and* his wheels *as* burning fire. A fiery stream issued and came forth from before him: thousand thousands ministered unto him, and ten thousand times ten thousand stood before him: **the judgment was set, and the books were opened** (Daniel 7:9, 10). In this prophetic prophecy Daniel sees the beginning of the judgment that takes place in heaven a short time in prophetic history prior to the second coming of Christ and the final judgment of every individual that has ever claimed the name of Christ. Here Daniel sees the Ancient of days **(our heavenly Father)** sit upon the "ark of his covenant" (Revelation 11:19), and then he sees Jesus, "*one* like the Son of man come with the clouds of heaven, and **came to the Ancient of days,** and they brought him near before him, (Daniel 7:13) to represent those from the time of Adam to the second coming, who have responded to the availability of the gospel in every generation since the fall of Adam.

Critical in understanding last day events is the marshaling of the nations of the world, in light of the judgment in the seventh, eighth, and ninth chapter of the book of Daniel. It is Daniel that saw the beginning of the judgment in heaven and the critical time it began in prophetic history. In chapter eight, Daniel sees the man of sin, the son of perdition, the mystery of iniquity (Daniel 7:11, 25; 8:11; 11:36; 2 Thessalonians 2:3-7), magnify himself as the prince of the host of heaven (Daniel 8:11), and in the beginning of his 1,260-year reign as the Vicar of Christ, he hides the divine priestly ministry of Jesus in the heavenly sanctuary (Hebrew 8:1, 2), from the focus and minds of the members of the Christian Church in Europe, the seat of his domain, during the dark ages.

It is in this timeframe of his **1,260-year reign** that the **Roman Catholic Church sets up a human priestly ministry in Catholicism as a central focus of salvation and forgiveness.** It is still today a canon code of the Papacy. In the Associated Press of December 12, 1984, the Pope urges Catholics to confess. "Pope John Paul II, depicting a 'world shattered to its very foundations' and threatened by social evils, on Tuesday **told Roman Catholics to seek forgiveness through the church and not directly from God.**" Still stubborn in apostasy, still trying to focus the minds of Christians on men instead of the God-man, Christ Jesus, Lord of life-giving righteousness (Revelation 1:12-15).

Daniel said by the false ministry of **men in black,** the truth of the gospel of Christ would be cast to the ground and the Catholic system would prosper and practice until the hour of judgment would begin in heaven (Daniel 8:12). And after the close of the judgment in heaven, the great red dragon, scarlet-colored beast system of church and state Christianity, who in the last days will exalt the principle doctrine of Roman Catholicism **(Sunday worship),** will be destroyed at the second coming of Christ (Revelation 19:19, 20).

It's with **prophetic insight** that the time of the beginning of the judgment in heaven is given to the prophet Daniel. In Daniel chapter eight, Daniel hears an angelic host speak. He says, "Then I heard one saint speaking, and another saint said unto that certain *saint* which spoke, How long *shall be* the vision *concerning* the daily **(administration of Christ in the heavenly sanctuary)**, and the transgression of desolation **(man's priestly ministry)**, to give both the sanctuary **in heaven (Hebrews 8:1, 2)** and the host to be trodden under foot?" Then the prophetic answer, "And he said unto me, unto two thousand and three hundred days; then shall the sanctuary be cleansed (Daniel 8:14).

Here we see a prophet of God critical in contemplating the plan of salvation and the sacrificial system given to Adam after the fall (Genesis 2:21), to Abraham at his calling (Genesis 15:6-10), to the Israelites of God after the Exodus from Egypt (Exodus 25:8). The earthly sanctuary service and its **ceremonial system** were given to the Israelites through the priestly ministry of the tribe of Levi (Deuteronomy 31:9). It was created for the principle purpose of revealing to man on earth the forensic work of God through the mediatory work of Christ in the heavenly sanctuary, in cleansing the universe of the malignancy of sin in heaven's judicial hall of justice, called the heavenly sanctuary (Hebrews 8:1-6). Sin originated in heaven, and it is in heaven's judicial hall of justice, where Christ presently dwells, that sin and all its characteristics will be judicially condemned and sentenced.

Daniel, knowing the principle purpose of the sanctuary on earth, that had been literally destroyed by Babylon about 605 B.C., was concerned as to its destruction and restoration to its meaning and purpose to the people of God. In his heartfelt desire to know and understand the time of its restoration, the time when its cleansing process would begin, Daniel is told, "And he said unto me, unto two thousand and three hundred days; then shall the sanctuary be cleansed (Daniel 8:14).

Again, critical in understanding time prophecy is the principle of thoughtful contemplation of the day/year principle scripture uses to calculate time prophecies (Numbers 14:34; Ezekiel 4:6). The two thousand and three hundred days, when the sanctuary would be cleansed (Daniel 8:14), is a **2,300-year prophecy**. The day/year timeline prophecy of Daniel 8:14, of "two thousand and three hundred days," represents 2,300 prophetic years of time predicted by Daniel when the sanctuary in heaven would begin its cleansing process. To Daniel is given the information necessary to those studying end-time events as to the time of the cleansing of the heavenly sanctuary of the recorded sins of God's professed people from the time of Adam's fall to the second coming of Christ.

In Daniel nine, after the long and heartfelt prayer of the prophet is critically highlighted (Daniel 9:4-19), the angel Gabriel is sent to give Daniel the information, skill, and understanding Christians would need to understand and calculate the time of the beginning of the 2,300 day/year prophecy of Daniel 8:14. Gabriel says, "**Know therefore and understand** *that* **from the going forth of the commandment to restore and to build Jerusalem**" (Daniel 9:25). Remember Jerusalem had been completely destroyed by the Dragon power of Babylon in the beginning of the sixth century B.C. (Jeremiah 51:34) because of continuous rebellion.

During the Babylonian captivity, Daniel understood through the prophecy of Jeremiah 25:11; 29:10, the reign of Babylon was coming to its end (Daniel 9:2). For seventy years Babylon was given, through the trials and experience of Nebuchadnezzar its king, ruling in the presence of God-appointed prophet Daniel, the time to understand and appropriate life-giving righteousness. Because Babylon rejected the righteousness of God, the next power in the biblical line of world-domineering nations defeated Babylon in 538 B.C., and in its time of power in the earth, Med-Persia would institute eventually the decree that would again establish Israel as a nation among nations for the salvation of the next generation of nations (Galatians 3:8). It was at the time of the reign of the Med-Persian Empire that Israel was afforded by God another period of influence in the Middle East to evangelize the people with life-giving righteousness.

It was in the autumn of the year 457 B.C., through heaven's providence, by the decree of Artaxerxes, then King of the Persian Empire, that the nation of Israel was again authorized as an independent nation. In Ezra 7:11-26, the decree issued by Artaxerxes documents the day (457 B.C.) when Israel received its autonomy. This is the date which also launched the beginning of the 2,300-year prophecy of Daniel 8:14, when *"know therefore and understand, that from the going forth of the commandment to restore and build Jerusalem"* (Daniel 9:25) was a pronouncement by Artaxerxes the king. Two thousand and three hundred years later in the autumn, October 22, 1844, the Day of Atonement (Acts 17:31), the fulfillment of the prophetic vision of Daniel 8:14, was complete. And Jesus came before the Father in the judgment hour of Revelation 14:6, 7 and began the judgment scene in heaven. Blotting out the sins recorded from the lives of those who in their lifetime have presented them in confession (1 John 1:9) through the merits of Jesus' precious atoning blood (Romans 5:11; 1 Peter 1:18, 19).

For over 160 years now the judgment has been going on in the heavenly Sanctuary (Hebrews 8:1-3), and will go on until the everlasting gospel message of Revelation 14:6-12 is appropriately given to every man, woman, and child on Planet Earth. The Remnant Seventh-day Adventist Church of Revelation 12:17 and Joel 2:32, placed in the midst of the New Testament Catholic Protestant Churches after the great disappointment of October 22, 1844, has now for more than 160 years been established to comprehend and convey to the world the direct and specific gospel all must believe and obey in order to have their sins blotted out of the sanctuary in heaven.

This is that specific time in prophetic history when Jesus is residing in the heavenly sanctuary during the prophetic judgment time, "the hour of his judgment" (Revelation 14:7), and blotting out of heaven's record books (Daniel 7:9) the confessed sin of God's people. Friends, now is the time, before it is ever too late, to register your name in the Lamb's book of life (Revelation 22:27) and receive the refreshing from the presence of the Lord (Acts 3:19). "To whom he said, this *is* the rest *wherewith* ye may cause the weary to rest; and this *is* the **refreshing:** yet **they would not hear**" (Isaiah 28:12).

Daniel said, "The judgment was set and the books were opened" (Daniel 7:10). Everything we have ever said and done in our lifetime, from the time of our birth to our death, is recorded in the books of heaven (Revelation 20:12). All is recorded, the place and time of our birth (Psalm 87:6), the positions we held, the settings and situations in our lives, but most specifically the era of each gospel truth presented in time to every generation since the fall. When the hour of his judgment began in heaven on October 22, 1844, the books were opened containing the recorded life records of every individual believer to witness the choices they made in their lifetime.

The apostle Peter describes the primary issue in the judgment and who the Lord of life begins judging in the judgment hour. "For the time *is come* that judgment **must begin at the house of God**" (1 Peter 4:17). Judgment begins **first** with those who have been represented as the house of God, the house of faith from the fall of Adam to our day. Principally, the first man scripture says was clothed with life-giving righteousness after the fall was Adam (Genesis 3:21; Isaiah 60:10). And principally, in the judgment hour everyone from Adam's day to ours **is** strictly scrutinized by "**the truth of the gospel**" in the life of the believer, pertaining to his or her "faith in the operation of God" (Colossians 2:12) appropriate to their generation.

Many in the judgment who have called on the "name of the Lord" (Romans 10:13) will find themselves without eternal life because they have **refused** to obey the sign of faith, the seal of imputed righteousness afforded their generation (2 Timothy 2:19). This truth is first critically displayed in the recorded life of Cain and Abel, repeated again and again in the lives of many believers, who have in their lifetime "gone the way of Cain" (Jude 1:11). While believing in Christ, they refused to obey heaven's forensic gospel. An example that must be significantly studied and understood by every generation of believers (Hebrews 11:4). Peter specified this issue when he said, "**And what shall the end be of them that obey not the gospel of God?**" (1 Peter 4:17). Friends, it's vital to study and accept gospel truth (receiving, believing, accepting, and obeying); the gospel of Christ is the first and primary issue in the judgment (Mark 1:15; 1 Corinthians 15:1; 1 Peter 4:17; 2 Thessalonians 1:7, 8).

Man may be a believer and commandment keeper to the fullest extent of the law revealed in the Decalogue of God or the Ten Commandments. But if man has not appropriated the imputed righteousness of Christ (Romans 4:11; Isaiah 8:16, 20) by obeying the "truth of the gospel" of their generation, our accounted righteousness will be denounced as illegal, immoral, blasphemous in the judgment. Exposed and found still in iniquity (Philippians 3:9-11; Matthew 7:23), or as iniquity is defined in scripture as in violation of the law. This may sound cruel and uninviting, but scripture says, "He that overcomes, the same shall be clothed in white raiment; and **I will not blot out his name out of the book of life,** but I will confess his name before my Father and before his angels" (Revelation 3:5).

Many a Christian in the judgment will not attain to what scripture calls "the resurrection of the dead (Philippians 3:11), the resurrection unto eternal life (Revelation 20:5), when Jesus comes, because Jesus cannot in **Divine righteousness** present them before the Father outside of gospel-imputed **righteousness.** They have **refused to obey the gospel message given in each generation from Adam to ours** (Revelation 14:6, 7; 2 Thessalonians 1:7, 8). Thus Jesus has no choice but to blot their names out of the Lamb's Book of Life (Revelation 3:5).

It's what's in the gospel; scripture constantly makes plain what God needs in the judgment hour to save us individually. Paul said, "For therein **(for in the gospel) is the righteousness of God revealed**" (Romans 1:17). What's in the gospel that God needs to save us is the **righteousness of Christ** produced by his perfect life, death, and resurrection, which contains the merits of the atonement necessary for our salvation. Peter also is critical in this issue of the judgment when he says, "And if the **righteous scarcely be saved,** where shall the ungodly and the sinner appear?" (1 Peter 4:18; Romans 1:18).

Of which Paul answers Peter's question emphatically about the ungodly sinner when he says, "But to them that are contentious, *and do not obey the truth,* but *obey unrighteousness,* **indignation and wrath, tribulation and anguish, upon every soul of man** *that doeth evil, of the Jew (command-ment keeper) first and also of the Gentile" (Romans 2:8, 9).* Friends, God needs the righteousness of Christ in the judgment to save all of us. The word **righteous** is used **225** times in scripture; the word **righteousness** is used **289** times. Do you think God is trying to say something emphatically specific to all of us **about righteousness?** Many a text in scripture asso-ciates directly the word righteousness with judgment and the issue that caused the rebellion in heaven to our present time.

"And I saw heaven opened, and behold a white horse; and he that sat upon him *was* called Faithful and True, and in **righteousness** he doth **judge** and make war" (Revelation 19:11).

"And he shall **judge** the world in **righteousness;** he shall minister judg-ment to the people in uprightness" (Psalm 9:8).

"Judge **me, O Lord my God, according to thy righteousness;** and let them not rejoice over me" (Psalm 35:24).

"And the heavens shall declare his **righteousness:** for God *is* **judge** himself" (Psalm 50:6).

"He shall **judge** thy people with **righteousness** and thy poor with judg-ment" (Psalm 72:2).

"Before the Lord: for he cometh, for he cometh to **judge** the earth: he shall **judge** the world with **righteousness,** and the people with his truth" (Psalm 96:13).

"Before the Lord; for he cometh to **judge** the earth: with **righteousness** shall he **judge** the world, and the people with equity (equally)" (Psalm 98:9).

"But with **righteousness** shall he **judge** the poor, and reprove with equity for the meek of the earth: and he shall smite the earth with the rod of his mouth, and with the breath of his lips shall he slay the wicked" (Isaiah 11:4).

"With my soul have I desired thee in the night; yea, with my spirit within me will I seek thee early: for when thy **judgments** *are* in the earth, the inhabitants of the world will **learn righteousness**" (Isaiah 26:9).

"My **righteousness** *is* near; my salvation is gone forth, and mine arms shall **judge** the people; the isles shall wait upon me, and on mine arm shall they trust" (Isaiah 51:5).

"Thus says the Lord, Keep ye **judgment**, and do justice: for my salva-tion *is* near to come, and my **righteousness** to be revealed" (Isaiah 56:1).

"But after thy hardness and impenitent heart treasures up to thyself wrath against the day of wrath and revelation of the **righteous judgment** of God" (Romans 2:5).

"Seek ye the Lord, all ye meek of the earth, which have wrought his **judgment**; *seek righteousness* seek meekness: it may be ye shall be hid in the day of the Lord's anger" (Zephaniah 2:3).

The judgment in heaven is now presently taking place, and **God needs the righteousness of Christ** according to gospel order in a sign sealed covenant contract, afforded man in this final generation and located in the message of Revelation 14:6-12. A covenant contract based on Christ our righteousness (Isaiah 24:5; 56:1-6), in order to justify and save us from the decree of unrighteousness (Romans 3:10; 6:16). For the last six thousand years of earth's history, God has worked through his chosen to relay specific truths to every generation since the fall.

All in their appointed time, revealing to their generation what God needs in the judgment from everyone to save them from, "It is written, there is none righteous, no not one" (Romans 3:10). On October 22, 1844, the judgment was open in heaven according to Daniel chapters seven, eight, and nine, and Jesus began judging **first** all throughout earth's history who have "called upon the Name of the Lord," in life-giving righteousness, revealed in their lifetime (Romans 10:13). Peter says, "For the time *is come* that **judgment must begin** at the **house of God**: and if *it* **first** *begins* at us, what shall the end *be* of them that obey not the gospel of God?" Peter also specifically says, "If the righteous scarcely be saved, where shall the ungodly **(unrighteous [Romans 1:18])** and the sinners appear?" (1 Peter 4:17, 18).

Critical is the standard of righteousness God needs in the judgment, exemplified in the life, death, and resurrection of Christ as a man in the nature of man after the fall. To reveal to the universe what God's universal creation would become if sin and unrighteousness is allowed to continue to exist. For six thousand years, God has revealed to the universe what the slightest molecule of sin would do if it is allowed to leaven the universe. Paul made it dangerously clear, "A little leaven leavens the whole lump" (Galatians 5:9).

Earth has been the theater of the universe, revealing the terrible ordeal in the lives of sinful humanity. Isn't it time to bring the narrative to its climax and begin the new as it should be in the everlasting kingdom of our Lord and Savior Jesus, the living Christ, whose kingdom is an everlasting kingdom of "righteousness and peace and joy in the Holy Ghost" (Romans 14:17).Whose principles are eternal in a vast universe of everlasting life. Especially to all the redeemed, whose earthly lives have seen what sin can do to an unbelieving creation fallen from the unquestionable glory of righteousness of God (Romans 3:23). Friends, I truly believe it's now time for us to take hold of God's glory, God's righteousness, and let's get our families and our loved ones off this miserable, terrible planet of sin.

⌒ *Chapter Twelve* ⌒
Heaven's Last Invitation to Life-Giving Righteousness

T wo thousand years ago, John the Baptist, in counseling his disciples prior to his imprisonment, said, "He that hath received his **(Christ) testimony** hath set to **his seal that God is true**" (John 3:33). Critical to this generation is the concept that from the fall of the human family God has always had a sign of faith and a seal of imputed righteousness afforded his people in every generation. Paul said, "Nevertheless the **foundation of God** stands sure, **having this seal**, The Lord **knows them that are his**, and let everyone that names the name of Christ depart from iniquity (depart from being in violation of the law because of Adam's sin)" (2 Timothy 2:19).

Just before Jesus comes again, the final sealing everlasting gospel message of Revelation 14:6, 7 and 7:1-3 will be given in the earth to prepare a specific group of Christians identified in scripture as the 144,000. Revelation 7:4 and 14:1-5 describes those who are called to stand and reflect like never before the divine character of their Lord and savior, Jesus Christ. The first-fruits unto God and to the Lamb, such as had never been known before in the universe. These are they who are called by the Father (John 6:44) and know not only Jesus by name but have the Father's own personal name written in their foreheads and intellect (Revelation 14:1). They are called to be a final voice from the many waters or peoples populating the earth (Revelation 17:5). Called to sing a song before the throne of God (Revelation 15:3, 4) never known or sung before in the annals of the history of the heavenly universe.

They have been called before the foundation of the world and have chosen of their own free will to **vindicate the Character of God** in redeeming man and securing all creation willing under the principles that God uses to govern life in His vast universe (Exodus 20:1-17). They testify before the **throne of God** in the **"judgment hour" (Revelation 14:7)**, before the whole universe that the throne of God, the righteousness of God, the law of God **cannot in the slightest molecule be compromised without anarchy in the universe.**

Friends, liberty of conscience has cost the Godhead (Colossians 2:9) an unimaginable price to create beings in His vast universe with the right to say yes or no to Christ's life-giving righteousness and the principles defined by the governing ideology distinguished as **Heaven's Universal Code of Conduct. The Law of God (Exodus 20:1-17) and the Gospel of Christ (Romans 1:16, 17)** are the governing ideology of God's throne and recorded epistle of His Divine character personified in the life, death, and resurrection of our Lord and savior Jesus, the living Christ, which will forever keep the universe safe and secure from sin ever rising its ugly head again to effect and destroy any part of God's universal creation (Nahum 1:7-9).

They, the 144,000, announce the Law and the Gospel to this final generation (Isaiah 42:21) and forever before the principalities and powers of the heavenly universe (Ephesians 3:10) reveal in character the full and final display of God's glorious conduct in saving his creation according to his eternal purpose he purposed in Christ Jesus (Ephesians 3:11). Never before has God called so many to say so much and reveal so much at a time when so much is at stake. It is at this time that the God of the universe is calling for the full and final display of the glory that will lighten the earth and the universe with Christ's everlasting life-giving purity of divine righteousness. And it is to you, friend, that God is calling to represent his full and final display of glory, or Christ's life-giving righteousness (Revelation 18:1), never before judicially characterized in the universe outside of the life of Christ.

The 144,000 resolve not to defile themselves with the doctrines of the 21st Century Apostate Woman, the Apostate 21st Century Christian Catholic Protestant Apostate Church (Revelation 17:3). They are biblically defined in scripture as virgins (Revelation 14:4) because they have believed, received, accepted, and obeyed **"the truth of the final gospel"** message given to this final generation (Revelation 14:6-12). In their mouth will be found no guile, no deceit or deception, no white lies, for they have been presented by Jesus without fault, divine righteousness before the throne of God (Jude 24; Revelation 14:1-5), and are converted to the purity of character with clean hands and pure hearts in the nature of heart Adam had before the fall, completely surrendered under the **protective power and guiding influence of the Holy Spirit of God** (Romans 14:17). They reveal in the light of the great controversy between Christ and Satan (Revelation 12:7) what God can do with a fallen race that is willing to "believe every word that proceeds out of the mouth of God" (Matthew 4:4) in an age when sin has taken its greatest hold on the human family (2 Peter 3:4, 5).

John says, "And after these things I saw another angel come down from heaven, having great power; and the earth was lightened with his glory" (Revelation 18:1). This verse in scripture is one of the central elements afforded the Seventh-day Adventist Remnant people of God just before Jesus comes again. It defines and empowers the final message that lightens the world with the final invitation to life-giving righteousness. It authorizes and empowers the Remnant Seventh-day Adventist Church (Revelation 12:17) with the same power afforded Jacob when he became Israel (Genesis 32:27-31), the apostles on the day of Pentecost (Acts 2:1-4). John says this angel has the **great power of God** and lightens the earth **with his glory.** This verse is critical in its application to the gospel of righteousness by faith unto Justification by faith into the imputed righteousness of Christ, in order for the Remnant Church to be empowered with the **power of God** to enlighten the earth with the **glory of God,** which must be understood collectively.

First, what does scripture say is the glory of God? One verse in scripture stands out above all others in the light of man's condition before God and the universe. One verse stands out in the light of the great controversy between Christ and Satan. One verse electrifies the whole problem between God and man, man and man, and the nature of man in the critical issue that will decide the destiny of every soul. "For all have sinned, and come **short of the glory** of God" (Romans 3:23). Friend, do you have the glory of God? I am not in any way trying to be bold or rude or critical. When Jesus comes again, if we do not have the glory of God, the righteousness of Christ, we cannot be saved nor receive the right to live in the Kingdom of God.

When the Revelation 18:1 angel lightens the earth with this **final message of life-giving glory** defined in Roman 1:16, 17 and Revelation 14:6, 7, whosoever for any reason refuses to comply with its divine instructions will negate any future right to everlasting life. Understanding what constitutes the glory of God (Psalm 97:6) will decide also who will be empowered by the angel of Revelation 18:1 to give the loud cry of the everlasting gospel message of the three angels of Revelation 14:6-12; in order to register all in righteousness in order to be saved when Jesus comes. Those empowered with the glory of God are symbolized as the kings of the east (Revelation 16:12; Daniel 11:44).

They will warn the world not to worship the woman that sits on the scarlet-colored beast (Revelation 17:3) by receiving the mark (**Sunday worship**) of the 21st Century Christian Catholic Protestant Apostate Churches. Who at that time sits upon the legislative and judicial powers of the nations of the world in the final world confederacy of church and state. Understanding, believing, receiving, accepting, and obeying the everlasting gospel of Christ (Revelation 14:6-12), which at that time will illuminate the glory of God, will afford the right to anyone who wants to "have the right to the tree of life," and to "enter through the gates into the city of God (Revelation 22:14).

Scripturally, the **glory of God** is the **righteousness of God (Psalm 97:6)**. When Adam sinned, he fell short of the glory of Christ, he fell short of God's glorious life-giving righteousness. **Officially, he fell short of legal forensic heavenly Righteousness and lost our heavenly Divine bill of rights**, a similar bill of rights in many ways comparable to the bill of rights we have here in the United States. When Adam sinned he took away any and all possibility for man to live or have any way for man to reconcile himself back to the purity of righteousness heaven demands, and live again under heaven's Bill of Life-Giving Righteousness. If it wasn't for Jesus intervening with heaven's plan of salvation from the foundation of the world (Revelation 13:8), we **could not** and **would not** have any way of being rescued from unrighteousness and the deceptive devices of the adversary of souls (Romans 3:10; 2 Timothy 2:26).

Isaiah says, "For when thy judgments *are* in the earth, the inhabitants of the world will **learn righteousness**" (Isaiah 26:9). We are seeing judgments taking place right now, terrible floods, fires, tornadoes, hurricanes, earthquakes causing "**men's hearts failing them for fear, and for looking after those things which are coming on the earth**" (Luke 21:26). But these judgments are minor compared to the judgments that will take place after the final everlasting gospel call to life-giving righteousness is given to the entire world (Matthew 24:14; Revelation 14:6, 7) and is rejected by most of the world and especially by most **professed** Christians.

Two thousand years ago Jesus came here as a man for man, to save man. He produced for every man in every generation since Adam all that every man in every generation, according to all the present truth (2 Peter 1:12) available in their day, all they need in the judgment hour (Revelation 14:7) to be saved. Because of Jesus' faithfulness in producing all that man needs in the judgment hour, God the Father has placed in Jesus' hands and his hands alone the right of judgment. "For the Father judges no man, but hath committed all judgment to the Son … And hath given him authority to execute judgment also, because he is the **Son of man**," born of a woman, "made under the law" (Galatians 4:3, 4; John 5:22-27), "**who did no sin, neither was guile found in his mouth**" (1 Peter 2:22).

Jesus alone has the right of judging every generation from the time of Adam's fall (Genesis 3:6) to the second coming, because he is the only man who has faithfully fulfilled every Divine act of obedience to the sign of faith, and seal of imputed righteous for every generation from Adam to the present time demanded by heaven's judicial code of conduct (Genesis 2:17; Exodus 20:1-17; Revelation 14:12; 22:14).

Jesus, the Son of God, the Son of Man
Alone has the Right of Judgment of all Men

For the Father judges no man, but hath committed all judgment to the Son … And hath given him authority to execute judgment also, because he is the Son of man.

Jesus, the Living Christ Has Alone Appropriated the
Right of Judging Every Man
In every generation
Acts 17:31

Because He has faithfully obeyed every Sign of Faith
&
Seal of Imputed Righteousness

<u>From</u>
Adam to Abraham
From the fall after Creation to Abraham **Sacrifice**
was the Sign, Seal of Imputed Righteousness
For even Christ our Passover is **sacrificed** for us (1 Corinthians 5:7)

<u>From</u>
Abraham to Jesus, Messiah the Prince
Sacrifice was Abram's seal of imputed Righteousness at the calling of his ministry (Genesis 12:1-8). But because of his blunders in his 24 years in his walk from faith to faith (Romans 1:17), **Circumcision** was given Him as His New Sign, Seal of Imputed Righteousness (Romans 4:1-22; recorded in Romans 4:11), **Jesus** the living Christ was **Circumcised** the eighth day, of the stock of Israel, *of* the tribe of Judah (Genesis 49:10; Luke 2:21; Philippians 3:5)

<u>From</u>
Messiah the Prince to October 22, 1844
Baptism was the Sign, Seal of Imputed Righteousness

"And Jesus, when he was **baptized**, went up immediately out of the water: and lo, the heavens were opened to him, and he saw the Spirit of God descending like a dove, and lighting upon him" (Matthew 3:16; John 6:27)

<u>**From**</u>
October 22, 1844, to Second Coming
The final Sign, Sealing of the Everlasting Gospel Message (Revelation 14:6, 7) to be given to the world containing heaven's Eternal, Universal, Never-Ending Sign, Seal of Worship and Rest in Righteousness, is **The 7th Day Sabbath (Luke 4:16)**

The gospel in this generation is "Saying with a loud voice, **Fear God, and give glory** to him; for the **hour of his judgment is come: and worship him** that **made heaven, and earth, and the sea, and the fountains of waters** (Revelation 14:7). If ever a verse in scripture reveals the ultimate issue in the universal conflict or the great controversy over Christ and Satan, righteousness or unrighteousness, creation or evolution, faith or presumption, life or death, the gospel of Christ or the gospel of man, this verse says it all. For approximately six thousand years the great controversy has raged on Planet Earth over "Know ye not, that to whom ye yield yourselves servants to obey, his servants ye are to whom ye obey; whether of sin to death, or of obedience to righteousness (Romans 6:16).

This great controversy is just about to come to its final conclusion in the light of the final and only gospel message revealed in the book of Revelation, calling the world after October 22, 1844, to yield to the authority and life-giving righteousness of our Lord and Savior, Jesus Christ. To this present generation, Daniel 11:44, 45 and Revelation 16:12-16 are illuminating lights and a billboard of warning to Christ's Remnant Church (Joel 2:32; Revelation 12:17), in the midst of the 21st Century Catholic and Protestant Churches (Revelation 13:1-18) in the gathering together of the nations of the world (Revelation 16:14; 2 Thessalonians 2:1). In which the Mystery of Iniquity (2 Thessalonians 2:7) is presently gathering MYSTERY BABYLON THE GREAT, THE MOTHER OF HARLOTS, AND ABOMINATIONS OF THE EARTH (Revelation 17:5) for the final erosion of life-giving righteousness.

Friends, for the past four years I have struggled to put in words what I have learned from scripture in the past thirty years of Bible study and prophetic interpretation (2 Peter 1:20, 21; Isaiah 28:9, 10). Many a day I have pleaded with God for assistance to help me convey in simple sentences what prophecy is revealing in the light of the final confederacy of church and state to envelope the earth. Writing this book has been the most difficult project of my entire life. Especially is this chapter most complex. For over a year I have prayed, reread, corrected, and double-checked, line upon line, precept upon precept (Isaiah 28:9, 10) how to present this chapter in words to make as plain as possible the truth of the final everlasting gospel message conveyed in Revelation 14:6-12 and Daniel 11:40-45.

It's most difficult for me to say in words, statements about Jesus, prophecy past and present, without reflecting upon Jesus anything that might reflect in any way something detrimental or unfavorable about His character and His divine method of operation. How difficult it is for finite man to literally express in words infinite characteristics about the God of the universe. This is something I, for myself, have had to contemplate in the expression. "And he said, draw not nigh hither: put off thy shoes from off thy feet, for the place where on thou stand *is* holy ground" (Exodus 3:5). My prayer to you, my friends, is that God may give you the understanding of what the issues are in the great controversy between Christ and Satan.

The gospel in this generation is as critical as it has ever been in the past. Much more so today because of the availability of the scriptures and the increasing light given in the Word of God revealing the final administration of Christ in attendance in heaven's Hall of Justice, called in scripture the heavenly Sanctuary (Hebrews 8:1-6). It reveals Jesus' presence before the Father, seated on the Ark of the Covenant (Daniel 7:9-14; Revelation 11:19), revealing to man after the great advent movement of the eighteen thirties and forties the final phases of Jesus' mediatorial work (1 Timothy 2:5) just before His second coming. It reveals Jesus in his official capacity in heaven, justifying (Romans 4:25) every born again son and daughter of God from the time of Adam to his glorious second return.

It is in the **Most Holy Place of the heavenly Sanctuary** where the Father sits on the Ark of the Covenant, containing the Ten Commandants written with the finger of Jesus on two tables of stone and placed in the earthly Ark of the Covenant by Moses (Deuteronomy 10:1-5). A copy and transcript of God's moral code of being and conduct that speaks to us collectively today about the final judgment of the human race and the standard in the judgment that affords eternal life (Ecclesiastes 12:13, 14). It's the **ceremonial system** of Israel (Leviticus 23) which enlightens this generation about the judgment in heaven and the corporate work of the Godhead in saving as many of the human family as is willingly receptive to receiving "the gospel, the commandments of God and the faith of Jesus (Revelation 14:12) that will be saved. The ark of God contains the Law of God, the Ten Commandments, the governing principles of God's universal identity and character which must be maintained in order for the universe to sustain life without conflict and controversy (Deuteronomy 10:1-5).

Justification by Faith

This final gospel message which **"lightens the earth with God's glory"** (Revelation 18:1; 14:6, 7; 7:1-3) contains the last sign, the last seal that will ever be given to mortal man just before Jesus comes again. Revelation 14:6, 7 says, "And I saw another angel fly in the midst of heaven, having the **everlasting gospel** to preach unto them that dwell on the earth and to every nation, and kindred, and tongue, and people, saying with a loud voice, Fear God, and give glory to him; for the hour of his judgment is come: and worship him that made heaven, and earth, and the sea, and the fountain of waters." Never in the past has the **gospel been called the everlasting gospel,** or has it been given in the full light of the issue that opened the great controversy in heaven, which began the conflict between Christ and Satan (Revelation 12:9).

Man is a created being, as are the angels that fell from heaven (Luke 10:18; 2 Peter 2:4; Jude 6), and whether we like it or not we will worship one thing or another (Romans 6:16). It is in this final dispensation of time that the everlasting gospel message is given to man that worship is one of the principle issues in the final message of life-giving righteousness. John says, "For the hour of his judgment is come: and **worship him that made heaven, and earth, and the sea, and the fountains of waters"** (Revelation 14:7). The everlasting gospel message of Revelation 14:6, 7 is calling this final generation to worship God in Spirit and in Truth (John 4:22-24). Men will either just before Jesus comes again worship the beast of Revelation 13:1-10; 14:9, 11; 15:2, or the God of the universe (Romans 6:16). There will be no middle ground, no fence-sitting when Jesus comes. And it is clear that Jesus, who created the universe, will only biblically be accepted and worshiped in "spirit and in truth" (John 4:22-24). It is in the phrasing **"worship him that made heaven, and earth, and the sea, and the fountains of waters"** that the final sign of faith, the final seal of imputed righteousness is symbolized if we are truly seeking and finding (Matthew 7:7) the pathway to eternal salvation.

Critical is the sensitivity of scripture in understanding the Book of Revelation in discerning "precept upon precept, precept upon precept, line upon line, line upon line, here a little, and there a little (Isaiah 28:10). This verse, Revelation 14:7, contains **"worship him that made heaven, and earth, and the sea, and the fountains of waters,"** a direct statement taken by John the Revelator from Exodus 20:8-11. "For in six days the Lord

(Jesus) **made heaven and earth, the sea, and all that in them is,** and rested the seventh day: wherefore the Lord blessed the *Sabbath day,* and hallowed it." David said, "Happy *is he* that *hath* the God of Jacob for his help, whose hope *is* in the Lord his God: **Which made heaven, and earth, the sea, and all that therein is:** which **keeps truth** forever" (Psalm 145:5, 6). For, "God *is* a Spirit: and they that worship him must **worship him** in **spirit** and in **truth**" (John 4:24; Genesis 1:1, 2).

Jesus said, "To those **Jews (Commandment Keepers [Psalm 60:10; Genesis 49:10])** which believed on him, If ye continue in my word, *then* are ye my disciples indeed" (And ye shall **know the truth, and the truth shall make you free [John 8:31, 32]).** There are many wonderful truths in the Bible, but the main truths essential to salvation in scripture are in greater jeopardy today than ever before. Paul said, God "will have all men to be saved and to **come to the knowledge of the truth**" (1 Timothy 2:4, 5). Many are "**ever learning and never able to come to the knowledge of the truth**" (2 Timothy 3:7). Bible truth is essential and eternally progressive. There are five essential Bible truths in scripture critical to the salvation of souls in this final generation.

Scripture is clear about salvation and the final issues in the great controversy (Jeremiah 25:31; Ecclesiastes 12:13, 14; 2 Thessalonians 1:7, 8) between God and the nations of this world.

First
Jesus is the Personification of Truth
He is the way, the truth, and the life (John 14:6). And Jesus must be believed on, (Acts 16:14) received (John 1:12), and obeyed (Heb.5:9).

Second
The Bible is the Manuscript of Truth
(John 17:17; John 8:31)
Which also must be believed (Acts 4:4) and
obeyed (2 Thessalonians 3:14).

Third
The Gospel is the Power of Truth
(Romans 1:16; Galatians 2:5, 14; Ephesians 1:13; Colossians
1:5) Which also must be believed (Mark 1:15), received (1
Corinthians 15:1), obeyed (2 Thessalonians 1:7, 8)

Fourth
Grace is the Gift of Truth
(John 1:14, 17; Colossians 1:6; 2 John 3; Romans
5:15, 17; Ephesians 2:8; 3:7; 1 Peter 4:10)
Which also must be believed (Acts 18:27), received, and obeyed (Romans 1:5)

Fifth
The Ten Commandments are the Principles of
Truth (Psalm 119:142, 151; 1 John 2:4)
Which also we keep, maintain, through the Gospel of Christ
by the indwelling power of the Holy Spirit (John 14:15; 15:10;
1 John 2:3; 3:22; 5:2, 3; Revelation 12:17; 14:12; 22:14).

As **Jesus** is the **Personification of Truth** he is also the
Personification of Righteousness (1 John 2:1).

As the **Bible** is the **Manuscript of Truth** it is also the
Manuscript of Righteousness (2 Timothy 3:16).

As the **Gospel** is the **Power of Truth** it is also the
Power of Righteousness (Romans 1:16, 17).

As **grace** is the **Gift of Truth** it is also the **Gift of
Righteousness** (Romans 5:17; Genesis 6:9; 7:1).

As the **Ten Commandments** are the **Principles of Truth** they are also
the **Principles of Righteousness** (Deuteronomy 6:25; Psalm 119:172).

These are the five main biblical truths this generation must believe, receive, accept, understand, and obey in order to be saved when Jesus comes
again. In order to stand in the day of his coming (Revelation 6:17). Paul
said, "And with all deceivableness of **unrighteousness in them that perish;**
because they **received not** the **love of the truth,** that they might be saved.
And for this cause God shall send them *strong delusion* (Isaiah 66:4; 8:19)
that they should **believe a lie:** That they all might be damned who **believed
not the truth,** but had **pleasure in unrighteousness**" (2 Thessalonians
2:10-12). Many a Christian in this generation is in jeopardy, believing that
one or two of these essential truths is all that is necessary in the plan of
salvation to save them at the second coming of Christ. But as Jesus, the

Bible, the Gospel, Grace, and the Ten Commandments biblically characterize truth and righteousness, all are distinct but not separate in the plan of salvation. When Jesus died on Calvary's cruel cross, "**Mercy and truth** met together, **righteousness and peace** kissed each other (Psalm 85:10).

Scripture Says

"Lord, who shall abide in thy tabernacle? Who shall dwell in thy holy hill? He that walks uprightly and works **righteousness** and speaks the **truth** in his heart" (Psalm 15:1, 2).

"**Truth** shall spring out of the earth; and **righteousness** shall look down from heaven" (Psalm 85:11).

"Before the Lord: for he cometh, for he cometh to judge the earth: he shall judge the world with **righteousness**, and the people with his **truth**" (Psalm 96:13).

"Thy righteousness *is* an everlasting **righteousness**, and thy **law** *is* the **truth**" (Psalm 119:142).

"*He that* speaks **truth** shows forth **righteousness**: but a false witness deceit" (Proverbs 12:17).

"And in mercy shall the throne be established: and he shall sit upon it in **truth** in the tabernacle of David, judging, and seeking judgment, and hasting **righteousness**" (Isaiah 16:5).

"And thou shall swear, The Lord lives, in **truth**, in judgment, and in **righteousness**; and the nations shall bless themselves in him, and in him shall they **glory**" (Jeremiah 4:2).

"And I will bring them, and they shall dwell in the midst of Jerusalem: and they shall be my people, and I will be their God, **in truth** and in **righteousness**" (Zechariah 8:8; Revelation 21:1-30).

"By the **word of truth**, by the power of God, by the **armor of righteousness** on the right hand and on the left" (2 Corinthians 6:7).

"For the fruit of the Spirit *is* in all goodness and **righteousness and truth**" (Ephesians 5:9).

"Stand therefore, having your **loins girt about with truth**, and having on the **breastplate of righteousness**" (Ephesians 6:14).

Many believe they have enough truth necessary for their eternal salvation, but truth that is not biblically connected with Bible righteousness cannot and will not at the second coming justify anyone with the right to everlasting life. In this final generation, the truth of the gospel has a new, distinct sign and judicial seal of imputed righteousness connected to the "law and to the testimony" (Isaiah 8:12, 20; 42:21; Revelation 7:1-3). For almost 6,000 years the enmity created in man because of Adam's sin, enmity that created the carnal mind hostile to the law of God and antagonistic towards the will of God (Romans 8:7), will now before the universe partake of its greatest test (Revelation 3:10).

It is not just the God of heaven that has been rejected of men but the principles that define the transcript of His Divine character, exemplified in the life, death, and resurrection of Jesus for the restoration of man to divine favor. Paul says man's carnal mind is contrary to God, for he is not subject to the law of God (Romans 8:7), which defines the character of God, because man has a created hatred, detestation for God's law, birthed by Adam's sin.

When Adam ate of the fruit of the tree of knowledge of good and evil (Genesis 3:6) he chose to create a hostile mind and inherited a hostile nature against God and the transcript of his moral character, defined by the written principles of the Ten Commandments (Exodus 20:1-17). When Adam sinned he willfully broke ("thou shalt not" [Genesis 2:17]) and rejected the ten principles that define and demand the moral righteousness of our Creator, the Lord Jesus Christ, the principles of purity that define the righteousness of Christ, in order for man to maintain the moral character of God by the complete, indwelled moral power of the Holy Spirit.

The Ten Commandments cannot be altered because they define in principle the unique, unprecedented character of God.

Scripture says
"Jesus Christ the same yesterday and today and forever" (Hebrews 13:8). When Adam sinned he rejected moral righteousness. *He rejected*

One
The Loyalty of God (Exodus 20:3)

Two
The Moral Spirituality and Divine Truth of God (Exodus 20:4-6)

Three
Reverence towards God's Name (Exodus 20:7)

Fourth
Righteous Rest in Moral Creative Power of our Lord Jesus, the living Christ, defined three times in the 4th commandment containing his Seal, the 7th Day Sabbath (Exodus 20:8-11)

Five
Respect for Authority (Exodus 20:12)

Six
Respect for Life (Exodus 20:13)

Seven
Purity of Heart (Exodus 20:14)

Eight
Honesty of Heart (Exodus 20:15)

Nine
Truthfulness of Heart (Exodus 20:16)
Ten
Contentment of the Heart (Exodus 20:17)

The Ten Commandments Reveal the Character of God As

1. Moral Loyalty of Character and Being (Exodus 20:3)

2. Morality in Spirit and Truth (Exodus 20:4-6)

3. Moral Reverence and Admiration (Exodus 20:7)

4. Moral Righteous Rest in Creation's 7th Day Sabbath Worship (Genesis 2:1-3; Exodus 20:8-11)

5. Moral Respect for Authority (Exodus 20:12)

6. Moral Respect for Life (Exodus 20:13)

7. Moral Purity of Heart (Exodus 20:14)

8. Moral Honesty of Heart (Exodus 20:15)

9. Moral Truthfulness of Heart (Exodus 20:16)

10. Moral Contentment of Heart and Character (Exodus 20:17)

All these Ten Principles represent and reveal the Character of God and what God designed man to be in character and nature of being from the beginning (Genesis 1:26, 27). Why does God ask us to **obey the gospel** (2 Thessalonians 1:7, 8; 1 Peter 4:17) and **keep his Commandments** (John 14:15; 15:10; Revelation 22:14)? **Because they are what He is in character and what He does in principle, and from this foundation we were created in His image, all with the capacity to obey the gospel and keep his commandments in principle (John 2:3, 4).**

We have to be obeying the gospel of Christ in order to appropriate the right to be Christlike in purity of character, because Adam placed us in an unrighteous **anti-gospel** condition. God **cannot morally save us without gospel rest in Christ our righteousness** (2 Thessalonians 1:7, 8). We then can keep his Ten Commandments through the indwelling power of the Holy Spirit (John 14:15, 16) because Christ lives out his character in us (Galatians 2:11). Man choosing what righteousness is in character and principle under God's divine principle of Liberty of Conscience. God wants us to keep his commandments because that's what He is and does. He never failed to exemplify them from the beginning of the great controversy in heaven and never will. These principles of righteousness were totally revealed in the life, death, and resurrection of Jesus Christ for the salvation of man in the human nature of man (Galatians 4:4). Heaven knows that without the purity of Christ's righteousness revealed and defined by the principles of the Ten Commandments (Exodus 20:1-17), heaven would be without a code of heavenly conduct, and the Universe would eventually become what Planet Earth has been for the last 6,000 miserable years of anarchy, destruction, and death.

In light of what's taken place in the three biblical areas of the Middle East, Europe, and the United States, the final gospel sign sealing message of Revelation 14:6-12 will soon be given to the world under the most terrible times and pressures man has ever seen. John says, "And after these things I saw four angels standing on the four corners of the earth, holding the four winds of the earth, that the **wind (*of strife*) should not blow on the earth**, nor on the sea, nor on any tree." John says, "And I saw another angel ascending **from the east**, having the **seal of the living God**: and he cried with a loud voice to the four angels, to whom it was given to hurt the earth and the sea, **Saying, Hurt not** the **earth**, neither the **sea**, nor the **trees**, till we have **sealed the servants of our God in their foreheads (*minds*)**" (Revelation 7:1-3).

As Abraham was given sacrifice at the beginning of his calling, he received 24 years later circumcision, a new sign of faith, and seal of imputed righteousness (Romans 4:11) about 1897 B.C.; As Jesus transferred the sign seal of circumcision to the sign seal of Baptism in A.D. 27 (Colossians 2:10-12; Galatians 3:26, 27; Mark 1:14, 15; 2 Peter 1:1). On October 22, 1844, Jesus, the Living Christ, entered the Most Holy Place (Hebrews 9:3) of the heavenly Sanctuary in order to initiate the final everlasting sign, sealing gospel message given in Revelation 14:6, 7 to the prophet John, and revealed to the Advent believers of the great Advent movement of the eighteen forties.

John says, "And I saw another angel fly in the midst of heaven, having the everlasting gospel to preach unto them that dwell on the earth, and to every nation, and kindred, and tongue, and people **Saying with a loud voice,** Fear God, and give glory to him; for the hour of his judgment is come: and **worship him that made heaven, and earth, and the sea, and the fountains of waters**" (Revelation 14:6, 7). Opening to our view the final biblical, scriptural sign seal to be given to this final generation just before Jesus comes again. The next chapter will reveal the sign seal authorized in heaven as to what this generation of believers must believe, accept, and obey in order to stand (Revelation 6:14-17) in the day when Jesus literally enters the atmosphere of this planet and resurrects His followers to the glory of everlasting life

⟿ *Chapter Thirteen* ⟿
Revelation's Everlasting Sign, Seal for Eternity

I was asked, "How does a fallen, sinful human being receive and maintain a personal relationship with our Lord Jesus Christ?" Many are struggling to understand what we all need, and God needs, in order to maintain this most precious and glorious union man had before the fall of Planet Earth (Genesis 3:7, 8). It is important to understand that the relationship we all want and need with the Father of the universe has one basic principle that initiates the union lost shortly after creation. Romans 5:10, 11 basically defines the whole of man's separation from our heavenly Father in two related words. The first is reconciliation, and the second atonement. It was the atonement of Christ (Romans 5:11) that restored man to the relationship (John 1:12) he had with his Creator before the fall, judicially produced only by the obedient life, death, and resurrection of our Lord and Savior Jesus Christ (Hebrews 5:7-9).

The word atonement is used 70 times in scripture and needs to be studied and understood in light of the cost of restoring and the redeeming of man. The word atonement means to restore, to reestablish two parties who have been separated by something critical. The atonement of Jesus restored man to divine favor with God, judicially reconciled man in the spiritual and moral state he had with God before the fall of humanity (Genesis 3:7). The word reconcile is similar to atonement except it critically conveys that in order for Jesus to restore man to his Creation relationship, He had to make provision for the lost righteousness which separated man from God through the unrighteous, willful act of Adam's sin (Romans 5:14; John 1:29).

Friend, the foremost critical ingredient in the atonement that reconciled man into the relationship with our wonderful Creator is the imputed life-giving righteousness of Christ; Christ our life-giving righteousness is the product of thirty-three years of Christ's sinless living, dying, and finally being resurrected to represent us as our advocate in heaven's judicial hall of justice. Righteousness is the foremost term of maintaining a personal relationship with Jesus. And where do we find the righteousness of Christ?

Paul says, "For there in, *for in the gospel message* is the **righteousness of God revealed**" (Romans 1:17).

If we want a relationship with God, and we must have one in order to be saved, we in this generation must comply with the biblical "truth of the gospel" of Christ. Paul said, "Awake to righteousness and sin not, for some have not the knowledge of God" (1 Corinthians 15:34). Shortly after creation, Adam's sin disconnected man from the righteousness of Christ and placed him under a decree of unrighteousness physically, spiritually defiling him, placing him under the decree of eternal death (Romans 3:10; 6:23). Since that time the adversary of souls has manipulated the critical concepts of how the gospel reinstates fallen humanity to his original identity and relationship in the beginning as sons and daughters of God (John 1:12), as citizens of God's heavenly Kingdom (Philippians 3:20).

Jesus said, "Go into all the world and preach the gospel to every creature (Mark 16:15). The **truth of the Gospel of Christ** (Colossians 1:5) must be believed (Mark 1:15), received (1 Corinthians 15:1), and then obeyed (1 Peter 4:17). Paul said when Jesus comes again, **those who are not obeying the gospel** of our Lord Jesus Christ "know not God" (2 Thessalonians 1:7, 8), have not awakened to the righteousness that justifies the believer from the error of his immoral condition, saves his soul from death, and covers (with the blood of Christ) a multitude of sins (James 5:20). Paul said, "Awake to righteousness and sin not," for without Christ, our life-giving righteousness, everything we do or say is polluted with sin and is sanctioned as sin. "Wherefore he says: Awake thou that sleeps, and arises from the dead and **Christ will give thee light**. See then that you walk circumspectly, not as fools, but wise (Daniel 12:3), redeeming the time, because the days are evil. Wherefore be not unwise, but understanding what the will of the Lord is (Ephesians 5:14-17; Daniel 12:3).

It is in the phrasing of Revelation 14:6, 7 the gospel message is conveyed for this time. The everlasting gospel in this generation is saying, "*With a loud voice,* **Fear God,** *and give* **glory** *to him; for the hour of his* **judgment** *is come: and* **worship** *him that made heaven, and earth, and the sea, and the fountains of waters*" (*Revelation 14:7*). These **four** critical words, *Fear, glory, judgment, and worship* are all given as a gospel issue in the light of "**him that made heaven, and earth, and the sea and the fountains of waters.**"

John says, with a loud voice, "**Fear God.**" Fear God if you do not have the life-giving righteousness of Christ, the righteousness God needs in the judgment hour in order to save every fallen son and daughter of Adam from the written decree of unrighteousness (Acts17:31; Romans 3:10;

Romans 6:16). Paul said in his day, "**Let us therefore fear**, lest a promise being left *us* of entering into his rest, any of you should seem to come short of it. For un**to us** was the **gospel preached**, as well **as to them**: but **the word preached** did **not profit** them, **not being mixed with faith** in them that heard *it*" *(*Hebrews 4:1, 2*)*.

This verse applies to every generation, especially to us today—before Jesus comes. The gospel to be preached in this final generation is bigger, broader, and greater than was given to any previous generation. It says something about God the Father, Son, and Holy Spirit that has never been said or known before. It introduces like never before the complete rest in the redemptive activity of God, planned before the foundation of the world by the creative and redemptive power of the Godhead (Colossians 2:9) working together for the salvation of the world (Matthew 3:16, 17; John 3:16, 17).

It is in this generation that the Lord has chosen to be "well pleased for His righteousness sake, and magnify the law and make it honorable" (Isaiah 42:21). It is in this generation that the law, "thou shall not" spoken at creation, and revealed in the 10 principles defining God's character, government (Genesis 2:17; Exodus 20:1-17), and the gospel (Romans 1:16, 17; Revelation 14:6-12) will be revealed to the universe, "to make all *(Creation)* see what *is* the fellowship of the mystery, which from the beginning of the world hath been hid in God, who created all things by Jesus Christ:

To the intent that now to the principalities and powers in heavenly places might be known by the church the manifold wisdom of God (Ephesians 3:10). That "the Lord is well pleased for his righteousness' sake; he will magnify the law (the written standard and purity of Christ's character), and make it (the moral code Exodus 20:1-17) honorable." In the light of the conflict, the great controversy between Christ and Satan, that began in heaven prior to the creation of this world (Ephesians 3:9, 10; Isaiah 42:21; Revelation 12:9). Never in the past has God used one of the Ten Commandments found in the Sacred Decalogue of His Holy Tabernacle as a witness (Matthew 24:14) in the gospel. Sacrifice, circumcision, and baptism have for nearly 5,800 years been the signs of precious faith (2 Peter 1:1), seals in past generations of righteousness by faith unto justification by faith in Christ given to the saints from Adam's fall through to October 22, 1844 (2 Timothy 2:19).

On October 22, 1844, when Jesus entered the Most Holy Place of the heavenly Sanctuary, Jesus Christ the Righteous (1 John 2:1) came before the Father (Daniel 7:9,13), who at that time sat on the throne of the Ark of the Covenant which was open in heaven (Revelation 3:8) and began the final phase of redeeming humanity (Revelation 11:19). In the light of that great judgment day, Revelation 14:6, 7; 15:1-5 opened to view the final gospel message to be given to this last generation living just prior to the second coming of Christ. Saying, with a loud voice, fear God and give glory to him; for the hour of is judgment has come. Worship him in the light of His creative and redemptive principle of life. The only principle that biblically defines the creative activity of Christ in creation (Genesis 2:1, 2; Mark 2:27, 28; Exodus 20:8-11) and the redemptive principle in His redemptive activity (rested in the tomb after his death on the cross) of rest found in the fourth commandment of the Sacred Decalogue (Exodus 20:8-11; Luke 23:53-56).

The everlasting gospel of Revelation 14:6, 7 calls this generation to a **spiritual righteous rest in the Seventh-day Sabbath,** which in this generation is a call to "worship him that made heaven, and earth, and the sea, and the fountains of waters" (Exodus 20:11). "In the beginning God **created the heavens and the earth.** David said, "Happy *is he* that *hath* the God of Jacob for his help, whose hope *is* in the Lord his God: **Which made heaven, and earth, the sea, and all that therein *is*:** which **keeps truth** forever" (Psalm 145:5, 6).

After August 11, 1840, the Middle East, Europe, and the United States, along with the rest of the world, was again prepared by God to receive the final presentation of the last Gospel message that would be given to man (Revelation 14:6, 7). As the second woe completed its work in subduing the antagonistic anti-gospel minds in Europe (Revelation 11:1-14), and the sixth trumpet the antagonistic anti-gospel mind in the Middle East (Revelation 9:12-21). John opens the tenth chapter of Revelation with the sound of the seventh trumpet.

"And I saw another mighty angel come down from heaven, clothed with a cloud: and a rainbow *was* upon his head, and his face *was* as it were the sun (*of righteousness*) and his feet as pillars of fire" (Revelation 10:1). He had in his hand a little book, pertaining to Daniel, and he set his right foot on the sea, a symbol for Europe, where the beast of Christianity **(Catholicism)** for over twelve hundred years sat on the powers of the state to enforce her religious beliefs (Revelation 13:1-10). He set his left foot on the earth, a symbol of the newly established area of the United States (Revelation 13:11-17) where the "loud cry" of the Advent movement began its greatest proclamation. John says this angel, who is a symbol for Christ, stands upon the two specific areas where Christianity has its greatest multitudes of influential believers, and He lifts up his hands to the heavens. "And swears by him that lives forever and ever, who created heaven, and the things that therein are, and the earth, and the things that therein are, and the sea, and the things which are therein, that there should be no dated time prophecy no longer (Revelation 10:6).

My fellow believer, Christ can and will come when the truth of the gospel of Revelation 14:6-12, along with the significance of the Seventh-day Sabbath sign of faith, Christ judicial seal of imputed righteousness, is presented and offered to every man, woman, and child on Planet Earth (Matthew 24:14; Exodus 20:8-11).

In Revelation 10:7, John says in the days of the sounding of the seventh angel, or the seventh trumpet, from the time he begins to sound the Mystery of God, the Mystery of the Gospel (Ephesians 6:19; Revelation 14:6, 7) should be finished upon the earth. The beginning of the sound of the seventh angel or the **seventh trumpet** originated "out of the east and out of the north" (Daniel 11:44) of the United States from the eighteen thirties to October 22, 1844. Unsealing the final prophecies revealed to the prophet Daniel to the generations living at the time of the end (Daniel 11:40-45; 12:4, 13).

Critical in the twenty-fourth chapter of Matthew, a timeline of prophecy given to the disciples beginning in the days of Jesus to the time of His all-important second coming is disclosed. In their desire to comprehend the future they ask Jesus, "Tell us, when these things shall be? And what shall be the sign of thy coming and of the end of the world (Matthew 24:3).

In His prophetic view of the future, Jesus gave insights to events that would take place in certain eras and places which would be repeated on larger scales. The destruction of Jerusalem reflects the destruction of the world. Famines, pestilences, and earthquakes in diver's places are in our day well nigh happening on a universal scale. The rise and claims of false Christ's are distinguished today by multiple Christian denominations existing in the last days, contrasted by individual apostasy leading to denominational apostasy, leading to earth's final united universal Christian apostasy of Church and State (Matthew 24:5, 24).

In the Savior's conversation with His disciples he describes a long period of great tribulation of the Christian Church. He said, "For then shall be great tribulation, such as was not since the beginning of the world to this time, no, nor ever shall be" (Matthew 24:21). This describes the long prophetic period of 1,260 years of Papal persecution that affected the Christian faith centered in Europe from A.D. 538 to A.D. 1798 (Revelation 11:2. 3; 12:6, 14; 13:5; Daniel 7:25; 12:7). Then Jesus said, "Immediately after the tribulation of those days shall the sun be darkened, and the moon shall not give her light" (Matthew 24:29); As the 1,260 years of great tribulation began to terminate, as it did in 1798, a half century earlier, according to Revelation 6:12, 13, three earth-shaking signs would be given preparatory to the great advent movement of the eighteen thirties and forties.

The first took place on November 1, 1755, known as the Lisbon earthquake, which shook Europe and its surrounding areas so violently that is was felt in America. The second was the great dark day of May 19, 1780. The great dark day in the eastern part of North America, symbolizing the spiritual darkness of the Christian people in Northeast America and the world. So great was the darkness in New England that people had to light candles at noonday in order to see. And until after midnight the moon, though at its fullest, gave no light, many believing that the Day of God was at hand. No satisfactory reason for this unnatural darkness of that era has ever been given, except the reason found in the prophecies of Jesus (Matthew 24:29; Revelation 6:12, 13).

The third was, "And the stars of heaven shall fall, and the powers of the heavens shall be shaken" (Mark 13:25). On November 13, 1833, one of the last signs given by Jesus appeared, which was promised by the Savior to the Christian Church as a sign preparatory to the Advent movement of the eighteen thirties and forties (Revelation 6:12, 13). John declared, as he saw in vision, the scenes that should announce the final preparation for the day of Jesus' return. "The stars of heaven fell unto the earth, even as a fig tree casts her untimely figs, when she is shaken of a mighty wind" (Revelation 6:13). This prophecy received a striking and inspiring fulfillment in the great meteor showers of November 13, 1833, in the American continent, and repeated again on November 25, 1833, in the European continent. Two locations in the earth where Christianity has its two most influencing, domineering Christians organizations on this planet, Catholicism and Protestantism.

How undeniable was this prophecy part of the fulfillment of prophetic events given by Jesus pertaining to the time men were raised up from different parts of the earth to announce the advent movement without any knowledge of one another's work in sounding the coming of Christ to all parts of the earth (Matthew 24:29).

After Scripture described these three events in prophetic time from November 1, 1755, to November 13, 1833, leading to the start of the great Advent movement of the eighteen thirties and forties, Jesus said, "And then shall appear **the sign of the Son of man** in heaven" (Matthew 24:30). This sign is none other than the sign asked for by the disciples on the Mount of Olives. It is the same "sign" question asked by the human heart from the time of Abraham (Genesis 15:8) to the first coming of Christ

(Matthew 12:38; Luke 11:29), to the very generation in which we live. Tell us, the disciples said, "**what shall be the sign of thy coming and the end of the world?**" (Matthew 24:3). The sign in this generation is as in every generation, the sign pertains to what the gospel is, says, and does as to one's evidence of faith in the presentation of the gospel from Adam to the second coming in light of one's faith in the "operation of God" (Colossians 2:12) for this generation.

The only **true divine sign** heaven affords to God's faithful in every generation is the timely gospel **sign that points to what Jesus had to do to save believers in every generation.** The first divine sign given to man after sin entered the world was **blood sacrifice**; about two thousand years later **circumcision** was introduced. About two thousand years after circumcision, **baptism was given.** And now in this generation, just prior to the second coming of Christ, **the final everlasting gospel sign of precious justifying faith** (2 Peter 1:1) **and Jesus' seal of imputed righteousness** is the 7th **Day Sabbath (Saturday** [John 3:33]). To be given to the world is found according as "to the Law and to the testimony if they speak not according to this word there is **(no gospel)** light in them (Isaiah 8:20). Jesus said, "And this gospel of the kingdom shall be preached in the entire world for a **witness** unto all nations, and then shall the end come" (Matthew 24:14).

The word *witness* in Matthew 24:14 is very specific. Of the 119 times the **word witness** is used in scripture, only in Matthew 24:14; Acts 4:33; 7:44; and James 5:3 is the word witness used to specifically point and apply to **evidence given** in the **Decalogue in the Sacred Tabernacle,** the Tabernacle in which Moses put the Ten Commandments in when he came down from the mountain after communicating with Jesus (Deuteronomy 10:1-5). The Greek word for witness in Matthew 24:14 means "evidence given, specifically referring to the two tables containing the Ten Commandments in the Decalogue in the sacred Tabernacle (**tables** [Hebrews 9:4]).

This evidence is none other than the 7th **day Sabbath of the fourth commandment**; The seal of God, the token sign of His authoritative right and power found in the fourth commandment, the only precept in the Decalogue that points to Jesus as Lord and Creator of the heavens and the earth (Exodus 20:8-11; Mark 2:27, 28). It clearly distinguishes **the true biblical day of worship** from all others. Throughout the scriptures, the Seventh-day Sabbath, God's only created rest day, is cited as the perpetual sign of Jesus creative and redemptive activity in human affairs (Mark 2:27, 28). It designates that Christ's authority is above all others in what day should be set aside as the day of spiritual rest and worship (Exodus 31:16, 17; Ezekiel 20:12, 20).

Today, the Seventh-day Sabbath is our sign of "precious faith … in the righteousness of God and our Savior Jesus Christ" (2 Peter 1:1). In the everlasting gospel of Revelation 14:6, 7, a witness unto all nations, and is the final evidence to be given in the Decalogue in the sacred Tabernacle, which says to all the world, we are not ashamed of the gospel of Christ (Revelation 14:6, 7; Romans 1:16). And the **Everlasting Gospel** (Revelation 14:6, 7) is **Righteousness by faith** (Romans 4:13) unto **Justification by faith** (Romans 5:1) through the imputed righteousness of Christ. Produced by Christ's Life, **Death,** and **Resurrection** (2 Timothy 2:8), of which the **Seventh-day Sabbath** (Exodus 20:8-11) is an **Everlasting Sign of precious Faith** (2 Peter 2:1) **and heaven's Judicial Seal** (Revelation 7:1-3) of its **Belief, Acceptance,** and **Obedience** (2 Thessalonians 1:7, 8) unto **Righteousness, Holiness** (Romans 6:19; Ephesians 4:24), and **Everlasting Life.**

"And he said unto me, unto two thousand and three hundred days; then shall the sanctuary be cleansed." "And I saw another sign in heaven, great and marvelous, seven angels having the seven last plagues; for in them is filled up the wrath of God." "And after that I looked, and, behold, the temple of the tabernacle of the testimony in heaven was opened: And the temple of God was opened in heaven, and there was seen in his temple the ark of his testament: and there were lightning's, and voices, and thundering, and an earthquake, and great hail (Daniel 8:14; Revelation 15:1; Revelation 15:5; Revelation 11:19).

It was after the passing of the time in 1844 that the great events from November 1, 1755, to November 13, 1833, to October 22, 1844 (Revelation 11:19), opened the eyes of the truly sincere Christian believer to the cleansing of the heavenly sanctuary transpiring in heaven. The "**open door**" message (Revelation 3:8) in light of Jesus entering the Most Holy Place of the heavenly Sanctuary to launch the beginning of the judgment hour message of Daniel 7:9-14 and Revelation 14:6, 7 given prior to October 22, 1844 (Matthew 24:29, 30). The decisive *7th trumpet everlasting gospel message* (Revelation 10:7) of *righteousness by faith of the first angel of Revelation 14:6, 7*; The critical message of the *second angel (Revelation 14:8)* revealing the fall of the Christian Churches, who by rejecting the judgment hour call of the first angel after October 22, 1844, completely disconnected their judicial right of being under the umbrella of Christ's life-giving righteousness.

And finally *the all inclusive third angel's (Revelation 14:9, 10) message of Justification by faith,* which concludes with "*they that keep the commandment of God and (keep) the faith of Jesus (Revelation 14:12).* Warning the world not to worship the beast, Catholicism (Revelation 13:1-10; 14:9), and his image, apostate Protestantism (Revelation 13:14, 15; 14:9), nor receive their mark of unity (Sunday worship). In light of Christ's final invitation to life-giving righteousness of which is inscribed, *"The commandments of God* (which includes Christ's fourth commandment)," *the 7th Day Sabbath worship day* (Revelation 14:7). Incorporated in the ten principles that define God's character (Exodus 20:1-17) in unity with the *"faith of Jesus"* (Revelation 14:12) that produced what the gospel is, says, and does for the believer. Illuminating the final *"truth of the* (**everlasting***) gospel"* message (Galatians 2:5; 14; Ephesians 1:13; Colossians 1:5; Revelation 14:6, 7) for this final generation.

These three end-time, all-important angels' messages (Revelation 14:6-12) envision our judicial relationship with God and those that biblically represent Him upon the earth after October 22, 1844. Today, the *Seventh-day Sabbath is the all-*inclusive gospel **sign of righteousness by faith,** the **everlasting seal of justification by faith** in the book of Revelation. Defined in the Decalogue of the sacred Tabernacle (Exodus 20:1-17) under the everlasting gospel message of Revelation 14:6, 7. Seen by the true gospel-believing, obeying people of God (1 Peter 4:17) as they contemplate the opening of God's Holy ark in heaven, containing the law of God that governs life in the universe (Revelation 11:19). *The light of the 7th Day Sabbath of the fourth commandment flashed its strong rays after October 1844, in the pathway of the Christian Churches transgressing the Sabbath day of rest of the fourth commandment, central in God's holy law (Exodus 20:8-11), upon those who are worshiping a manmade day of anti-gospel rest, called Sunday worship.*

In the book of Revelation, the prophet John describes the scenes of this Gospel age. He sees in heaven the ark of the testimony from where God speaks to his representatives (Exodus 25:21, 22; Numbers 7:89; Exodus 33:9-11; Leviticus 1:1). There the Holy Law of God shines in holy decorum, just as when Jesus wrote it with his own finger on tables of stone (Deuteronomy 10:1-5). John describes the work that will be done in the last days, when the Protestant churches, the image to the beast (Revelation 13:15) in the United States, confederates with Catholicism in Rome, the first beast of Revelation 13:1-10, and works against God's final sign, seal of life-giving righteousness (**the 7th day Sabbath**). Against those who "keep the commandments of God and have the testimony of Jesus" (Revelation 12:17; 19:10). John says, "And the dragon, **(the voice of civil government in the United States)** was wroth with the woman, and went to make war with the remnant of her seed, which keep the commandments of God, and have the testimony of Jesus Christ (Joel 2:32; Revelation 12:17).

The biblical gospel light is shining forth today upon the fourth commandment of the Sacred Decalogue; God is opening the understanding of many to see that they have been breaking the Lord Jesus' 7th Day Sabbath (Mark 2:28). My fellow Christian, the temple door of God is opened in heaven (Revelation 3:8) and there is seen in His temple the ark of His testament (Revelation 11:9). Calling you and me to be aware of the critical relationship the everlasting gospel (Revelation 14:6, 7, 12) has to the law of God (Isaiah 42:21). This holy principle, **Seventh-day Sabbath rest**, covered by the mercy seat, in which the holy angels are represented as looking reverentially into (Exodus 25:21, 22; Hebrews 9:4, 5), will decide the true relationship between God and His people, and foremost the destiny of most Christians living just before Jesus comes again.

What a responsibility is ours to comply with God's principle that governs righteous rest in the universe. The Principle that **confirms Justification unto eternal life in the judgment** (Acts 17:31; Revelation 14:6, 7) in this generation and forms characters in harmony with the law that defines the character of God. We are drawing nearer and still nearer to the solemn event of our Lord's second coming. And every man that hath this hope in him purifies himself, even as He **(Christ)** is pure (1 John 3:3).

John says, "And I saw another angel ascending from the east, having the **seal of the living God**: and he cried with a loud voice to the four angels, to whom it was given to hurt the earth and the sea, Saying, Hurt not the earth, neither the sea, nor the trees, **till we have sealed the servants of our God in their foreheads**" (Revelation 7:2, 3). What is the seal of God? The word of God gives only one definition to what constitutes the seal of God. The seal of God contains the name of God, Jesus Christ the Lord, the Creator of heaven and Earth, distinguished in the fourth commandment of the **evidence in the Decalogue of the Sacred Tabernacle,** defined in the Ten Commandments (Exodus 20:8-11; Ezekiel 12:12, 20; Hebrews 4:9; 9:4).

"Nevertheless the **foundation of God** stands sure, having this seal, **the Lord knows them that are his**" (2 Timothy 2:19; Revelation 13:8). This seal of God, the Seventh-day Sabbath, is a sign of approval, a biblical attestation of truth and genuineness, a mark of authority and ownership in righteousness, a proof of one's quality in relationship with his Creator. When Jesus was sealed (John 6:27), he was sealed in, "Bind up the testimony, seal the (righteousness) of law among my disciples" (Isaiah 8:16). "And Jesus, when he was baptized, went up straightway out of the water; and, lo, the heavens were opened unto him, and he saw the Spirit of God descending like a dove, and lighting upon him. And lo a voice from heaven saying this is my beloved son in whom I am well pleased" (Matthew 3:16-17).

When Jesus was sealed by his heavenly Father, an attestation from His Father in truth and genuineness in righteousness was given him. A sign of authority and mark of ownership, as proof from his Father qualifying Jesus' humanity, in the quality of righteousness and relationship with his father, witness heard and confirmed from scripture (Matthew 3:16, 17). Those who are sealed like Jesus are also attested with the same quality of relationship, and are filled with the indwelling power of the Holy Spirit, sanctified by Him in obeying the truth of the gospel of Christ (Acts 5:29-32). Those who "keep the commandments of God, and have the faith of Jesus" (Revelation 14:12) are counted as God's children. They "grieve not the Holy Spirit of God, whereby they are sealed unto the day of redemption (Ephesians 4:30). "Bind up the testimony, seal the law among my disciples" (Isaiah 8:16; 2 Timothy 2:19). Jesus was sealed in the law as a man for man. God does not call anyone into Christianity without establishing him or her in gospel righteousness. Again, what are the biblical principles of God's righteousness? "All thy commandments are righteousness" (Psalm 119:172; Exodus 20:1-17). God-written code of universal conduct written with the finger of Jesus (Deuteronomy 9:10) personified in Jesus' day as a man called the righteousness of God for the salvation of the world (John 2:1).

Again, the seal of God in the law is the Seventh-day Sabbath of the fourth commandment, and is evidence to us today that we believe the gospel in the Spirit of truth (John 4:23; Ephesians 1:13). Jesus said to His disciples, "*If ye love me, keep my commandments. And I will* pray the Father, and he shall *give you another Comforter* that he may abide with you forever; even the *spirit of truth;* for he dwells with you, and shall be in you. But the comforter, which is the Holy Ghost, whom the Father will send in my name, *he shall teach you all things and bring all things to your remembrance" (John 14:14-17:26).*

Rest in Righteousness

Jesus said, "Come unto me, all ye that labor and are heavy laden, and I will give you rest" (Matthew 11:28). On Friday at dusk, as the seventh-day Sabbath comes upon us, we are reminded, "There **remains** therefore a Sabbath (rest) to the people of God" (Hebrews 4:9). Although the seventh day is critical for all of us to keep, we must remember and contemplate that the promise of Christ in giving us rest is not in just keeping a day because it is stipulated as a judicial principle (Exodus 20:8-11). The rest that Jesus has promised us is Jesus' rest, *God's righteous rest.*

As a man cannot truly rest until his work is finished, even so it is a biblical principle in the creation account. When Jesus finished creating this world, finished creating it in six working days, then and only then did He rest from all he had created and made. He rested in the fact that after creation order, He would have no more to establish in order to create abundant life on this planet. It would flow from what He had established at Creation. This is a biblical principle in the character and creative nature of God, Jesus the life-giving, Omnipotent Christ, "in that he rested from all his work which God created and made" (Genesis 2:1-3).

In turn, it is true that man overturned God's plan in creation and began its downward course of destruction, but scripture reveals that Jesus interceded through His forethought plan of salvation to rescue and redeem man anew (Revelation 13:8), in which He will eventually recreate the earth made new (Isaiah 65:17; Revelation 21:1-5).

Just as the seventh day was given after creation as a sign of God's rest, God's righteous rest (Genesis 2:1-3; Hebrews 4:3-5), the seventh-day Sabbath still occupies a prominent place in the record of God dealing with his people. From the beginning of time, and as it has always been, **the seventh-day Sabbath is a rest issue in the eyes of God,** which will continue throughout all eternity (Isaiah 66:22, 23). Just as Jesus ended His work of the creation of our world by resting on the seventh day (Genesis 1:31), so too He ended the sixth day of the week by hanging and dying on the cruel cross for the salvation and redemption of man. He was then laid in the tomb by His faithful followers (Luke 23:50-54), where he **rested in the tomb on the seventh day** from His perfect work of redeeming man (Luke 23:56).

The seventh-day Sabbath still remains from the time of Eden, and is a gospel pledge from God to us in this generation as our sign of faith in the righteous rest of Christ in creation and redemption. It is not just given to us today as just a creation issue. It is scripturally declared in the book of Revelation as a gospel issue to the remnant people of God (Revelation 12:17; 14:6, 7). Scripture is crying, screaming for the Church to understand what constitutes today's *righteous rest*, gospel rest (Romans 1:17) in the righteousness of Christ. The everlasting gospel message to be given to the world in this generation is a fear God, give him glory, judgment hour, and **seventh-day Sabbath issue in Christ our righteousness**.

The seventh-day Sabbath is to us today a day of intimacy and righteous relationship with the Creator of the universe. A legal, forensic, judicial gospel message saying to each one of us, *You belong to me, says the Lord* in righteous rest and redemption. Friend, I don't know about you, but what the seventh-day Sabbath says to me excites me today as much as the day when my wife and I sealed our marriage with a kiss. It puts happiness and joy in my heart that cannot be defined or expressed! Let us all really contemplate what scripture is truly telling us about what a difference a day makes in the eyes of the Lord (Isaiah 56:1-6). Brethren, rest and rejoice in the Lord, and again I say, *REJOICE!*

And I saw another angel ascending from the east, having the seal of the living God: and he cried with a loud voice to the four angels, to whom it was given to hurt the earth and the sea, Saying, Hurt not the earth, neither the sea, nor the trees, till we have **sealed the servants of our God in their foreheads**" (Revelation 7:2, 3). "And the third angel followed them, saying with a loud voice, if any man worship the beast and his image, and receive **his mark in his forehead,** or in his hand *(Sunday worship)* the same shall drink of the wine of the wrath of God" (Revelation 14:9, 10).

There will be two classes of Christians just before Jesus comes, one with the seal of God *(Seventh-day Sabbath worship)* in their foreheads, the other with the mark of the beast *(Sunday worship).* As Adam had a choice in his test of life-giving righteousness and chose the wrong tree (Genesis 2:17). As in the test of **righteousness by faith** between Cain and Abel in bringing the right sacrifice (Hebrews 11:4; Genesis 4:3-16), as in the test of righteousness by faith in Noah's day of entering the ark or ending up in the water (Genesis 7:1; 1 Peter 3:20). As in the test of righteousness given to literal Israel in the judgment hall of Christ in A.D. 31, between Christ or Caesar (John 19:15), so shall a test be given to this final generation just before Jesus comes again in the clouds of heaven.

Revelation says, "because thou hast kept the word of my patience, I also will keep thee from the hour of temptation, which shall come upon the entire world, **to test them that dwell upon the earth**" (Revelation 3:10). Friend, God cannot keep us in the future "**hour of temptation**" unless we believe Revelation's gospel message conveying to this generation the truthfulness of the seventh-day Sabbath gospel message ordained for this final generation (Revelation 14:6, 7).

As two trees before the fall, two sacrifices shortly after the fall, an ark or water before the great flood, two men represented in a judgment hall in Jesus' day (A.D. 31), were past examples of crisis times for the people of God, so to today the final crisis of what a difference a day makes in the eyes of God will determine the fate of many professed Christians. This test will be totally based on what scripture says in the context of faith as to what day God has established as the Sabbath rest to the people of God (Hebrews 4:9). The believing and keeping of the Seventh-day Sabbath over the believing and keeping of Sunday sacredness in the light of Christ our righteousness in the future legislated worldwide Christian Sunday law will determine in this final generation who believes (John 14:29) and bares the true credentials of Christ our Righteousness (Malachi 3:16-18).

The believing of the Seventh-day Sabbath rest will, just before Jesus comes again, be the final point of controversy in the issue of establishing a man in obedience to "the truth of the gospel" (Galatians 2:5, 14; Ephesians 1:13; Colossians 1:5) and the gospel message of righteousness by faith unto Justification by faith (Romans 5:1; Revelation 14:6-12). By setting apart the seventh-day Sabbath at Creation, Jesus established a memorial of conception and recognition of his divine power and authority as Creator. There is nothing in the Sabbath that restricts it to any particular nation, tongue, or people. It was created for all man (Mark 2:27, 28) in the contemplation of the works of God in creation order.

John says, "In the beginning was the Word, and the Word was with God, and the Word was God. The same was in the beginning with God. **All things were made by him**; and without him *(Jesus)* was not anything made that was made" (John 1:1-3). Jesus said, "If ye love me, keep my commandments. And I will pray the Father, and he shall give you another Comforter that he may abide with you forever; even the Spirit of truth**; whom the world cannot receive, because it sees him not, neither knows him: but ye know him; for he dwells with you, and shall be in you** (John 14:15-17). Will we choose to be numbered with the righteous when the final "truth of the gospel" message is given to the world (Revelation 14:6, 7), or be numbered with those who chose to "receive not the love of the truth" (2 Thessalonians 2:10) and be blinded by the deadly deceptive power of the enemy (2 Corinthians 4:3-5).

Friend, God will assuredly call this world to judgment for the death of his son in the light of Justification by faith, and the Seventh-day Sabbath truth will decide in this generation who will appropriate the right to eternal life. Shall we choose the mark the world is preparing the Christian Church to keep, **Sunday worship** (Revelation 13:16; 14:9; 15:2)? Or receive the seal of God (Revelation 7:1-3) defined in Revelation's final gospel message to the world, the **critical issue in 7th Day Sabbath Worship** (Revelation 14:6-12).

Gospel Order

If there was ever a time when gospel order should be established in Christ's last day, 7th-Day Remnant Adventist Church (Revelation 12:17), it is now in light of what is taking place in the three areas of the world where Bible prophecy is presently being fulfilled. To those who profess to be teachers of righteousness, a representation of Christ's piety, meekness, and humility must be present in the soul character of those presenting "present (*gospel*) truth" (2 Peter 1:12). In order to establish (Isaiah 54:14) precious souls in the righteousness of Christ in this generation. Brethren, it is critically important to bear in mind that we are handling precious words of inspiration, and the truth of the gospel must be presented in the order represented in the life of Jesus at the beginning of His ministry (A.D. 27) to its closure (A.D. 31) at the time of his gospel commission to his disciples (Matthew 28:18-20; Mark 16:15. 16).

Not all ministers are biblically presenting the first (Revelation 14:6, 7), second (Revelation 14:8), and third angel's messages (Revelation 14:9-11) of Revelation 14:6-12 in time order, gospel order. The gospel for this final generation must have a continuous gospel outline from Genesis to Revelation, defined from Adam to Abraham, from Abraham to Jesus, from Jesus to the Reformation, from the Reformation to the Great Advent Movement, from the Great Advent Movement to the final mighty cry of Revelation 18:1-5. Many ministers do not have in place the critical understanding of the gospel outline that constitutes this generation's final everlasting gospel message (Revelation 14:6-12).

There needs to be a greater understanding of gospel order among ministers and congregations to arouse them to the critical, sensitive message of righteousness by faith into justification by faith unto life. There is a present danger taking place since September 11, 2001, in light of the scenario that took place during the Great Advent Movement of the eighteen thirties and forties in the drying up of the river Euphrates (Revelation 13-21). The prophetic chart, according to Habakkuk 2:1-4, given to the Advent messengers reveals although "it tarry" in the end "it shall speak."

Did not Jesus at the beginning of His ministry exemplify gospel order in the orderly process of believing, receiving, and obeying the gospel? He instructed His lone evangelist, John the Baptist, to present "present truth" "in the way of righteousness" (Matthew 21:32; Luke 7:29, 30). "By faith in the operation of God," in transferring circumcision, which was the old covenant sign of faith, to water baptism, the New Testament sign of faith (Colossians 2:9-12). Circumcision was Abraham's sign of "precious faith," his legal seal of imputed righteousness (Romans 4:11; 2 Peter 1:1).

John the Baptist then fulfilled the born again commission of Jesus (John 3:5) in the experience of water baptism. This was gospel order in Jesus' day, critical in order for a candidate for heaven **in that generation** to receive gospel righteousness (Romans 1:16, 17), gospel peace (Romans 10:15, 16; Ephesians 6:15). Giving the individual the right to be indwelled by the divine power of the Holy Spirit (Romans 5:1-5; Ephesians 1:13), exemplified at the baptism of Christ in the beginning of His ministry (Matthew 3:13-17).

Brethren, could Jesus enter the kingdom of heaven *as a man, for man,* in order to represent man, for the salvation of man, if He did not appropriate gospel righteousness through gospel order? **The answer is an unequivocal** *no.* Paul said the kingdom of God is first "**righteousness,** and second **peace,** and third **joy in the Holy Ghost**" (Romans 14:17). And any gospel message that is given outside of this orderly process hinders heaven's judicial process of saving mankind and does injustice to the gospel of Christ and to the individuals who are "hungering and thirsting after **(life-giving) righteousness**" (Matthew 5:6). The first message Jesus gave to Israel at the beginning of His ministry was, "The kingdom of God is at hand, repent you, and believe the gospel" (Mark 1:16). "For therein (for in the gospel) is the **righteousness** of God revealed" (Romans 1:17). Christ's righteousness is the primary ingredient in obtaining eternal life and citizenship in God's eternal kingdom (Philippians 3:20).

Jesus said, "Seek ye *first* the kingdom of God and **His righteousness.**" How many Christians today have ascribed to the righteousness of religious leaders (Matthew 5:20) ministries in a stupor as to a sinner's heavenly rights in obtaining divine power in overcoming the sinful, deplorable nature we all personally live in? Paul said, "Wherefore take to you the whole armor of God that ye may be able to withstand in the evil day, and having done all, to stand. Stand therefore, having your loins girt about with **(gospel)** truth, and having on the breastplate of **righteousness**; and your feet shod with the **preparation of the gospel of peace**" (Ephesians 6:13-15).

My fellow Christian, a minister of Christ may appear pure in conversation and action. He may be educated in the greatest Christian schools of our day. He may be called by men in ministerial authority eloquent in speech and stature, but this does not represent the fact that the **"truth of the gospel" (Galatians 2:5, 14; Ephesians 1:13; Colossians 1:5)** is in place. The gospel given by Jesus was pure and simple, until the apostle Paul revealed the presence of a perverted gospel entering the Christian Church (Galatians 1:6, 7; 2:14). Men perverting the gospel, preaching half truths and skepticism developing the spiritual darkness today far exceeding the darkness pervading in Jesus' day (Luke 2:79). As the apostle Paul said, "O, full of subtlety and all mischief, thou child of the devil, thou **enemy of all righteousness**, wilt thou not cease to **pervert the right way of the Lord?**" (Acts 13:10).

For almost two millennia, the real "truth of the gospel" of Christ has been hidden beneath the rubbish of error, at times its light almost making a recovery. Soon it will, brethren, soon it will. And the **glory of the Seventh-day Sabbath gospel message of Revelation 14:6-12 will encircle the earth** with a message so pure and so precious that thousands will walk away from all this world has to offer, clothed in the precious faith Peter said is only obtained "through the righteousness of God and our Savior Jesus Christ" (2 Peter 1:1).

Brethren, "the light of the glorious gospel of Christ" (2 Corinthians 4:4) is shining today in a greater beauty and capacity than has ever been presented in any past generation of religious history. This message has been conveyed to this generation through the three angels' messages of Revelation 7:1-3; 14:6-12. *Defining and defending the everlasting gospel of righteousness by faith into justification by faith. Forever stamping and securing the Seventh-day Sabbath sign, seal in the hearts of the universe (Ephesians 3:9-11), revealing eternally the incredible eternal love of God.*

Will you join with the Godhead (Colossians 2:9), the Holy Heavenly Angels, and God's appointed agencies in presenting this message to this final generation in the light of the "judgment hour," prior to the second coming of Christ, and "speak the same thing when it comes to the truth of the gospel" (Revelation 14:7; 1 Corinthians 1:10)? Please, brethren, let's finish the gospel commission in gospel order Jesus gave to us to present to this generation (Matthew 28:18-20). How critical will the judgment reveal the work of the minister who has failed to present these golden truths, the golden merits of Christ's atonement that initiates true Justification unto life. Please, brethren, "the time is fulfilled, the kingdom of God is at hand" (Daniel 8:14). It's time to repent and believe the **"truth of the gospel of Christ"** (Mark 1:15; Ephesians 1:13; Colossians 1:5)

∽ *Chapter Fourteen* ∽
Day Short of Righteousness

"Behold, the Lord makes the earth empty, and makes it waste, and turns it upside down, and scatters abroad the inhabitants thereof. And it shall be, as with the people, so with the priest; as with the servant, so with his master; as with the maid, so with her mistress; as with the buyer, so with the seller; as with the lender, so with the borrower; as with the taker of usury, so with the giver of usury to him. The land shall be utterly emptied, and utterly spoiled: for the Lord hath spoken this word. The earth mourns *and* fades away, the world languishes away, the haughty people of the earth do languish. The earth also is defiled under the inhabitants thereof; because they have **transgressed the laws, changed the ordinance, broken the everlasting covenant**" (Isaiah 24:1-5).

These five verses in Isaiah 24 depict the deplorable result of man's reign on the earth from the time of Adam's fall to the final result of his total annihilation of his unrighteous state of being (Jeremiah 17:9; Romans 3:10) at the second coming of Christ. One verse in these five verses outlines and depicts the whole of man's futile endeavor to rule himself in the last six thousand years of earth history. "The earth also is defiled under the inhabitants thereof; because they have transgressed the laws, changed the ordinance, broken the everlasting covenant (Isaiah 24:5).

It was shortly after the creation of this world that Adam chose to "**transgress the Law** (of Christ [Romans 5:14]) by rejecting life-giving righteousness (Romans 9:37). It was shortly after the death of the twelve apostles that the New Testament Christian Catholic Universal Church "**changed the ordinance**" in the Law, the Seventh-day Sabbath commandment (Exodus 20:8-11) to the first day of the week, creating Sunday sacredness and worship. It was then the New Testament Christian Catholic Universal Church "speak great words against the most High, and shall wear out the saints of the most High, and **think to change times and laws**" (the fourth commandment [Exodus 20:8-11]), and they **(the world)** shall be given into his hand until time and times and the dividing of time" or for 1,260 years (Daniel 7:25; Numbers 14:34; Ezekiel 4:6).

It was after the death of the apostles, about the middle of the second century A.D., that the New Testament Christian Universal Church began its diabolical work of transferring the Seventh-day Sabbath rest to Sunday observance (Revelation 13:5-7). And soon as the world breaks the everlasting gospel covenant recorded in Isaiah 56:1-8, when they reject the final everlasting gospel message of Revelation 14:6-12 by uniting the world in a united confederacy of church and state **through legislated Sunday sacredness,** Isaiah's prophecy will say, "Therefore hath the curse devoured the earth, because they that dwell therein are desolate (**of life-giving righteousness**) and therefore the inhabitants of the earth will be burned" (Isaiah 24:6).

How undeniable to see and recognize in these three phases of Isaiah 24:5 the deplorable condition depicting the whole of man's historical defilement in his 6,000 years of chronicled reign. First, when Man or Adam **"transgressed the laws"** in the Garden of Eden, in the area of the world known as the Middle East. Secondly, when Man **"Changed the Ordinance"** in Europe, the area of the world where the New Testament Christian Catholic Church took its seat of Ecclesiastical authority over the then-known world from A.D. 538 to 1798 and heralded to the nations during that time, the change of the Seventh-day Sabbath rest to Sunday worship, the first day of creation week.

And finally, when man, deceived by the image of the beast (Revelation 13:15), unites with "the beast out of the sea" (Revelation 13:1-10) and **breaks the everlasting covenant** he will end his reign on earth when the United States, the Dragon's voice (Revelation 13:11; 16:12), **legislates (Revelation 17:13) Sunday worship** in honor of the beast out of the sea (Revelation 13:1-10), the Roman Catholic Church. How undeniable is this prophecy being seen and fulfilled in the area of the world where Christianity has had it greatest religious freedom of expression, the United States of America. The last biblical head of the seven-headed, ten-horned beast (Revelation 17:3), who takes control of the world just before Jesus comes and initiates the final blasphemy that instigates final world apostasy.

This whole description of gospel apostasy unto blasphemy against God (Revelation 13:6) in our day is depicted in Isaiah 24 and 25, along with Jeremiah 4 and 25:30-38, outlined in John's prophecy of the seven last plagues in Revelation 16:1-21. These plagues are God's judgments on man's willful transgression and violation of His divine principles (Exodus 20:1-17) that describe His character and governs life in His Universal Kingdom through the imputed righteousness of Christ. Each plague has a specific meaning and purpose as to specific locations that have in the past caused man's willful, sinful decline throughout the ages.

John says, "And I heard a great voice out of the temple saying to the seven angels, go your ways, and pour out the vials of the wrath of God upon the earth (Revelation 16:1). These plagues fill up the wrath of God in man's final rejection of the last gospel message (Revelation 14:6, 7; Romans 1:16-18) that has encircled the earth. Especially upon those Christians who have led out in rejecting God's final eternal sign of faith, God's eternal seal outlined in the fourth commandment. Defining the 7th day Sabbath; Jesus' everlasting sign, His everlasting seal of imputed justifying righteousness (Revelation 7:1-3; 2 Peter 1:1).

Soon, very soon, man in this final generation will, with the Bible in their hands, willfully choose and legislate on a global scale **Sunday worship, the mark of the beast (Revelation 13:16; 14:9-11; 15:2; 16:2)**. Over the Bible Seventh-day Sabbath rest, **the day Jesus created (Mark 2:27, 28) and kept, "leaving us an example**, that we should follow is his footsteps" (Luke 4:16; 1 Peter 2:21, 22). John says, "And after that I looked, and, behold, the temple of the tabernacle of the testimony in heaven was opened … And the temple was filled with smoke from the glory of God, and from his power; and **no man was able to enter into the temple**, till the **seven plagues of the seven angels were fulfilled**" (Revelation 15:5-7).

The temple of God in heaven is the only place where sins can be forgiven and blotted out (Hebrews 8:1-5; Acts 3:19, 17:31). And those who chose not to believe and obey the everlasting gospel of Christ, recorded in the fourteenth chapter of the book of Revelation, before he comes, to fear his name, and worship him in imputed gospel rest, will then understand too late what it means, "for thy judgments are made manifest" (Malachi 3:16-18; Revelation 15:4).

These plagues are dreadful, but more so meaningful to the Christian living in this critical time in earth's history. They depict the now critical movements in the three areas of the world where the Dragon, the beast, and false prophet are now presently working together for world civil and religious domination (Revelation 16:13, 14). And it shall be, as with the people, so with the priest; as with the servant, so with his master; as with the maid, so with her mistress; as with the buyer, so with the seller; as with the lender, so with the borrower; as with the taker of usury, so with the giver of usury to him. *The land shall be utterly emptied, and utterly spoiled: for the Lord hath spoken this word (Isaiah 24:2)*.

John said, "And I heard a great voice out of the temple saying to the seven angels, go your ways, and pour out the vials of the wrath of God upon the earth. And the first went, and poured out his **vial upon the earth**; and there fell a noisome and grievous sore **upon the men** which had the **mark of the beast** and upon them which **worshiped his image"** (Revelation 16:1, 2). This first plague falls foremost on the earth, a biblical symbol for the United States of America (Revelation 13:11), where the greatest civil and religious constitution that has ever existed outside of the one given to literal Israel shortly after the Exodus (Exodus 10:4, 5; 31:24-26). It's the "beast out of the earth," the United States of America (Revelation 13:11; 16:13), that speaks like a dragon and gives its legislative and law enforcement power (Revelation 17:13) to the image of the beast (Revelation 13:14, 15). The apostate Protestant Churches of the United States, a parallel to the time when Babylon's reign on the earth (Jeremiah 51:34), when she legislated religion on the then-known world (Daniel 3:1-7; 9:2). These church and state unions will in our day begin the final work of apostasy in this country, legislating Sunday Worship in reverence to the beast out of the sea, the Roman Catholic Universal Church (Revelation 13:1-10), which also has encircled the whole earth.

This plague is a "noisome, a grievous sore," which enrages the professed Protestant and Catholic Churches of this country because they have become contentious (Romans 2:8, 9) in not obeying the sign sealing everlasting gospel message of Revelation 14:6, 7 by uniting to legislate religion. Their version of the Papacy's day of spiritual rest and worship (Revelation 17:13). Anyone who does not comply and convert to the 21st Century Christian Catholic Protestant Church's principle doctrine (**Sunday Worship**) will be subject to this generation's universal death decree (Revelation 13:15), so long used by the Papacy during the dark ages of Catholic history. Alternately, anyone who does not comply and convert to Revelation 14:6-12 final everlasting gospel messages will be subject to heaven's future universal punishment and eventually the death decree recorded in Revelation 20:14.

The second plague or vial falls "upon the sea" (Revelation 16:3), the area of the world where "the beast out of the sea" (Revelation 13:1-10), Catholicism, has had its greatest stronghold. This plague truly defines and declares that souls die (Genesis 3:19; Ezekiel 18:4, 20; Ecclesiastes 3:18-20). When a person dies, they're dead until their life's record appears before the judgment seat of Christ (2 Corinthians 5:10; Revelation 20:12). Then, when Jesus comes again, He raises them up for eternal judgment (Hebrews 9:27; Revelation 14:7; 20:4, 5, 12), whether "they have done good unto the resurrection of life (Revelation 20:5) or whether they have done evil, unto the resurrection of damnation" (Revelation 20:14, 15). They are judged and then sentenced accordingly for either obeying or rejecting the gospel covenant of their era (Isaiah 24:5; 56:1-5; Hebrews 10:26). Then those who are found unrighteous will be finally annulled of life (John 5:29; Hebrews 9:27; 2 Corinthians 5:10; Romans 14:10; Ezekiel 18:4, 20; Revelation 20:12-15).

Europe suffers the second vial of God's wrath as the waters of Europe (Revelation 17:15) turn to blood in view of the fact that Revelation 16:3 says, "Every living soul died in the sea." Both man and beast (Ecclesiastes 3:18-20) begin the ultimate process of earth's inhabitants dying; Zephaniah says, "I will utterly consume all *things* from off the land, says the Lord. I will consume man and beast; I will consume the fowls of the heaven, and the fishes of the sea, and the stumbling blocks with the wicked; and I will cut off man from off the land, says the Lord. I will also stretch out mine hand upon Judah, and upon all the inhabitants of Jerusalem; and I will cut off the remnant of Baal from this place, *and* the name of the **Chemarims (idolatrous priest who are scripturally void of righteousness, passion, love, and kindness, in darkness to the gospel of Christ)** with the priests; And them that worship the **host of heaven (Horoscopes** [Deuteronomy 17:3; Jeremiah 8:2]) upon the housetops; and them that worship *and* that swear by the Lord (Romans 10:13, one verse believers) and that swear by Malcham (the national **idol** of the Ammonites, or idolaters) and them that are turned back from the Lord; *and those that have **not sought the Lord**, nor **enquired for him**" *(Zephaniah 1:2-6; Matthew 6:33; Zephaniah 2:3; Philippians 3:9).*

It's because Catholicism has hid and withheld the **"truth of the gospel"** (Romans 1:18) from the nations of Europe and the world for the last fifteen hundred years and set up idols in the Christian faith. This second plague falls in the European theater because most believers have not personally established the Papacy's doctrinal teachings through biblical or scriptural evidence. They have chosen to accept the Papacy's philosophy or the teachings of men instead of the word of God (Psalm 146:3; Acts 17:11; 2 Timothy 2:15, 3:16).

She, since 1798 without a government to enforce her faith, "says in her heart, **I sit a queen**, an am no widow" (Revelation 18:7), **as the kings, leaders of the earth** are now again in the final generation, enforcing her day of worship. She will begin her punishment by this second plague because of her willful apostasy, and this plague begins the final work of smiting her of followers, and then finally she will be annihilated of life by the armies of heaven (Revelation 19:11-16; Daniel 11:45).

"And the third angel poured out his vial upon the rivers and fountains of waters; and they became blood (Revelation 16:4). The third plague is similar to the second. But it falls in a different area of the world, the Euphrates, a biblical symbol for the Middle East, the inhabitants, or waters

(Revelation 17:15), of the religion of Islam (Revelation 17:15). They represent the descendants of Abraham and Lot. Those living today with the mindset of Ishmael (Genesis 16:11, 12) "Edom and Moab and the chief of the children of Ammon" (Daniel 11:41), who rejected the gospel message of their day and set up an anti-gospel message in the Middle East to counter any biblical teachings of Christianity (Revelation 9:1-18). They became a bottomless pit (Revelation 9:1, 2) of rebellion and terror against themselves and the world after Christianity was driven out of the Middle East during the reign of the old Roman Empire.

These waters are symbols of Old Testament nations (Isaiah 8:7; 17:12, 13; Jeremiah 46:1-8) and are symbolized in the book of Revelation as the people of the Euphrates (Revelation 16:4, 12; 17:12-15), or the Middle East. They are the present work of the Dragon's voice of the United States (Revelation 13:11) in order to dry up or subdue the killing fringes of Islam (Genesis 16:11, 12). To restrain them until they all unite, Catholics, Protestant, and Islam in a global civil and religious legislation, or legislated Sunday law. Backed by the mystery of iniquity who has set up MYSTERY BABYLON THE GREAT, MOTHER OF HARLOTS, Catholicism and her HARLOT DAUGHTERS, Apostate Protestantism, centered in the United States and Europe. United with the Arab world, the ABOMINATIONS OF THE EARTH (Revelation 17:5; Deuteronomy 18:9-14).

These first three plagues fall in a reverse pattern where the Lord from Abraham's day to ours has centered the proclamation of the gospel of Christ in different eras of time. First, after the great flood, for almost two thousand years, the gospel was proclaimed in the Middle East through the faithful descendants of Abraham; Then centered in Europe through the preaching of the apostles; and finally just before Jesus comes, initiated in the Northeast corner of the United States through the great Advent Movement of the eighteen thirties and forties.

These Plagues do not fall at the same time or in the same place, but begin in the areas and strongholds of those who have united and initiated the final world apostasy. Accordingly, these plagues begin to fall first in the United States, then Europe, thirdly in the Middle East, symbolized by the earth the United States, the sea Europe, and then "upon the rivers and the fountain of waters" symbolized as the peoples of the Middle East (Revelation 16:2-4). Reversing the punishment in the areas of gospel light from the time of Abraham's calling (Genesis 12:1-4) to our day.

Then, in Revelation 16:5-7, the prophet John records in his hearing the approval of the universal; "Thou art righteous, O Lord, which art, and was, and shall be, because thou has judged thus. For they have shed the blood of saints and prophets, and thou has given them blood to drink; for they are worthy, And I heard another (angel) out of the altar say, Even so, Lord God Almighty, true and righteous are thy judgments (Revelation 16:5-7). Since the crucifixion of Christ, the universe has been amazed at the purity, holiness, and righteousness of God in his dealings with the unrighteousness of men as the four beasts of Revelation, and the twenty-four elders (Revelation 4:8-11) bow down in constant adoration before the throne of God as they witness the constant work of God in the sanctuary for the redemption of defiant humanity.

It's the fourth plague that speaks specifically to this final generation. John says, "And the fourth angel poured out his vial **upon the sun**; and power was given to him to **scorch men with fire.** And men were scorched with great heat, and **blasphemed the name of God**, which **hath power over these plagues**: and they repented not to give him glory" (Revelation 16:8, 9). How relevant and important are these two verses to the born again (John 3:7), remnant people of God. To be biblically studied, believed, and understood in the light of Revelation 14:6, 7, everlasting gospel, seventh-day Sabbath message. "For precept must be upon precept, precept upon precept; line upon line, line upon line; here a little, and there a little" (Isaiah 28:10). Brethren, the world is about to be converted to **Sunday worship** through a universal, global Sunday law backed by the Dragon, Beast, and False Prophet of Revelation 16:13.

Received and deceived by "spirits of devils," working in the minds of men, especially the civil and religious leaders of this final generation (Revelation 16:13, 14). No one is going to leave this planet until after the seven last plagues fall on Planet Earth (Revelation 15:8) and have done their decisive work on this generation, especially on the men who have rejected the everlasting gospel message of Revelation 14:6-12; Above all upon the ministers who have withheld the truth of the gospel of Christ in unrighteousness (Romans 1:18, 25; 2 Corinthians 11:13-15).

The Bible is vitally clear, unless the people of God, His last-day Remnant Church (Joel 2:32; Revelation 12:17), study, believe, understand, and obey what is symbolized by **"the name of God which had power over these plagues"** (Revelation 16:9), they will have no Divine power (Revelation 16:9) to overcome the seven last plagues that inundate the earth. John says men **"blasphemed the name of God,"** which is not difficult to understand what God in the past has associated with His Name, which must be understood according to Bible principle of interpretation (Isaiah 28:9, 10).

The Name of God

Ezekiel twenty is one of the most comprehensive chapters in scripture that defines what God associates with His name. Scripture says, "But they rebelled against me, and would not hearken unto me: they did not every man cast away the abominations of their eyes, neither did they forsake the idols of Egypt: then I said, I will pour out my fury upon them, to accomplish my anger against them in the midst of the land of Egypt. But I wrought for **my name's sake**, that it should not be polluted before the heathen, among whom they *were*, in whose sight I made myself known unto them, in bringing them forth out of the land of Egypt. Wherefore I caused them to go forth out of the land of Egypt, and brought them into the wilderness. And I gave them my statutes, and shewed them my judgments, which *if* a man do, he shall even live in them. **Moreover also I gave them my Sabbaths** (Exodus 16:23-30) to be a sign between me and them, that they might know that I *am* the Lord that sanctify them. **But the house of Israel rebelled against me** in the wilderness: they walked not in my statutes, and they despised my judgments, which *if* a man do, he shall even live in them; and **my Sabbaths they greatly polluted**: then I said, I would pour out my fury upon them in the wilderness, to consume them.

But **I wrought for my name's sake**, that it should not be polluted before the heathen, in whose sight I brought them out. Yet also I lifted up my hand unto them in the wilderness, that I would not bring them into the land which I had given *them*, flowing with milk and honey, which *is* the glory of all lands (Exodus 12:41; 13:5) 1491 B.C.

Because they despised my judgments, and walked not in my statutes, but **polluted my Sabbaths**: for their heart went after their idols. Nevertheless mine eye spared them from destroying them; neither did I make an end of them in the wilderness. But I **said unto their children in the wilderness**, Walk ye not in the statutes of your fathers, neither observe their judgments, nor defile yourselves with their idols: I *am* the Lord your God; walk in my statutes, and keep my judgments, and do them; **And hallow my sabbaths**; and they shall be a sign between me and you, that ye may know that I *am* the Lord your God. Notwithstanding **the children rebelled against me**: they walked not in my statutes, neither kept my judgments to do them, which *if* a man do, he shall even live in them; **they polluted my Sabbaths**: then I said, I would pour out my fury upon them, to accomplish my anger against them in the wilderness. Nevertheless I withdrew mine hand, and wrought for **my name's sake**, that it should not be polluted in the sight of the heathen, in whose sight I brought them forth I lifted up mine hand unto them also in the wilderness, that I would scatter them among the heathen and disperse them through the countries; Because they had not executed my judgments, but had **despised my statutes**, and had **polluted my Sabbaths**, and their eyes were after their fathers' idols" (Ezekiel 20:8-24).

This whole chapter defines the detour, blaspheme (Ezekiel 20:27), and laxity literal Israel came to that caused their destruction and captivity in Babylon about 605 B.C. A precursor to the final character of the New Testament Christian Catholic Protestant Churches that causes the falling of the seven last plagues on this planet and the second coming of Christ (Revelation 19:11-16; 1 Corinthians 10:11).

It is also the laxity the "nobles (leaders) of Judah" (Nehemiah 13:17) took towards the Sabbath in the rebuilding of the temple after their captivity in Babylon was accomplished (Daniel 1:1, 2; 9:2). Nehemiah said, "In those days saw I in Judah *some* **treading wine presses on the Sabbath**, and bringing in sheaves, and lading asses; as also wine, grapes, and figs, and **all** *manner of* **burdens, which they brought into Jerusalem on the Sabbath day**: and I testified *against them* in the day wherein they sold victuals. There dwelt men of Tyre also therein, which brought fish, and all manner of ware, and **sold on the Sabbath unto the children of Judah**, and in Jerusalem.

Then I contended with the nobles of Judah, and said unto them, what evil thing *is* this that ye do, and profane the Sabbath day? Did not your father's thus, and did not our God bring all this evil upon us, and upon this city? **yet ye bring more wrath upon Israel by profaning the Sabbath**. And it came to pass, that when the gates of Jerusalem began to be dark before the Sabbath, I commanded that the gates should be shut, and charged that they should not be opened **till after the Sabbath**: and *some* of my servants set I at the gates, *that* **there should no burden be brought in on the Sabbath day**. So the merchants and sellers of all kind of ware lodged without Jerusalem once or twice. **Then I testified against them**, and said unto them, why lodge ye about the wall? If ye do *so* again, I will lay hands on you. **From that time forth came they no** *more* **on the Sabbath. And I commanded the Levites that they should cleanse themselves, and** *that* **they should come** *and* **keep the gates, to sanctify the Sabbath day**. Remember me, O my God, *concerning* this also, and spare me according to the greatness of thy mercy" (Nehemiah 13:15-22).

All these warnings were "written for our admonition" (1 Corinthians 10:11), made known from generation to generation, from Adam to our time (Romans 15:4). All given to us for the restoration of humanity (Isaiah 58:11-14), to the state of being God planned for man to preserve from creation (Genesis 2:26, 27; Hebrews 4:1-11). And those who chose not to reverence and obey the Bible's description of what God associates with His name, **the 7ᵗʰ Day Sabbath,** that has power over these plagues (Revelation 16:9), will find themselves in the final scene of earth's history without life-giving righteousness and the right to eternal life.

It's in Isaiah 56 that the final message of Revelation 14:6, 7 is defined to those who want and choose to be numbered with the people of God in the final everlasting gospel covenant contract afforded this final generation. Isaiah says, "Thus says the Lord, Keep ye judgment, and do justice; for **my salvation is near to come**, and **my righteousness to be revealed**. Blessed is the man that doeth this, and the **son of man (the unconverted or unborn again man [John 3:5-7])** that lay's hold on it, that **keeps the Sabbath from polluting it**. And keeps his hand from doing any evil (Isaiah 56:1, 2). In these two verses we find judgment, justice, righteousness to be revealed, of which righteousness is the primary gospel factor from Genesis through Revelation (Romans 1:16, 17; Galatians 3:8). The keeping of the seventh-day Sabbath has always been a principle sign in God's dealing with his people from the time of creation (Genesis 2:1-4; Hebrews 4:1-9; Revelation 14:6, 7) to our time.

Yet, Isaiah is not finished in this chapter. He says in verses 4-6, "For thus says the Lord unto the eunuchs **that keep my Sabbaths**, and choose *the things* that please me, and **take hold of my covenant;** Even unto them will I give in mine house and within my walls **a place and a name better than of sons and of daughters**: I will give them an **everlasting name**, that shall not be cut off. Also the sons of the stranger, **that join** themselves to the Lord, to serve him, and to **love the name of the Lord**, to be his servants, every one that **keepeth the sabbath from polluting it, and taketh hold of my covenant** (Isaiah 56:4-6).

Only those who study the scriptures (Matthew 4:4; Acts 17:11; 2 Timothy 2:15) in order to understand, believe, accept, and obey the principle issues in the great controversy between Christ and Satan will be numbered with the redeemed when Jesus comes. The 7ᵗʰ Day Sabbath (**Saturday**) is God's day of rest and worship, and is of intimate significance between God and man. Those who choose to rebel from this one principle God has chosen as a **gospel issue** for this generation will be "found wanting" (Daniel 5:27) and separated from the Kingdom of God (Exodus 20:8-11; James 2:10). When the last life-giving gospel message in Revelation 14:6-12 is given to this final generation just before Jesus comes (Revelation 22:20, 21).

The fourth plague is given on behalf of man's rebellion to the true Bible issue when it come to what day God has created (Genesis 2:1-3) and made

(Mark 2:27) in behalf of man's need to rest under God's provisions for the benefit of his physical, spiritual, mental, and moral needs. Man and beast are **"scorched with great heat"** (Revelation 16:8, 9) because men have chosen to worship the *"day of the Sun" (Sunday)* and set up a world union of church and state. Contentious (Romans 2:8) to what a difference a day makes in the eyes of God (Isaiah 55:8, 9; 56:1-6; 58:12-15; Hebrews 4:1-11). This plague is a direct decree from heaven for the formation of the world apostasy and rebelling against God's Holy day of gospel rest and worship in Christ our righteousness (Revelation 14:6, 7).

The fifth plague falls on the "seat of the beast and his kingdom was full of darkness" (Revelation 16:10). This plague is a direct parallel to the darkness that fell on Egypt (Exodus 10:21-23). It's main purpose is to protect God's people from the death decree (Revelation 13:15) legislated upon God's remnant who will not compromise the truths of the everlasting gospel message. Darkness covers the earth because men have been given legislative authority after a universal mandate to take the lives of those who would not relinquish the biblical truths conveyed to them by heaven's providence (Revelation 13:15, 16; 14:9-11). This darkness is beyond comprehension upon those **"whose names are not written in the book of life of the Lamb slain from the foundation of the world (Revelation 13:8)**. They are fully intent on eradicating from the earth those who will not compromise their faith and keep **Sunday worship**. The earth at this time is the legislated "seat of the beast" (Revelation 16:10) and has marked the world with blaspheme pertaining to what biblically represents the name of God (Revelation 13:6). The fifth plague clothes the world in darkness so great that God's remnant cannot be located to be killed or annihilated from this planet.

It's the sixth plague that the unsaved begin to understand they have been deceived into believing the Mystery of Iniquity (2 Thessalonians 2:7), which has produced MYSTERY BABYLON THE GREAT (Revelation 17:5) throughout the world. Civil and church leaders, ministers which have been deceived into working with "spirits of devils, working miracles, which go forth unto the kings of the earth and the whole world to gather them to the battle of that great day of God Almighty" (Revelation 16:14). Too late they see that there is "a famine in the land, not a famine of bread, nor a thirst for water, but of hearing of the words of the Lord" (Amos 8:11). Too late they see, as in Noah's day (Matthew 24:37-39; Genesis 7:5-7), that probation has closed on this generation.

Then scripture declares the beginning of the final battle of Armageddon, and man is prepared for the final battle scripture calls Armageddon, or the Mountain of slaughter. Fathers against sons, daughter-in-law against mother-in-law, family members against families; and a man's foes shall be they of his own household (Matthew 10:35, 36), which includes the households of faith. Members of church organizations who now turn on their members and ministers with "wailing and gnashing of teeth" (Matthew 13:42).

It's at the seventh plague that the condemned people of God (Joel 2:32; Revelation 12:17; 14:12; 19:7-9) hear the voice of the Father announcing the time of the appearing of Christ's second coming and the time of their deliverance (Revelation 16:17, 18; Acts 1:11). Then the trinity of apostasy, the mystery of iniquity, the dragon, the beast, and the false prophet, the leaders in the union of Church and State universal legislation, will be divided (Revelation 16:13; 17-21), broken up and destroyed (Isaiah 13:6-13). Then the elements of the world will inundate the final destruction of the earth (19:11-21) and the second coming of Christ will take place for the deliverance of Jesus' people, who are sealed for eternity (Zephaniah 3:20; Revelation 7:1-3; Revelation 16:18-21).

In truth, the Savior of the world has been rejected of men as much in this generation as has ever been in the past in the light of the truth of what the gospel is, says, and does for fallen humanity. Was it not "the commandments of God and the faith of Jesus" that demanded the demonstration of the cross of Christ (Romans 3:31)? The glory of the cross of Christ is as misunderstood and misapplied by the Christian world today as it was in Jesus' day. Jesus counseled Adam before the fall, saying, "Thou shall not," and if you do, "Thou shall surely die." Did Jesus not have a standard and foundation for His statement to Adam (Genesis 2:17)? When will we understand that the standard and foundation for Jesus' words to Adam before the fall were the commandments of God and the faith of Jesus (Genesis 3:11)? The commandments of God are the governing principles and foundation of His eternal government. The faith of Jesus was, is, and will always be the standard of righteousness that the commandments of God demand before any of God's Ten Governing Principles can be kept.

The religious leaders in Jesus' day declared in their own ignorance, "He saved others; Himself He cannot save" (Matthew 24:42). They did not understand that He could not, in truth and righteousness, save himself without putting Himself and his governing principles of life forever in eternal jeopardy. Principally rejected and ignored by most of humanity, which has left our planet in total ungovernable anarchy and death. People are dying in unrighteousness, and the only one that can save them is the righteousness of God that hung on the cross two thousand years ago in shame and scorn. The righteousness of God must be totally understood in the light of the glorious gospel of Christ, "who hath abolished death, and **has brought life and immortality to light through the gospel**" (2 Timothy 1:10). There are bottles of fermented, perverted gospel wine everywhere, many drinking decayed gospel matter when the fresh fruit of the Tree of Life is again being ignored and replaced by another tree, another gospel (Galatians 1:6, 7).

Isaiah said, "Arise, shine; for thy light is come, and the glory of the Lord is risen upon thee. For, behold, the darkness shall cover the earth, and gross darkness the people: but the Lord shall arise upon thee, and his glory (His righteousness [Psalm 97:6]) shall be seen upon thee" (Isaiah 60:1-3). I wish everyone who claims to believe the truth of the gospel of Christ would take seriously the wonderful things presented in these verses. There are many today on dangerous ground. Let all understand that the "truth of the gospel" either saves or hardens the heart unto eternal perdition. There is no middle ground. The rejection of the light of "truth of the gospel" (2 Timothy 1:10) will condemn many a Christian when Jesus comes again (2 Thessalonians 1:7, 8). Skepticism and infidelity are increasing everywhere. Precious light has been hidden under a bushel of error, and many neglect their responsibility when they see a neighbor "sin a sin which is not unto death," which, if it is not corrected before Jesus comes, will become a "sin *(of unrighteousness)* unto death" (1 John 5:16).

Let all see and understand the responsibility placed on God's people to "preach the word, be instant in season, out of season; reprove, rebuke, exhort with all longsuffering and doctrine" (2 Timothy 4:1). God has given sufficient evidence in scripture as to what to say and how to say it. Paul said, "I am not ashamed of the gospel of Christ: for it is the power of God unto salvation ... for therein is the righteousness of God revealed" (Romans 1:16, 17). Who are truly the subjects of Christ's Divine Kingdom? Only those who by faith have taken hold of Christ's heavenly "gift of divine righteousness" (Romans 5:17), through the gospel of peace (Romans 10:15), and received in the heart, joy by the indwelling power of the Holy Ghost. Paul says, "For the kingdom of God is not meat and drink; but righteousness and peace and joy in the Holy Ghost" (Romans 14:17). We belong to God by creation and redemption. And we individually must, because of our human condition (Romans 3:23), transfer our present citizenship (Philippians 3:20) from this planet to Jesus' Universal Kingdom of unprecedented divine righteousness (Hebrews 1:8).

It is by faith in the gospel of Christ that the righteousness of God saves every son and daughter of Adam (Romans 1:16, 17). Many may believe that righteousness is by faith alone, but scripture says faith is not heavenly faith without legal forensic righteousness. Peter said under divine inspiration as an apostle of Christ, "to them that have **obtained like precious faith** with us **through the righteousness of God** and our Savior Jesus Christ" (2 Peter 1:1). Righteousness may be received by faith, but it is not true legal heavenly faith that leads to Justification by faith unto eternal life (Romans 5:1) until it is stamped as Abraham was with divine righteousness, and then tested (Revelation 3:10) in a sign seal covenant contract afforded him in his generation (Romans 4:11; James 2:20-23; Genesis 22:12; Isaiah 56:1-8; Revelation 14: 6-12).

James said, "Even so faith, without works is dead, being alone" (James 2:17). Brethren, in order to be saved when Jesus comes we must all contemplate our human position and take the necessary steps in present truth (2 Peter 1:12). As Abraham did in gospel order of his day to obtain the "righteousness and peace and joy in the Holy Ghost" that **God needs** to make us part of his heavenly kingdom. The apostle Paul said, "If we are not obeying the gospel (Revelation 14:6, 7) when Jesus comes the second time, we shall be punished and separated from the presence of God and the glory of His life-giving power forever (2 Thessalonians 1:8, 9). This fact should in our day stir every soul in contemplating Christ, our lift-giving righteousness (Romans 4:19-24).

How many a restless heart would be content today if the **fruit of righteousness** where truly understood by the people of God; How many today are defining the gospel as just good news, leaving many void of what the "truth of the gospel" truly conveys to the human heart. Did not the apostle Paul say, "Stand therefore, having your loins girded about with *truth*, and having on the breastplate of *righteousness*; and your feet shod with the *gospel of peace* (Ephesians 6:15).

Adam, in the beginning, negated the righteousness and peace man had with his Creator by his willful sin shortly after creation (Romans 5:12). And has not the God of peace for thousands of years endeavored with heaven's entire abundant grace tried to convey to man the meaning and purpose of righteousness and the fruits of righteousness through the *gospel of peace*? Paul said, "I beseech you brethren, by the name of our Lord Jesus Christ, that ye *all speak the same thing*, and that there be no divisions among you; but that ye be perfectly joined together in the same mind and in the same judgment" (1 Corinthians 1:10).

In his statement to the Hebrews, Paul said, "It is appointed unto men once to die, but after this the judgment" (Hebrews 9:27). And did not Peter answer this statement by saying the principle issue in the judgment is obeying the gospel of peace (1 Peter 4:17)? Jesus produced the gospel of peace that affords us the right to believe and receive the righteous peace, that we may all stand in righteousness when our names come up in the judgment seat of Christ (2 Corinthians 5:10).

Paul said, "For I am jealous over you with godly jealousy: for I have espoused you to one husband that I may present you as a chaste virgin to Christ. But I fear, lest by any means, as the serpent beguiled Eve through his subtlety, so your minds should be corrupted from the simplicity that is in Christ" (2 Corinthians 11:2, 3). Has not this text found its fulfillment among many in the household of faith? Has not the subtlety of Satan crept in among God's people and preached another Jesus; Whom Paul said, "We have not preached," or another spirit, "Which we have not received," or another gospel, "Which we have not accepted" (2 Corinthians 11:4)? Brethren, how many versions of the gospel are there among us? There was only one gospel in Jesus' day, and when Paul saw Peter was starting to walk not uprightly according to "the truth of the gospel," he contended with him as to its message and truth (Galatians 2:14-16).

Friend, *how long* before we humble ourselves together and plead for a unity that will truly exalt what God wants the gospel to say to the human heart, which is now void of the peace man truly needs with his maker? *How long* before we truly commit, "for the hope which is laid up for you in heaven, whereof ye heard before in the word of **the truth of the gospel**" (Colossians 1:5). *How long* before a covenant commitment is made between God and His remnant people for the true proclamation of the gospel of Christ? *How long* before the gospel of the kingdom is *preached for a witness* unto all nations, "saying with a loud voice, Fear God and give glory to Him" (Revelation 14:6, 7)? *How long, Oh Lord, how long?*

Is it not time for the gospel message to ring though our churches? Should not our members plead for the increased faith and knowledge we all need from Him, who is our only source of power and strength, the Lord Jesus, the living Christ? Upon each one of us rests the responsibility of warning the world of the coming confederacy in a future global union of Church and State. There is among us a fearful lack of the sympathy that must be felt for souls, that the apostle Paul said we "must give account" (Hebrews 13:17). God is waiting and watching for men and women to awake to their responsibility to proceed and be no longer indifferent in the work of God.

The everlasting gospel is to be preached to every nation, kindred, and tongue, and people (Revelation 14:6-12). The world can only be convicted and convinced, not just by what is said in the pulpit on Sabbath morning, but by that which the church members do and say by their corresponding lives according to gospel order in their community. As it is *the minister's responsibility and duty to define the theme of "the truth of the gospel of*

Christ" to the households of faith. It is also equally critical that the members constituting the body of Christ consciously and biblically acknowledge what the everlasting gospel is, says, and does for every individual who takes hold of its **scriptural truth**.

Brethren, it wasn't softly muffled sounds that heralded the gospel messages of many past generations. We have a message direct from the Lord to bear to the world. Let us remember we are pilgrims and strangers on a planet void of the righteousness of Christ, and we must testify to all around us what constitutes righteousness, peace, and joy in the Holy Ghost for the salvation of souls. Paul said, "I am not ashamed of the gospel of Christ: for it is the power of God unto salvation to everyone that believes … for therein is the righteousness of God revealed from faith to faith: as it is written, The Just (**the made right with God**) shall live by faith" (Romans 1:16).

Today, the "**truth of the gospel**" (Ephesians 1:13; Colossians 1:5) is defining the salvation message as "The **Everlasting Gospel** (Revelation 14:6, 7) is **righteousness by faith** (Romans 4:13) into **Justification by faith** (Romans 5:1) through the **imputed Righteousness of Christ** (Romans 4:11). Produced by Christ's **life** (Romans 5:10), **death,** and **resurrection** (2 Timothy 2:8). Of which the **Seventh-day Sabbath** (Exodus 20:8-11) is **Heaven's official Sign of righteousness by faith** (2 Peter 1:10). **Jesus' Everlasting Seal** (Revelation 7:1-3) of **Justification by faith,** in light of its **belief, acceptance,** and **obedience** (2 Thessalonians 1:7, 8) into **righteousness** unto **holiness** (Romans 6:19; Ephesians 4:24) and **everlasting life**. This is the critical message that must go to every kingdom, nation, tongue, and people before Jesus comes again (Matthew 14:14; Revelation 14:6-12).

Friend, for over the past four years I have endeavored to convey to all the enormity of our condition and what God needs to save each one of us. It's critical to understand that evil prevails and will continue to prevail until godly ministers are biblically *grounded in the* **truth of the Gospel,** and act to the enormity of their godly calling. Although at times some may have found my manuscript a little difficult to understand, I have done all at this time to convey to you the most wonderful gospel message that constitutes eternal life in the judgment hour message for this final generation. It is my prayer that what may seem difficult to believe, understand, and obey may not overwhelm you.

Please pray for divine guidance with a heart willing to meet God on his terms for the salvation of your soul and the souls of others. It only took one sin (Romans 5:12) to place us in this deplorable condition we are all in. It took Jesus thirty-three years of sinless living (1 Peter 2:22), then dying on a cruel cross, and Jesus' resurrection into God's heavenly Temple of Judicial Justice, where He now presides, to remedy our sinful condition (2 Timothy 2:8; Hebrews 8:1-6). Please, brethren, I leave you with this final statement and pray it will impress and fill your heart.

Call to Righteousness

It is critical that man understand his condition before God. It is not our work to deal with the specific sins of men until we first deal with the explicit sin that has put him in this condition: his present state of unrighteousness (Romans 3:10). Man may take necessary steps of putting away many bad habits of sinfulness, but the decree of unrighteousness placed on him by Adam's willful sin (Romans 5:12) has only one remedy. It is by beholding the "Lamb of God which takes away the sin **(decree of unrighteousness)** of the world" (John 1:29) which is imperative to believing (Mark 1:15), receiving (1 Corinthians 15:1), and obeying (1 Peter 4:17) the gospel of Christ (Romans 1:16). It is only through the **purity of Christ's life-giving righteousness** that man can attain the character and purity of holiness God demands as a standard of life in His universal Kingdom (Exodus 20:1-17). "This is the truth of the gospel" (Romans 1:17; Colossians 1:5).

Jesus said, "For I say to you, that **except your righteousness** shall **exceed** *the righteousness* **of the scribes and Pharisees**, ye shall in **no case enter into the kingdom of heaven**" (Matthew 5:20)

Paul said, "As it is written, there is **none righteous**, no, **not one**" (Romans 3:10).

Jesus said, "But seek ye **first the kingdom of God**, and **his righteousness**, and all these things shall be added to you" (Matthew 6:33).

Paul said, "For the **kingdom of God is** not meat and drink; but **righteousness**, and peace, and joy in the Holy Spirit" (Romans 14:17).

Paul said, "And be found in him, **not having mine own righteousness**, which is of the law, but that which is through the faith of Christ, the **righteousness which is of God** by faith" (Philippians 3:9).

Isaiah said, "**In righteousness shall thou be established**: thou shall be far from oppression; for thou shall not fear: and from terror; for it shall not come near thee." "This *is* the **heritage of the servants** of the Lord, and their **righteousness *is* of me, says the Lord**" (Isaiah 54:14, 17).

Peter said, "Nevertheless we, according to his promise, **look for** new heavens and a new earth, **wherein dwells righteousness**" (2 Peter 3:13).

Isaiah said, "For as the earth brings forth her bud, and as the garden causes the things that are sown in it to spring forth; so the Lord GOD will **cause righteousness and praise to spring forth** before all the nations" (Isaiah 61:11).

Jesus said, "The time is fulfilled, and the **kingdom of God is at hand**: repent ye, and **believe the gospel**" (Mark 1:15).

"And this **gospel of the kingdom** shall be **preached** in all the world, for a witness *(in the Sacred Decalogue)* unto all nations; and **then shall the end come**" (Matthew 24:14).

Paul said, "For therein *(for in the gospel)* is the **righteousness of God revealed** from faith to faith: as it is written, the just *(the made right by the righteousness of Christ)* shall live by faith" (Romans 1:17).

Paul said, "For he will **finish the work**, and cut *it* short in righteousness: because a short work will the Lord make upon the earth" (Romans 9:28).

Peter said, "What shall be the end of them that obey not the gospel of God" (1 Peter 4:17)?

Paul said, "And to you who are troubled rest with us, when the Lord Jesus shall be revealed from heaven … **in flaming fire, taking vengeance** on them that know not God, and that **obey not the gospel** of our Lord Jesus Christ: Who **shall be punished** with everlasting destruction" (2 Thessalonians 1:7-9).

John said, "And I saw another angel fly in the mist of heaven, having the **everlasting gospel to preach** unto them that dwell on the earth, and to every nation, kindred, and tongue, and people, **Saying with a loud voice**, Fear God, and give glory to him; for the hour of his judgment is come: **and worship him that made heaven, and earth, and the sea, and the fountains of water**" (Revelation 14:6, 7; Exodus 20:8-11).

Called to be Witnesses

Many today are crying for the revelation of Jesus Christ in the person of his saints. God desires and needs his people to represent before the world a holy people, because the world can and will only be saved by the light of the glorious truth of the glorious gospel of Christ (Ephesians 1:13; 2 Timothy 1:9, 10). It's the message of present gospel truth (2 Peter 1:12) that is to call men out of darkness into God's marvelous **gospel light**, given to His commandment-keeping remnant people (Joel 2:32; 2 Timothy 1:10; Revelation 14:6, 7). It will **give Pentecostal power** to many lives, and as they bear witness to the gospel's biblical truth, true justification unto sanctification of the Holy Spirit will take place. God desires His people to place themselves in a gospel relation to Him that they shall bear to every nation, kindred, and tongue what it means to do justly, to love mercy, and to walk humbly with the Lord (Micah 6:8). Paul said, "I am not ashamed of the gospel of Christ: for it is the power of God unto salvation to everyone that believeth; to the Jew (commandment keeper) first, and also the Greek (Romans 1:16.)

For there in (Romans 1:17), for in the Everlasting Gospel (Revelation 14:6, 7) is **righteousness by faith** (Romans 4:13) unto **Justification by faith** (Romans 5:1) into the imputed (attributed) **righteousness of Christ** (Romans 5:20-25). Produced by Christ's **life, death** (Romans 5:10), and **resurrection** (2 Timothy 2:8). Which the **Seventh-day Sabbath** (Exodus 20:8-11), **heaven's official seal** (Revelation 7:1-3), to be given to all "them that have obtained like precious faith (2 Peter 2:1) ... through the righteousness of God, and is to witness as Christ's official judicial evidence in the Sacred Decalogue (Matthew 24:14) of its belief, acceptance, and obedience (2 Thessalonians 1:7, 8) into **righteousness** unto **holiness** (Romans 6:19; Ephesians 4:24) and **everlasting life.** This is the critical message that must go to every kingdom, nation, tongue, and people before Jesus comes again in the clouds of heaven (Revelation 14:6-12).

Friend, I leave with you on the last pages of this volume five Bible inserts, plus an end-time covenant contract pertaining to present truth. And as you see these upcoming biblical events, you may of your own free will decide through biblical interpretation between righteousness or unrighteousness, Christ or Satan, eternal life or the second death (Revelation 20:14).

Now, the God of peace that brought again from the dead our Lord Jesus, that great shepherd of the sheep, through the blood of the *everlasting covenant*, make you perfect in every good work to do his will, working in you that which is well pleasing in his sight, through Jesus Christ to whom be glory forever and ever. Amen (Hebrews 13:20, 21). "Wherefore the rather, brethren, give diligence to make your calling and election sure: for if ye do these things, ye shall never fall: For so an entrance shall be ministered to you abundantly into the everlasting kingdom of our Lord and Savior Jesus Christ. Wherefore I will not be negligent to put you always in remembrance of these things, though ye know *them,* and be **established in the present truth**" (2 Peter 1:10-12).

Jesus said, "And this gospel of the kingdom shall be preached in all the world, for a testimony to all nations; and then shall the end come" (Matthew 24:14).

"And the Lord answered me, and said, write the vision, and make *it* plain upon tables, that he may run that reads it. For the vision *is* yet for an appointed time, but at the end it shall speak, and not lie: though it tarry, wait for it; because it will surely come, it will not tarry" (Habakkuk 2:2, 3).

WRITE THE VISION, AND MAKE IT PLAIN ON TABLES
(Habakkuk 2:2, 3)
70 Weeks or Years of Prophesy of Daniel 9:24-27

70 Prophetic years of probation *Upon Israel as a Nation*
457 B.C.--34 A.D.
   Decree to Rebuild 490 Years Stoning of Stephen
  Ezra 7:11-17-------------------------------------Acts 7:57-60

457 B.C.---------**69 Weeks *To Messiah the Prince*** ---------- A.D. 27
Decree to Rebuild Jerusalem--- 483 Years to---Messiah the Prince
   Ezra 7:11-17 Matthew 3:13-17

Final week, or 7 Last Prophetic years for literal Israel
A.D. 27--- Gospel to the Jews ---A.D. 34 (John 15:22)
A.D. 34--- Gospel to the Gentiles (Acts 13:45-47)

2,300 Years prophecy of Daniel 8:14
457 B.C.----2,300 Prophetic Years---- October 22, 1844

THE FINAL SCENARIO
The seven heads are seven mountains on which the woman sits.
(Revelation 17:3; 18:7)

She, the woman
The 21ˢᵗ Century Christian Catholic Protestant Universal Church
Sits in
Full legislative and Judicial Control
On the Seven biblical Apostate Heads of
Of

C	C	C	C	C	C	C R	C	R
1.	2.	3.	4.	5.	6.	7.8.	9.	10.
Egypt	Assyria	Babylon	Medo-Persia		Greece	Rome	United States	
Egypt	Syria	Iraq	Iran		Greece	Rome	United States	
—————Middle East—————					——Europe——		——America——	
————House of Islam————					—Catholicism—		—Protestantism—	
—Beast from Bottomless Pit—					—Out of Sea—		—Out of Earth—	
—Rev. 9:1-2—					—Rev 13:1-10—		—Rev.13:11-18—	

Who does the Bible say saves us?

"For God so loved the world, that he gave his only begotten Son, that whosoever believeth in him should not perish but have everlasting life." "Neither is there salvation in any other: for there is none other Name under heaven given among men, whereby we must be saved." "That if thou shalt confess with thy mouth **the Lord Jesus**, and shall believe in thine heart that God hath raised him from the dead, thou shalt be saved." "For with the heart man believeth unto righteousness; and with the mouth confession is made unto salvation" (**John 3:16; Acts 4:12; Romans 10:9, 10**).

What does the Bible want us to do about Jesus?

"He became the author of eternal salvation unto all them that **obey him**." (**Hebrews 5:9**)

What does the Bible say saves us?

"Who will have all men to be saved, and to come unto the knowledge of the truth (**1 Timothy 2:4**). "For the hope which is laid up for you in heaven, whereof ye heard before in the word of the **truth of the gospel** (**Colossians 1:5**). "Moreover, brethren, **I declare unto you the gospel which I preached unto you, which also ye have received, and wherein ye stand; By <u>which also you are saved</u>**" (**1 Corinthians 15:1, 2**).

What does the Bible want us to do with the gospel?

"For the time is come that judgment must begin at the house of God; and if it first begin at us, what shall the end be of them that obey not the gospel of God." "And to you who are troubled rest with us, when the Lord Jesus shall be revealed from heaven with his mighty angels, in flaming fire taking vengeance on them that know not God, and **obey not the gospel of Christ**" (**1 Peter 4:17; 2 Thessalonians 1:7, 8**).

How does the Bible say we are saved?

"But we believe that through the **grace of the Lord Jesus Christ** we shall be saved." "For by **grace** are ye saved through faith; and that not of yourselves: it is the **gift of God**" (**Acts 15:11; Ephesians 2:8**).

What does the Bible want us to do with grace?

"**But grow in grace**, and in the knowledge of our Lord and Savior Jesus Christ. To him be glory both now and forever." "And I saw another angel fly in the midst of heaven, **having the Everlasting gospel** to preach unto them that dwell on the earth, and to every nation, and kindred, and tongue, and people" (**2 Peter 3:18; Revelation 14:6**).

Ten Glorious Gospel Merits

Jesus Produced for us by His Faithful Life
1. A bill of rights for all Mankind (2 Timothy 4:8).

2. Our new Title or Identity as Children of God. (John 1:12).

3. A Judicial right to be saved by grace through the righteousness of Christ (Romans 5:1, 2, 21; 2 Peter 1:1, 2).

4. The right to be sealed with the Holy Spirit. (John 3:5-8; Ephesians 1:13; 4:30)

5. The right to repentance and acceptance in the Judgment hour (Daniel 7:9-13; Acts 17:30, 31; Revelation 14:6, 7).

By His Faithful Death
Jesus Produced
6. A Death Certificate in our Name (Galatians 2:20).

7. Peace with our heavenly Father through the shedding of the blood on his cross (Colossians 1:20).

8. A Bill of Sale for all of our sins (1 Corinthians 15: 1-3; 1 Peter 1:18, 19)

9. Justification by faith through the imputed righteousness of Christ that covers the sins of the World. (Rom.4:1-8; Jn.15:22; 1Jn.1:9; 2:1-2)

By His Resurrection
10. An Advocate with the Father at Judgment time (Daniel 7:9-14; 8:14; Revelation 14:6, 7)

**Justifying for us a Rite of Passage or a Passport into the
Kingdom of God when Jesus comes again.
(Hebrews 4:14; 1 Thessalonians 4:13-16; 2 Peter 1:11; 1 John 2:1)**

*If you continue in my word you shall know
the Truth, and the Truth shall make you Free* (John 8:32)

Jesus is the Personification of Truth
He is the way, the truth, and the life (John 14:6)
Jesus must be believed (Acts 16:14), received (John 1:12),
Obeyed (Hebrews 5:9)

The Bible is the Manuscript of Truth
(John 17:17; John 8:31)
Which also must be believed (Acts 4:4) and obeyed (2 Thessalonians 3:14)

The Gospel is the Power of Truth
(Romans 1:16; Galatians 2:5, 14; Ephesians 1:13; Colossians 1:5)
Which also must be believed (Mark 1:15), received (1 Corinthians 15:1),
Obeyed (2 Thessalonians 1:7, 8)

Grace is the Gift of Truth
(John 1:14, 17; Colossians 1:6; 2 John 3; Romans
5:15, 17; Ephesians 2:8, 3:7; 1 Peter 4:10)
Which also must be believed (Acts 18:27),
Received, and obeyed (Romans 1:5)

The Ten Commandments are the Principles of Truth
(Psalm 119:142, 151; 1 John 2:4)
Which also we **_keep_**, maintained through the Gospel of Christ
by the indwelling power of the Holy Spirit (John 14:15; 15:10;
1 John 2:3; 3:22; 5:2, 3; Revelation 12:17; 14:12; 22:14)

As **Jesus** is the **Personification of Truth,** He is also
the **Personification of Righteousness** (1 John 2:1)
As the **Bible** is the **Manuscript of Truth**, it is also
the **Manuscript of Righteousness** (2 Timothy 3:16)

As the **Gospel** is the **Power of Truth,** it is also
the **Power of Righteousness** (Romans 1:16)

As **Grace** is the **Gift of Truth,** it is also
the **Gift of Righteousness** (Romans 5:17)

As the **Ten Commandments** are the **Principles of Truth,** they are also
the **Principles of Righteousness** (Deuteronomy 6:25; Psalm 119:172)

Revelation 14:6, 7 Everlasting Gospel
The **Everlasting Gospel of Christ** *is* **Righteousness by faith** *(Romans 4:13)*
into **Justification by faith** *(Romans 5:1) through the Imputed Righteousness*
of Christ (Romans 5:20-25). Produced by Jesus' **Life,** **Death,** *and*
Resurrection *(2 Timothy 2:8). Of which the* **Seventh-Day Sabbath** *(Exodus*
20:8-11) **is heaven's** *Everlasting Sign of precious Faith (2 Peter 1:1),*
Christ's Everlasting Judicial Seal *(John 6:27; Revelation 7:1-3) of its Belief,*
Acceptance, and **Obedience** *(2 Thessalonians 1:7, 8) into* **Righteousness**
unto Holiness *(Romans 6:19; Ephesians 4:24) and Eternal* **Life.**

What is the biblical truth of the Gospel?
Righteousness by faith into Justification by Faith
(Galatians 2:14-16; 3:8; Colossians 1:5; Romans 1:16, 17; 3:26; 5:18)

What did Jesus have to do to produce what the Gospel is?
1. Live a perfect life without sin (1 Peter 2:21,
22; Hebrews 4:15; 1 John 3:5)
2. Died (Romans 5:8, 9) **3.** Was Resurrected (2 Timothy 2:8)

How important is it to understand the truth of the Gospel?
Scripture says at the second coming of Christ, God's
vengeance will be poured out on those who do not know
God and obey not the Gospel (2 Thessalonians 1:7-9)

How do we biblically Believe the Gospel?
To believe the gospel means to obey it, and obey Jesus
(1 Peter 4:17; Hebrews 5:9). In the judgment, salvation begins
with obedience to the gospel of Christ (Romans 10:16).

How do we obey the Gospel in the 21ˢᵗ Century?
Revelation pictures the final gospel message of justification by
faith to this fallen world. **Saying with a loud voice,** "Worship
him that made heaven, and earth, and the sea, and the
fountains of waters" (Isaiah 56:1-6; Revelation 14:6, 7).

How do we worship him that made heaven, earth, and the sea?

The phrase "made heaven and earth, the sea" is taken from Exodus 20:8-11, which means to keep the Seventh-day Sabbath as a sign of obedience to the gospel of Christ (Exodus 31:16, 17).

Which New Testament verses associate the Gospel with the Seventh-day Sabbath (Hebrews 4:1-11)

Neglect this great salvation; despise this glorious gospel offer of justification through the righteous blood of Christ, and sanctification through the cleansing power of the Holy Spirit, and there remains no more sacrifice for sins (Hebrews 10:26-30). But sanctify the Lord God in your hearts: and be ready always to give an answer to every man that asks you a reason of the hope that is in you with meekness and fear (Hebrews 5:7-9; 1 Peter 3:15).

Heaven's Official Passport into Jesus' Universal Kingdom of Everlasting Righteousness
Revelation 7:1-3; 14:6, 7, Sign, Seal of Everlasting Gospel

Sign, Seal of Creator of Heaven and Earth

7th Day Sabbath, Seal of Citizenship

Sign, Seal of the Everlasting Covenant (Isaiah 56:6)

7th Day

And because ye are children, God hath sent forth the Spirit of his Son into your hearts, crying, Abba, Father
Sabbath

And I saw another angel fly in the midst of heaven, **having the everlasting gospel to preach** to them that dwell on the earth, and to every nation, and kindred, and tongue, and people, **Saying with a loud voice, Fear God**, and **give glory to him**; for **the hour of his judgment is come**: and **worship him that made heaven, and earth, and the sea, and the fountains of waters** (Revelation 14:6, 7).

And there were sealed a hundred *and* forty *and* four thousand of all the tribes of the children of Israel. And, lo, a Lamb stood on the mount Zion, and with him a hundred forty *and* four thousand, having his *Father's name* written in their foreheads (**Revelation 7:4; 14:1**).

Here is the patience of the saints: here are they that keep the commandments of God and (keep) the faith of Jesus (Revelation 14:12).

Covenant Sign of Faith, Seal of Righteousness
Sign, Seal of God, Creator of heaven and Earth
7th Day Sabbath
Sign, Seal of the Everlasting Covenant between God and his Creation

I Covenant with the **Lord, JESUS CHRIST,** by accepting and receiving Christ's **7th day Sabbath,** an **Everlasting Sign of Citizenship,** Heaven's **Official Seal and Bill of Rights,** as my Official Decree of obedience to the Everlasting Gospel of Jesus Christ (Revelation 14:6, 7). This Official Covenant Seal establishes me as an authorized Citizen of the Kingdom of God, a Commandment Keeper with Certified rights to the Tree of Life, and entrance through the Gates of the City of God (**Revelation 22:14).**
"**Remember** the **Sabbath day**, to keep it holy. Six
days shall thou labor, and do all thy work:
But the **seventh day** *is* the **Sabbath of the Lord** thy God: *in it* thou
shall not do any work, thou, nor thy son, nor thy daughter, thy
manservant, nor thy maidservant, nor thy cattle, nor thy stranger that
is within thy gates: For *in* six days **JESUS** made heaven and earth, the
sea, and all that in them *is*, and **rested the seventh day:** wherefore the
Lord blessed the Sabbath day, and hallowed it" (**Exodus 20:8-11).**

"And I saw **another angel** ascending from the east, having the **seal of the living God**: Saying Hurt not the earth, neither the sea, nor the trees, **till we have sealed the servants of our God in their foreheads (Revelation 7:2, 3).** Therefore shall ye **lay up these my words in your heart** and **in your soul,** and **bind them for a sign** upon **your hand,** that they **may be as frontlets between your eyes**" (**Deuteronomy 11:18).** "Also the sons of the stranger, that **join themselves** to the Lord, **to serve him,** and to **love the name of the Lord,** to be his servants, **every one that keeps the Sabbath** from polluting it, **and** <u>takes hold of my covenant</u>" (**Isaiah 56:6).**

If you have found this gospel message Biblically beneficial and would like to share it with others, copies are available

From

Pastor Edmond G. Labbe
P.O. Box 1553
156 Buxton Road
Saco, ME 04072
Phone: 207-571-4846 Cell: 207- 408-1223
righteousness@maine.rr.com

WARNING! WARNING! WARNING!

It's critical today to understand the United States of America is presently fulfilling her destiny as the last world power in the long line of prophetic nations who would arise prior to the second coming of Christ. According to biblical symbols, our country is presently in the position to fulfill her final destiny in a geo-political religious confederacy now taking place in world affairs. This great nation that was once based on religious liberty is now uniting the kings of the earth for the final erosion of truth. The United States will, in the near future, lead a world alliance that will <u>biblically reject life-giving righteousness.</u> The symbols in Daniel and Revelation define the times, events, locations, and the principle characters that are presently preparing the world for the final conflict. These two prophetic books reveal events and decisions that the 21st Century Christian Church today will face in the final hours of earth's history. These events parallel the events that took place in Jesus' final hours before the cross. The Church is reaching the pinnacle of corruption and confusion that mirrors that which happened in Jerusalem two thousand years ago. This book is written in a biblical format to define the nations, events, and issues that face this generation; and, friends, it's not for the faint of heart. It is based on thirty years of critical Bible study, from Genesis to Revelation. It will biblically challenge all believers to understand how specific truths revealed in past generations apply in our present day, symbols revealing an urgent gospel message to you and me. If you are looking for a simple understanding of issues pertaining to past and future events which apply to you, this book is for you. Come, friends, learn about the final deception by world powers just before Jesus returns. It's our future in the light of what it has cost the Lord Jesus Christ, and eternal price of our creation and redemption.